1598235

Dawn Powell

Twayne's United States Authors Series

Joseph M. Flora, Editor

University of North Carolina, Chapel Hill

TUSAS 715

DAWN POWELL

Dawn Powell

Marcelle Smith Rice

North Carolina State University

Twayne Publishers
New York

Twayne's United States Authors Series No. 715

Dawn Powell
Marcelle Smith Rice

Twayne Publishers
1633 Broadway
New York, NY 10019

Library of Congress Cataloging-in-Publication Data
Rice, Marcelle Smith.
    Dawn Powell / Marcelle Smith Rice.
        p. cm. — (Twayne's United States authors series ; TUSAS 715)
    Includes bibliographical references (p.) and index.
    ISBN 0-8057-1602-5 (alk. paper)
    1. Powell, Dawn—Criticism and interpretation.   2. Women and literature—United States—History—20th century.   3. New York (N.Y.)—In literature.
4. Ohio—In literature.   I. Title.   II. Series.
PS3531.O936 Z89 2000
813'52—dc21   99-059564

This paper meets the requirements of ANSI/NISO Z3948-1992 (Permanence of Paper).

10 9 8 7 6 5 4 3 2 1

Printed in the United States of America

For David, Benjamin, and Katharine,
who shared their lives with this book.

Contents

Preface

Five years after I began my search for Dawn Powell's works, I met Tim Page, who, it turns out, had been pursuing the same quest at about the same time. For hours during that first meeting, we talked of our discoveries, of our research, of our passion for Powell. It was such luxury to talk of her without having to preface it with, "No, that's D-A-W-N—like the break of day—Powell" ("Yes, I know I have the name of an unsuccessful stripper," Powell admitted. "It is my strong suit.")[1] Later, as we drove down Interstate 40 toward Chapel Hill, Tim said quietly, "You know, not everybody likes her." We silently chewed on this thought, Tim's words echoing back along the dismal years of Powell's puzzling critical neglect.

Since that moment, I have met a few of those people who question the value of Powell's works, and I am still puzzled. I like Powell's works because they make me laugh out loud. I like Powell because she wrote *in* America *about* America during a time when other American writers fled to Europe. With a rare blend of wit and empathy, Powell captured a time and a people caught in the frenetic web of early twentieth-century progress in America.

As Powell once wrote, her novels "follow the mass life of America as well as the individual life [in order to] record the lives of these people now [rather] than wait till the glacier has destroyed them and left only a statistical clue."[2] Powell strove to create a modern novel of manners that allowed her to denounce the prevailing evils of the world while maintaining the comic equilibrium necessary to continue living in a perpetually fragmenting world. "I am the only person who is doing contemporary social satire," Powell wrote in her diary in 1943.[3] Her satire is neither harsh nor frivolous; "I believe true wit should break a wise man's heart," she wrote. "It should strike at the exact point of weakness and it should scar. It should rest on a pillar of truth and not on a gelatine base, and the truth is not so shameful that it cannot be recorded."[4] Powell wielded her pen in order to expose people inside and out; "[the] sense of a frame briefly imprisoning life is what a good portrait should be and I should be able to do that in words," Powell wrote (*Diaries,* 317). Powell was criticized for these portraits—not because they are not true but because they are too true.

At the centennial of Powell's birth, her "portraits" finally received recognition. Until the mid-1990s, her papers were not easily accessible. In her dissertation on Powell, Judith Faye Pett laments the recalcitrance of Powell's executor, Jacqueline Miller Rice, saying that her "refusal or inability to respond calls into question whether the role of the literary executor is to protect an author's papers *for* or *from* the interests of posterity."[5] Tim Page has done much to rectify this situation through the publication of Powell's diaries and letters. Until 1989, all her books were out of print; now 11 novels and several of her short stories have been reprinted. Gore Vidal was instrumental in sparking the Powell revival in 1987 with an essay in the *New York Review of Books.* John Updike pushed it along with a lengthy essay on Powell in the *New Yorker.*[6] And her revival was made official with a National Public Radio piece to mark the release of *Dawn Powell At Her Best* (1994), a collection of two novels and several short stories. Thirty years and a week after her death, Powell made the cover of the *New York Times Book Review* with the headline: "Dawn Powell, a writer once buried alive, is back in town."[7]

In her lifetime, Powell had a loyal, if small, band of admirers, including Ernest Hemingway, Edmund Wilson, John Dos Passos, and Van Wyck Brooks. Attracted to Powell by her wit, they stayed for her insight. Drawing on her Ohio upbringing, Powell had a pragmatic, that is to say, Midwestern, approach to writing. She wrote about the people and places she observed, rather than trying to emulate the model du jour. Many of her novels received favorable reviews, and *The Wicked Pavilion* was given the plum cover spot in the *New York Herald Tribune* Sunday book review in September 1954. Although Powell herself said that her work was "neither literary nor intellectual,"[8] in 1964, she was awarded the Marjorie Peabody Waite Award for lifetime achievement; such an honor was the very thing she had dreamed of as a child in rural Ohio.

Powell wrote throughout her life, adjusting her process as she juggled the writing of 15 novels with more mundane writing tasks, such as book reviews. The novels provided Powell with advances, but she frequently was without money, so she would dash off short stories and reviews, accumulating hundreds of both; 18 of her stories were collected in *Sunday, Monday and Always* (1952). In addition, she wrote several dramas—two were published—several musicals, screenplays, reviews, and a huge number of letters.

But of all her writing, the novel was her chosen form—everything else was a distraction. "The novel is my normal breath," Powell wrote. "I feel I've never done anything on plays or short stories and in working on them I feel insecure, unsatisfied, hysterically delighted at best"(*Diaries,* 69). Critics divide Powell's novels rather neatly into an Ohio cycle of five novels published between 1928 and 1934 and a New York cycle published between 1936 and 1962; however, Powell also published an Ohio novel in 1944 and her first novel, *Whither* (1925), is set in New York City. Her diaries underscore the fact that the division is not really neat, as they evidence a continual tension between her Midwestern background and her New York present; this tension tugged at her on many levels, and she sometimes worked simultaneously on an Ohio novel and a New York novel. Powell's Ohio background wrapped itself around her life in Greenwich Village, informing her outlook and her writing. Her Ohio novels feature glittering glimpses of the big city; her New York novels feature Midwesterners trying to overcome their low beginnings. Malcolm Cowley once commented that Powell "had always done two things—the sentimental and the satirical" (*Diaries,* 385); this, too, is reductive, as one finds gentle satire in the "sentimental" Ohio novels and, beneath the broad-stroke satire of the New York novels, one finds an honest affection for this world that treats its people so badly at times.

Several years have passed since Tim and I headed down that highway together. And after all the reading, all the research, all the writing, Powell still has the power to amaze. Recently, Tim told me, with a bit of surprise, or maybe awe, in his voice, "I still like her." If the first readings took my breath away, later readings engage, like an old friend. I, too, am surprised and awed when I leaf through a book I know well to find myself laughing out loud—again. Our journey has brought us not to a state of exhaustion but to a renewed passion and enriched appreciation for Powell and her works.

Acknowledgements

Much appreciation and gratitude goes to Tim Page, who generously shared his resources, knowledge, and passion for Powell.

Thank you to Jack Sherman for sharing his memories and allowing them to be printed here.

Grateful acknowledgement is given to the following universities and publishers for permission to cite from the noted texts:

To the University of Minnesota Press, excerpts from Bakhtin, M. M. (Mikhail Mikhailovich), 1895–"Problems of Dostoevsky's Poetics" (Theory and history of literature, v. 8), Edited and Translated by Caryl Emerson, Copyright © 1984 by the University of Minnesota.

To the University of Virginia Library Special Collections Department, excerpts from The John Dos Passos Papers.

To Steerforth Press, excerpts from *The Diaries of Dawn Powell,* and from the following works by Dawn Powell: *The Bride's House, The Happy Island, A Time to Be Born, My Home Is Far Away, The Wicked Pavilion, The Golden Spur, Dance Night, Come Back to Sorrento, Turn, Magic Wheel, The Locusts Have No King, A Cage for Lovers,* and "What Are You Doing in My Dreams?"

Excerpts from the works of Dawn Powell by arrangement with the Estate of Dawn Powell.

Chronology

1896   Dawn Powell born November 28 in Mount Gilead, Ohio.

1903   Powell's mother, Hattie Sherman Powell, dies December 6.

1907   Roy Powell marries Sabra Stearns Powell, August.

1910   Powell runs away from home to Shelby and the home of Orpha May Sherman Steinbrueck.

1914   Begins study at Lake Erie College, Painesville, Ohio.

1915   Writes Woggs diary.

1918   Graduates from Lake Erie College. Moves to Pomfret, Connecticut, then to New York City.

1920   Marries Joseph R. Gousha.

1921   Joseph (Jojo) R. Gousha Jr. born August 22.

1925   *Whither* published.

1928   *She Walks in Beauty* published.

1929   *The Bride's House* published.

1930   *Dance Night* published.

1932   *The Tenth Moon* published.

1933   *Big Night* produced by the Group Theater.

1934   *The Story of a Country Boy* and *Jig Saw* published. *Jig Saw* produced by Theatre Guild.

1936   *Turn, Magic Wheel* published.

1938   *The Happy Island* published.

1940   *Angels on Toast* published.

1942   *A Time to Be Born* published.

1943   *The Lady Comes Across* produced.

1944   *My Home Is Far Away* published.

1948   *The Locusts Have No King* published.

1952   *Sunday, Monday and Always* published.

1954   *The Wicked Pavilion* published.

1956   *A Man's Affair* (abridged paperback version of *Angels on Toast*) published.

1957   *A Cage for Lovers* published.

1960   Awarded honorary Doctor of Literature by Lake Erie College.

1962   Joseph Gousha dies February 14. *The Golden Spur* published October 5.

1963   *The Golden Spur* nominated for National Book Award.

1965   Powell dies November 14.

1973   Matthew Josephson writes first posthumous review of Powell's work, in *The Southern Review.*

1987   Gore Vidal writes "Dawn Powell: The American Writer."

1989   Powell omnibus (*Angels on Toast, The Wicked Pavilion, The Golden Spur*) published by Quality Paperback Books.

1994   Powell's papers released. *Dawn Powell at Her Best* published.

1995   *The Diaries of Dawn Powell,* edited by Tim Page, published.

1998   *Dawn Powell: A Biography,* by Tim Page, published. Joseph R. Gousha dies Christmas Day.

1999   *Selected Letters of Dawn Powell,* edited by Tim Page, published.

Introduction: "The Oxygen Of Laughter"

"I . . . cannot exist without the oxygen of laughter," Dawn Powell wrote (*Diaries,* 419). Indeed, Powell's laughter permeated both her conversation and her writings. Unlike the well-recorded bon mots of her contemporary Dorothy Parker, Powell's verbal witticisms largely evaporated in late-night alcoholic fumes. "She was certainly the wittiest person I have ever known, with a rapid-fire running commentary," recalled Rosalind Baker Wilson, daughter of Edmund Wilson. "Dawn was as witty as Dorothy Parker, but she was difficult to quote."[1] Powell endured frequent comparisons to Dorothy Parker, but the broad scope and purpose of Powell's satiric novels far exceeded Parker's witty verbiage and focused, ironic stories.

Individually, Powell's novels focus on the lives of everyday people; as a whole, the novels trace the movement of these people from the provinces to the city. Her early novels show the restless stirrings that indicate the move away from the small town. The roots of this movement, as Powell shows, are found in individual desires, rather than in a groundswell of social unrest. Powell asserted that her works, even when set outside of the Midwest, were based in provincial Ohio.

> As a member of a family rooted in Ohio for nearly 150 years my observations have been concentrated on such people's struggle against or in defense of their inherent provincialism. My novels have followed this trail—the provincial in the city eager to trade his naivete for a sort of Hollywood culture, the other provincial American determined to keep his roots in a rootless environment, then the provincial returning to his roots with cosmopolitan messages.[2]

Powell's early works—five novels written between 1928 and 1934—are set in Ohio, a state she had left in 1918, writing later that "There's something about farm life that gives you the strength to run anywhere in the world."[3] Powell ran to New York City, where she stayed for more than four decades, calling herself a "permanent visitor." Her departure from Ohio made her a permanent visitor to that home also. She was outsider and insider in both the Midwest and New York. In her haunting memoir "What Are You Doing in My Dreams?" Powell wrote: "It's as if the day I left Ohio I split in two at the crossroads, and went up both roads, half of me by day here in New York and the other half by night with the dead in long-ago Ohio" (*Best,* 447). Powell's novels are rooted in this dualistic outlook.

"It is both natural and sensible that the place where we have our roots should become the setting, the first and primary proving ground, of our fiction," Eudora Welty wrote in *The Eye of the Story.*[4] In fact, Powell's first novel, *Whither,*[5] is set in New York City. But the novel's lukewarm reception forced her to recognize that she was not ready to let characters live in a place that she was just coming to know, so she turned to the provinces of her youth for a setting. Coming on the heels of the provincial movement in American literature, Powell's early works were quickly dubbed "regionalism," a tag that confused her: "My work—rigidly classified as 'accurate photography' when a study of feeling . . . could not possibly be done by photography, nor could those people be so cheerfully listed as 'small town types.' . . . I don't see at all that I am a 'regional writer' " (*Diaries,* 57). It is possible to consider Powell a regional writer, but not in the narrow sense of that term. Powell put her characters in places she knew. In her early career, this meant placing her characters and their stories in "long-ago Ohio." Later, she wrote about her adopted home, New York City, which itself became nearly a character in the novels.

Place causes characters to act and react. Even after moving to New York, Powell, and her characters, responded to Ohio's pull. Welty explains the complexity of the relationship between the "new home" and the place left behind:

> There may come to be new places in our lives that are second spiritual homes—closer to us in some ways, perhaps, than our original homes. But the home tie is the blood tie. And had it meant nothing to us, any other place thereafter would have meant less, and we would carry no compass inside ourselves to find home ever, anywhere at all. . . .
>
> [T]hose writers who for their own good reasons push out against their backgrounds nearly always passionately adopt the new one in their work. Revolt itself is a reference and tribute to the potency of what is left behind. (Welty, 131)

Powell also recognized the "potency of what is left behind." The setting, however, does not make the novels "regional." As Welty notes, " 'Regional,' I think, is a careless term, as well as a condescending one, because what it does is fail to differentiate between the localized raw material of life and its outcome as art. 'Regional' is an outsider's term; it has no meaning for the insider who is doing the writing, because as far as he knows he is simply writing about life" (Welty, 132).

One test for regionalism is to ask whether the story could be set in another place or whether it must be set in that locale. By that test, all fiction would be regional because the story is a product of the relationship between character and place: "Place . . . has the most delicate control over character too: by confining character, it defines it" (Welty, 122). In the Ohio novels, place defines character. Powell consciously allowed her characters the freedom to respond to place and, occasionally, reviewers recognized this symbiosis:

> Harold Stearns [gives] . . . an excellent, understanding review [of *The Tenth Moon*] crediting me with a fusing of the new stream-of-consciousness school and the directly realistic. This is definitely what I set out to do—to crash down new dimensions in character work, to make and know my people so that their past, present, future, wishes, regrets, dreams, and actualities were enclosed spirally in a conch-shell sort of growth, all braided simultaneously with time into one fused portrait which was not the image but the reality. (*Diaries,* 53)

In other reviews, slight plots are perceived as flaws, as Powell records here: "Found some reviews—by [Orville] Prescott of *Time to Be Born* and another of *My Home Is Far Away* by [Harvey] Breit and both hit on my chief fault: fine scenes, dialogue, people, but the chief story is thin, weak, or trivial if indeed present at all" (*Diaries,* 385). Powell reveals here an awareness of structure that clearly deviates from the model of dramatic action rising to a climax and falling to a resolution. The lack of theme and compelling plot are incidental to the marvel of the unfolding of the tale. The novels show how place shapes character and how character shapes place. Powell's early novels, erroneously read as examples of regionalism, seem slight, lacking depth of plot and scene. But when read as experimental forays into characters' response to place, as shown in chapter 2, the novels reveal insight into the human spirit.

Powell's satires received more acclaim in her lifetime. "I am the only person who is doing contemporary social satire," Powell declared in 1943 (*Diaries,* 213). This is a daring statement in view of her contemporaries Sinclair Lewis, Mary McCarthy, Tess Slesinger, Clare Booth Luce, and, of course, Dorothy Parker, but Powell's words are defensible. Lewis satirized Middle America, sacred ground for Powell, whose Midwestern stories exhibit humor tempered by the sepia-toned landscape drawn from Powell's childhood memories. Lewis's influence is evident in Powell's Ohio novels, especially in *The Story of a Country Boy* (1934), her story of a reluctant Babbitt. In it, Powell invites a punning comparison to Lewis when an uppity provincial character inquires of another, "Don't you think Sinclair Lewis is a little unfair to us in the main?"[6] Powell spares her characters the sneering omniscient superiority that marks Lewis's fiction, and she spares her readers the occasional lofty didacticism. Powell simply presents the scene; her readers may sneer if they so desire.

Where McCarthy's works focus on upper-class society, Powell's focus on the middle class. The satiric gaze upon the middle class is crucial to Powell's motive because she wanted to hold up a mirror to her middle-class readers. It is too easy to laugh at other people, Powell maintained, and the real challenge lies in recognizing our own foibles. Powell admired McCarthy's potential, but she lamented McCarthy's insistence on jabbing her "good punch" at "studied academosis" rather than at the larger social scene, as Powell did (*Diaries,* 395). Slesinger's lone novel, *The Unpossessed,* a portrayal of New York City intellectuals, displays a spare satiric style. In a brief comparison of her own work-in-progress to the work of Slesinger, Powell wrote, "Cannot tell about this book . . . it seems barish but not as bare as Tess Slesinger's stuff" (*Diaries,* 103). Clare Booth Luce wrote extensively in reportage and fiction, dramas and screenplays, and she had the power of the press on her side. Powell had little respect for Luce, a fact made abundantly clear in her scathing satire of Luce in *A Time to Be Born* (1942). Luce shared with Powell an ability to laugh at her own sex, as evidenced in the play and movie *The Women,* but Luce was rather more of a feminist than Powell was.

Parker's work is simply different. Parker excelled in the close, ironic look at a single character in a short story; Powell needed the broad canvas of the novel to paint her larger satires. Parker herself denied that she was a satirist: "If I'd been called a satirist there'd be no living with me," she told an interviewer. "But by satirists I mean those boys in the other centuries. The people we call satirists now are those who make cracks at topical topics and consider themselves satirists—creatures like George S. Kaufman and such who don't even know what satire is."[7] As far as writing a novel, Parker said, "I wish to God I could do one, but I haven't got the nerve" (Capron, 117). Powell did have the nerve. So Powell may well be accurate in saying that she was the only writer doing her form of satire.

But even Powell's most devoted fans often misunderstood her form of satire. In his 1973 reintroduction of Dawn Powell, Matthew Josephson, a critic and a longtime friend of Powell's, wrote,

Readers who acquired a taste for her fictions were evidently able to thread their way through her lightly spun and seemingly frivolous or aimless plots and enjoy many pages illuminated by her quick intelligence and irrepressibly comic spirit. The good humorists dealing with the comedy of manners play a most useful part in helping us to see that which is real and that which is sham in our social behavior. Casually, in a tone of levity, her books told the plain truth about the changing mores of the urban American during a long span of time extending from the 1920s through the 1950s. Rereading her, one finds her novels have a considerable historical interest for us—the humor and the shrewd observations of her contemporaries have not dated, they are all there. (Josephson, 18)

That Josephson, a fan of Powell's works, characterized her novels in this way is a bit disturbing. He seems to have liked the novels *despite* their lightness, ignoring the role of Powell's "casual" language, which is the very essence of her work, capturing as it does the movement of natural language, which in turn creates the sense of reality and history that was central to Powell's mission for writing.

Edmund Wilson, a longtime friend of Powell's, noted and appreciated Powell's ability to capture the surfaces of everyday reality: "[Powell] has imagined and established for her readers her own Greenwich Village world, which is never journalistic copy and which possesses a memorable reality of which journalistic fiction is incapable."[8] Wilson does not attribute this quality to any particular aspect of Powell's writing. Powell's narratives display an enticing readability that belies the force of the satire underlying the "lightly spun and seemingly frivolous or aimless plots" Josephson described. Powell herself was astonished at the way her books were promoted as light reads or not promoted at all. She vented this frustration in a letter to the famed editor Max Perkins:

I do not like at all the approach called to my attention recently in *Publisher's Weekly,* which refers to [*A Time to Be Born*] as "slightly wacky" and uses other deprecatory phrases that would come better from an angry reviewer than from the publisher. There is nothing wacky in the book, nor is there anything to be gained by suggesting it is a jolly little book for the hammock. It is serious satire in the way Dickens and Thackeray built satire—the surface may be entertaining but the content is important comment on contemporary affairs. There are very few American writers today who are writing satire on the present age—or on any age for that matter—and if I did not think such work was important I would not engage in it. I am sure there must be readers for a novel whose mood follows the tempo of the news they are reading, even though, like the news, it does not always take the point of view they would prefer. That is why I think the book's contemporary scene value should be stressed, and if it is "slightly mad," it is merely reflecting the times.[9]

Powell conveyed a sense of reality in her New York novels by re-creating the language of a shaping reality. That is, one comes to know the place and the characters by what they say and do. The chaos of a bar, for instance, may be conveyed by a barrage of conversational snippets that may seem aimless and that confuse the reader. The reader thus enters the chaos of the scene and shares with the characters the sensory overload that often accompanies initial entry into a bar. Powell's methodology is drawn from Menippean satire, an eclectic form that reveals plot through a series of seemingly random patterns. Only when viewed from the distance of completion does the overall movement become apparent. Chapter 3 explores this movement in five New York novels.

Midway through her career, Powell startled critics and readers of her New York satires by publishing an autobiographical novel set in Ohio. Far from being a throwback to her earlier sentimental novels, however, *My Home Is Far Away* (1944) is strengthened by her forays into satire, and a closer look at the novel and its predecessors shows that it has a natural place in the development of Powell's body of work. Chapter 4 provides a close look at this novel and at autobiographical elements in Powell's other novels.

In a couple of novels, Powell stepped beyond the bounds of Ohio and New York. *Angels on Toast* (1940) is a rollicking journey with American businessmen under high pressure, who race across the country to make big deals in big cities and make small deals of love affairs and marriages. Sharp, witty, and biting, the novel is one of Powell's best. Arguably Powell's worst novel, *A Cage for Lovers* (1957), is set in Paris and upper-state New York. This novel, along with *A Man's Affair* (1956)—a gutted version of *Angels on Toast*—are instructive in their weaknesses because they help to point up the strengths of Powell's other writings. These "out of place" novels are discussed in chapter 5.

Powell's final New York novel, *The Golden Spur* (1962), shores up fragments of Powell's themes and characters as she takes a fond valedictory look at her beloved New York City. In chapter 6, this final novel is contrasted with her first representation of the city in *Whither* (1925) to highlight the sharpening of her gaze. In *The Golden Spur*, Powell draws her themes together in a final reckoning of her lifelong affair with the novel.

Throughout her life, Powell responded ambivalently to criticism of her work: On one hand, she wanted to be appreciated; on the other hand, she was committed to presenting her vision in whatever form best accommodated it. She recognized the difficulty in reconciling the two ends: "Usually after [writing] a novel I see a glaring fault growing on me that I must run from. I keep trying to make a conventional sympathetic character but they elude me because I find the reverence for the conventional almost criminal in life" (*Diaries*, 375). This ambivalence permeates her personal writings, as she struggled to reconcile her satiric vision with the critical strictures of the novel. When Powell lashed herself, she was struggling with the collision between form and audience expectations. Despite her self-criticism, Powell persisted in pursuing her vision, as her writing seemed to find its own form. She reminded herself: "You must remember that you don't know what people find in your work so there's no sense in trying to repeat it. You can only *do,* in the way that seems best to you" (*Diaries*, 305). The final chapter of this study considers Powell's legacy, the way in which she did what seemed best to her.

Throughout Powell's lifetime of writing, the oxygen of laughter sustained her. After a bleak childhood, she escaped to New York and lived a life punctuated by tragedy and only occasional triumphs. Late in life, she wrote: "I learned early that the best way to be alone with your own thoughts is to be funny. Laughter is a curtain behind which you can live your own life and think as you please—a sort of sound barrier" (*Diaries*, 409). This study begins with a look behind the curtain at Powell's life, in order to set the stage for an enriched reading of her novels.

Chapter One

"Permanent Visitor": Dawn Powell's Life

Powell's dreams of New York began forming when she was a young child being shuffled from relative to relative across central Ohio. At that time, her dream was an insistent yearning to escape Ohio. Like Marcia Willard in *My Home Is Far Away,* Powell was "the kind of person who was always glad going away instead of coming home."[1] Once Powell left Ohio after college, she did not return except for very brief visits. "There is really one city for everyone just as there is one major love," Powell wrote. "New York is my city because I have an investment I can always draw on—a bottomless investment . . . of building up an idea of New York—so no matter what happens here I have the rock of my dreams of it that nothing can destroy" (*Diaries,* 326). Assuming the role of "permanent visitor," Powell was never far from the fear of failure that might force her to return to her native land.

Growing Up in Ohio

Dawn Sherman Powell was born in Mount Gilead, Ohio, on 28 November 1896,[2] the second of three children—all girls—born to Roy King Powell and Hattie Sherman Powell. Powell's father was a traveling salesman who frequently left young Dawn, her mother, and her two sisters, Mabel and Phyllis, to fend for themselves. After their mother's death when Dawn was seven, the girls were shuffled off to various relatives, who became increasingly reluctant to take on the responsibility of three girls who received little financial support from their father.

When Dawn was 10, her father married Sabra Stearns and gathered up the girls to live on a farm with this stepmother, "who didn't know what to do with us," Powell wrote, "so she put us outdoors after breakfast and locked all the doors" (*Best,* 444). In interviews, Powell occasionally alluded to this brief, miserable time with her detested stepmother, but the few details about this time that are available are found in her diaries, as she gathered the memories that would be shaped into *My*

Home Is Far Away. Only here, from the distance of more than three decades, does Powell record the litany of "stepmother's rules for us":

> *Never* Come in the Parlor—*Never* Sit in the Living Room Chairs—and if unavoidable because a guest urges this violation of property, Do Not put Sweaty, Dirty, Leprous little hands on the nicely polished wood or allow Filthy Shoes to brush the nap of the rug, and above all Do Not Stand in Doorway, looking with anxious terrified eyes at Said Stepmother, thus revealing the horror under which you lived. The daily chilling misery of being unwanted, in the way. (*Diaries,* 186)

In addition to this apparent mental and emotional abuse, there were also episodes of physical abuse:

> The time one girl had tonsillitis and Step M. put rag dipped in coal oil around neck. In night anguish of fiery throat so great all three girls wake up but with one accord did not call Step M. to do anything as they were so resignedly sure this was her intention. In the morning she tore off the cloth, part of the skin coming with it, and she giggled at her mistake in not putting Vaseline on first. (*Diaries,* 187)

Powell endured this life for about a year, staying out of her stepmother's way by slipping away from the house to write in old ledgers she had found. One day Powell looked under the front porch for the hidden ledgers and could not find them. " 'No use looking,' our stepmother called out from the other side of the locked screen door. 'I burned all that trash you were writing' " (*Best,* 444). After this episode, Powell ran away—taking with her all of the money (90 cents) that she had earned picking berries—to Shelby, her mother's hometown.[3] There, she was welcomed into the home of Orpha May Sherman Steinbrueck, the older sister of Powell's mother and a woman before whom Powell's stepmother "cringed" (*Diaries,* 186).

"Auntie May" was a sort of ur-mother for young relatives. Over a few decades, she raised a dozen or so Sherman cousins in her home by the Big Four railroad track in Shelby, where she had moved after her divorce from Otto Steinbrueck. Along with her daughter Gretchen, Orpha May ran a boardinghouse with a host of permanent and transient residents. "Her home was a haven for children and other family members in need of help, as well as lucky hoboes riding the rails of the hundreds of freight trains passing through Shelby," wrote John F. Sherman, Powell's favorite cousin, who moved in with Aunt May some 15 years after she took in

Powell and her sisters.[4] The three girls spent their adolescent years with Aunt May, and long after Powell left Ohio, Aunt May remained a strong force in her life. On a visit in 1933, Powell wrote that "It so chanced that the conditions at Auntie May's were so nearly like those I left— with . . . Auntie May and I content as always to talk about all things all day, never bored with each other" (*Diaries*, 72). Aunt May became the model for the wise and gentle Aunt Jule in *She Walks in Beauty* and for the heroic figure of Aunt Lois in *My Home Is Far Away*.

The ghosts of Powell's erratic childhood make several bleak appearances in Powell's novels. A ragged troupe of outcast children appears in *The Bride's House*. The most clearly drawn portrait of the gray days of her childhood is found in *My Home is Far Away*. Powell's counterpart in this novel is Marcia, a seemingly stoic child with "intense sensations" who is chastised for not crying at her mother's funeral. In an oddly distant yet intimate view, Marcia muses on her feelings:

> The little girl named Marcia could be pinched or bruised without feeling pain, because she was filled with the numbing fragrance of death, an immense thing by itself, like a train whistle blowing far off, or an echo in the woods. There were no people in it, not even Mama, here or gone. But nobody knew this. Nobody knew it but Marcia's secret self, and it filled her to the brim with such a tangle of desperate wonder there was room for nothing else. (*Home*, 105)

Throughout her life, Powell commanded a calm, removed visage, at odds with the strife of her life and inner turmoil revealed throughout her diaries. This apparent stoicism seems to have developed out of her fragmented youth. Powell wrote:

> I do not remember crying much as a child except as a private secret luxury of overwhelming *weltschmerz*. I was braced against hurts and pains but wallowed in black philosophic bogs of tears alone, especially in my teens. I do recall my surprise at tears popping out (as if I was an ordinary child, I thought—rather proud) when I opened my first jack-in-the-box on a Christmas tree and I cried for shame, really, that I had expected something nice and here was a joke. (*Diaries*, 423–24)

The move to Aunt May's provided the first steps to Powell's eventual escape from the hurts and pains inflicted by Sabra Stearns Powell. She would continue to move farther from home.

In 1914 Powell won a scholarship to Lake Erie College in Painesville, Ohio. From the retrospect of 44 years, Powell recalled,

> I arrived at Lake Erie College in September of 1914 with a delirious sensation of having been shot from a cannon into a strange, wonderful planet. All summer long I had been working for this great day. In the little factory town where I had lived I saved every cent, working on the newspaper by day, ushering in a movie house by night. . . . The world of girls seemed mysterious and infinitely fascinating after my town full of factory-men. It is a rich, illuminating experience to discover the thousand different ways girls can be girls, and still be nothing like yourself.[5]

Even with "every cent" saved from working, Powell had to work her way through college, and after graduation she still owed $800. But the debt was worth it to Powell because of the spirit and worldview that it gave her:

> There were girls who were slowly becoming conscious that they were not just girls, but part of a great world outside, a world of war and noble deeds waiting to be done. Five of us, linked by a common passion to break through to that outside world, marched down to the new Dean's chambers one night imploring an answer to our great question, as burning as it was vague. "Tell us what we can do," we begged her. "Things are happening everywhere and we can't just sit in classrooms. Tell us what to do." The tiny little woman in her blue wool dressing-gown looked at us gravely and then opened her door wider. "Supposing you come in and tell me what *you* think," she said. Whatever was said—we all talked at once—we tiptoed back to our rooms that night with the breathless conviction that we had received a revelation. I cannot remember what Miss Brownfield could have said to us, but I still remember the glorious sense of power she gave us. We were free. All roads were open to us. There was nothing we could not do and we would know the right moment when it came. Such were the peaks from which we sought to soar.[6]

The prosaic peaks from which Powell soared at Lake Erie included being editor of the college magazine and of an underground newspaper. Her roommate, Eleanor Farnham, said in an oral history of the college, "I was sorry for any Lake Erie students who were not there at the time of Dawn Powell. Dawn turned everything upside down . . . [She] stimulated me to question, which is part of going to school."[7] Powell began to "break through to that outside world" after graduating from Lake Erie College in 1918, when she promptly moved to New York City.

New York City: The Early Years

Upon arriving in New York City, Powell embarked on a variety of jobs unrelated to writing. One of her first jobs was a stint as a traveling booster for the suffragette movement. Her "zeal in this direction was excited . . . by the knowledge that I was to draw Big moneys," she wrote to her college friend Charlotte Johnson. "For a dollar I'd go on an anti-suffrage beat."[8] She joined in the war effort by enlisting in the Navy, a job that suited her meager income, she wrote to Johnson, as "the uniform solves the clothes problem to a great extent."[9] When peace broke out, Powell whirled through the next couple of years with various part-time jobs, including work at the Red Cross and in the public relations office at the Interchurch World Movement. For three days in 1919, she even did some acting—as an extra in "Footlights and Shadows."[10] Throughout this time, she reserved her evenings for writing.

In these years, Powell published several short stories and essays in such magazines as *American Agriculture* and *Southern Ruralist*. At this time—and later in her life—she was encouraged by the fact that she could raise money in this way with little effort on her own part. Of the story "Impressions of a First Voter," published in 1919 in the New York *Sun,* Powell wrote, "As it only took me fifteen minutes to write the thing—it was just what had happened so all I needed to do was exaggerate it a little—I think it was easy money and I intend to do a lot of it."[11] In these early writings, she frequently published under the gender-neutral name D. Sherman Powell.

Powell was committed to making a living in New York, but she was ambivalent about her lifestyle. In 1918 she wrote to Johnson: "I've been 'doing the Village' quite consistently lately and feel that sooner or later I'll be among 'em."[12] Just a month later, she qualified this: "I don't care for living quarters in the Village—Bohemian they may be but they're draughty and dirty and no bathrooms mostly. . . . Bohemian I be but I prefer to boheme in normal surroundings because bohemian atmosphere makes me feel normal."[13] For reinforcement of normalcy, Powell occasionally visited her Ohio home and reported with similar ambivalence:

> Just back from 13 days home. Do you know I learned more in those 13 days? I feel all tender and lovely towards all my relations and I love all my friends bitterly and would die for any of 'em providing it were painless and free. . . . But glad as I was to see everyone, I had not the slightest desire to be always among 'em. No. My happiness was highlighted by the consciousness of being able to fly out into the World again at once.[14]

Thus Powell lived her first few years in the city, working odd jobs, writing small pieces, and coming to know this city that would play such a large role in her writing.

"Women can't get down to their real work till the man thing is settled—not for material urge or status, just possession," Powell once told Lake Erie College graduates (*Diaries,* 463). It was at this point in her life that Powell settled her own "man question." Much of her writing in 1920 was devoted to "The Book of Joe," a very personal collection of writing about Joseph Roebuck Gousha, a music critic from Pittsburgh. Powell and Gousha married on 20 November 1920, at the Little Church Around the Corner in New York City. Charles Norman, a poet, wrote of his meeting Powell in a bookshop: "She was pretty, slender, and shy; the tragedy that was to oppress her life and her husband's was still in the future—the near future—and the wit for which she was to become famous was not yet in evidence. Her husband was the wit."[15] But, according to Norman, Gousha claimed, "I married a girl with more talent than I have, and I think she should have the chance to develop it" (Norman, 31). Powell and Gousha were each convinced that the other possessed superior talent. This mutual admiration both bonded and distanced them. Eventually, it was Powell who rose higher.

The tragedy began just a year after the wedding, when Powell gave birth to their son, Joseph Roebuck Gousha Jr. After the birth, Powell wrote to her sisters: "I didn't know till two days afterward that they didn't think the baby was going to live. I had a terrible time and it was just as hard on the baby. He is awfully husky but being born was a tough business for him and just before he came out his heart went bad. . . . Poor little lamb had a clot on his brain that caused a sort of convulsive paralysis."[16] Even in the midst of this moving account, the diminutive Powell retained a sense of humor as she added: "He is unusually tall. Got that from me."

Jojo, as they called him, added a greater dimension to Powell's ambivalence. Her great joy and her great sorrow, Jojo was required to spend most of his life in institutions. Powell was alternately awed by Jojo's moments of lucidity and appalled at his lapses into incoherence and, occasionally, violence. The label of the time for Jojo was "retarded," but later diagnoses indicated autism, possibly complicated by schizophrenia, and cerebral palsy. Powell's diaries and letters are threaded with plans to improve Jojo's life—usually suggesting a move to the country. Powell tended this dream for decades, but it never came to fruition. Powell was born to write, but she was compelled to do her duty because of Jojo's need for costly supervised care. She never complained of the financial and emotional cost of Jojo's care, and many friends didn't even meet Jojo until he was an adult. She told a few close friends, "Do you know whom I love best in this world?—Jo-Jo. He is really very intelligent and just *different* from other people" (Josephson, 49). The incredible stress of Jojo's difference left its mark in her diaries and letters, as she struggled to understand what doctors themselves did not understand. At one point, a doctor recommended a lobotomy as the only way of dealing with Jojo, and Powell nearly agreed to it. But, as she wrote to her sister, "my friend Dos Passos in Baltimore (with close associates at Johns Hopkins) came rushing up and said I must not permit it, that the results were still unsatisfactory, and not to let them make a guinea pig of Jojo. Result was my undying gratitude to Dos, for a psychoanalyst appeared at that time who did more than anyone for Jojo."[17] When Jojo appeared in Powell's nighttime dreams, they lived in a country house (*Diaries,* 358) and Jojo was always four (*Diaries,* 313), the age of innocence before Powell admitted that her son was significantly and seriously different from other children.

This revelation came during the summer of 1925, when Powell and her son stayed with relatives in Ohio after an apparent rift between Powell and Gousha, caused in part by Jojo's erratic behavior. Powell wrote to Gousha: "Unlike their children, [Jojo] has to be watched every second. The few minutes yesterday when I wasn't watching he had almost kicked a second-story screen out and was sitting on the sill ready to fall out in another second. And he vaulted the porch railing. . . . He is—as you have suspected before—totally unmanageable."[18] This trial separation ended earlier than planned, again because of Jojo's behavior, but also because, as Powell avowed to her husband, "We mustn't tear ourselves apart this way, must we, dear? I'm glad in a way that we did this once so that [we] could see what a fizzle that theory is."[19] The few diary entries for 1925 reveal that this was a turning point for the family: "Joe and I decide to readjust our lives," Powell wrote on 19 October (*Diaries,* 6), and on 21 October, she simply noted, "All day with my child. . . ." (*Diaries,* 6). By 1930, Jojo was under full-time supervised care at an institution. Powell, like most writers, frequently mined her relationships for character bases, but no recognizable semblance of Jojo makes an appearance in her novels.

During these early years, Powell began to forge lifelong friendships, most notably with John Dos Passos, whom she met in 1926, and with John Howard Lawson, a playwright with whom Powell had a passionate

relationship that teetered between love and hate, appreciation and dis-
gust. She wrote in 1932, "It seems to me I could be happy just with Dos
and Jack as friends—the two people to be lost on a desert island with"
(*Diaries,* 58). But, she wrote, "I vary in hating and despising Jack (for
his mental and emotional cowardice in his work and in his life) to admir-
ing him beyond reason (for his occasional flashes of heroic courage or
strength)" (*Diaries,* 64). Powell also dined with Theodore Dreiser, drank
with E. E. Cummings, and cowrote jokes with Dwight Fiske, another
longtime friend. "Those first years in New York I was perfectly happy,"
Powell wrote, "including Jojo's first two years, in spite of his sickness. I
should know now that happiness for me consists of three things—
1) having people I like like me, 2) being in the place I want to be (New
York, usually), 3) being able to write what I want. Ability to live luxuri-
ously, pay bills, have material things, really doesn't come into this so it's
illogical for me to sacrifice my three necessities" (*Diaries,* 24–25).

The Washington Square Table

Powell lived at various addresses in Greenwich Village, which in the
1920s, '30s, and '40s was a center for literary and artistic activity.
"[The] Village is my creative oxygen," she wrote (*Diaries,* 391). The
liveliness of the Village informed Powell's writing, as she noted: "One
importance of living in the Village for a writer is that it keeps him more
fluid generally—more *au courant* with the life around him. For a historical novelist it might not be good—constant struggle between contemporary life and a set dead pattern" (*Diaries,* 383). Powell felt oppressed
by domestic duties, and she hated going to other people's houses where,
she said, "you have to eat or drink what they have, and if the company is
dull you are *trapped* for the evening" (Josephson, 23). So she frequently
went out in the evenings, and her primary social venue was the Washington Square Table that convened at the Brevoort and at the Hotel
Lafayette, an old-fashioned hotel near Washington Square. "For years,"
Powell said, "I lived so close to the Lafayette that I could look down
from my apartment window and see my own checks bouncing there"
(Josephson, 23). As contrasted with the Algonquin Round Table,
Josephson says, "[Powell's] own show was more informal, spontaneous
and private; it was for fun and not for publicity" (Josephson, 20). In the
evenings, Josephson writes, Powell would hold forth at the Lafayette:

From her corner table [Powell] could keep in view the three entrances to that spacious room, and she used to rise to greet acquaintances as they arrived or sat down at other tables, sometimes bringing them over to join her own group as if she were the hostess there. What went on about her within the walls of this café was, after all, the spectacle of life; these were men and women in their hours of leisure engaged in the pursuit of happiness in "love and art," as Edmund Wilson said; and that was what mainly occupied Dawn Powell. (Josephson, 24)

Those who contributed to "the spectacle of life" included literary friends—John Dos Passos and Edmund Wilson—and artists—Niles Spencer, Stuart Davis, and Reginald Marsh. "If you knew Dawn Powell, you didn't need to know anyone else," Jacqueline Miller Rice said. "People came to her."[20] The group could often be found loitering until the wee hours. They were so much a fixture through the 1930s that they merited a mention in *The WPA Guide to New York City:* "The Hotel Lafayette, founded in 1883, at the southeast corner of Ninth Street, is known for its French cuisine, while its café, like that of the Brevoort, is a meeting place of intellectuals, American and foreign."[21] Powell mourned the passing of the Lafayette, which was razed in 1953, in *The Wicked Pavilion,* which closes with these words: "The Café Julien [aka Lafayette Hotel] was gone and a reign was over. Those who had been bound by it fell apart like straws when the baling cord is cut and remembered each other's name and face as part of a dream that would never come back."[22] Powell hearkens to her Midwestern past with the strawbale, as she expresses her own presence in this urban upheaval.

Powell moved easily among social circles. She was equally good (and bad) friends with both men and women, and her appearance made her approachable: "She was small and somewhat plump, with black hair and brown eyes set off by skin of unusual pallor, and had finely shaped hands. . . . Her expression was at once puckish and alert, her eyes never stopped moving, dancing" (Josephson, 21). In addition to being in the middle of bohemians and, later, beatniks in Greenwich Village, her plays were produced by the Group Theatre, a notably leftist group; she also corresponded with mainstream American authors, including Ernest Hemingway. On occasion, she traveled uptown to dine with Dorothy Parker. "Friends are like food," Powell wrote, "one's palate and capacity and preference changes with education, travel, ulcers, and better opportunities for choosing" (*Diaries,* 269).

Those "foods" that Powell retained a taste for, with just occasional indigestion, included Edmund Wilson. Wilson's daughter, Rosalind Baker Wilson, wrote that "[Dawn Powell] was the first person my father and Dos called up when they went to New York, supplanting even girl-friends" (R. B. Wilson, 199). Their friendship lasted 35 years, riding the ups and downs that accompany such a long relationship. After an outing with Wilson in 1943, Powell wrote, "Curious effect a day with Bunny Wilson had on me—balanced me so that I remembered again the nat-ural pleasures of the mind—reading, thinking and working, all of which are canceled by drinking" (*Diaries,* 215). Another time she wrote: "Bunny Wilson is funny. He appears to ask questions but pays no atten-tion to answers, though later they emerge. Now that his mind has enlarged into such a vast organization, it's as if conversation has to wait in the lobby till the message has been routed through the proper depart-ment. Sometimes it has to come back Monday" (*Diaries,* 142). Powell's friendship with Wilson also satisfied her hunger for home without her actually having to return home, as she frequently spent weekends at Tal-cottville, Wilson's house in upstate New York. Rosalind Baker Wilson wrote that "[Dawn Powell] was the only one of my father's friends who ever came to Talcottville for more than a few nights who really enjoyed it and who understood the pleasure of sitting on the front porch, watch-ing the hamlet go by, and of driving around. . . . To Dawn, Talcottville was just a continuation of her Ohio childhood" (R. B. Wilson, 198–99). As the two old friends strolled into the 1960s, Wilson told Dawn that his wife had noted that Dawn was one of his only "real friends. She said, 'The reason for that is that there's never been anything between us.' I agreed."[23] When Powell died, Wilson wrote in his diary: "I have felt that some part of my own life was gone" (E. Wilson 1993, 490).

Powell's friendship with Dos Passos was sustained through frequent correspondence and occasional meetings, frequently at other people's houses. Dos Passos wrote that "It was at Esther's [Andrews] I first met Dawn Powell, one of the wittiest and most dashingly courageous women I ever knew."[24] Dos Passos allied Powell with the "Greenwich Village exiles," as he dubbed those people who lived their lives on the fringes, quietly producing their art with no desire for celebrity. Dos Pas-sos, who envied this quiet performance, as he was not able to escape the celebrity that was thrust upon him, was a frequent guest at Powell's home. On a night when Powell had Dos Passos and Coby Gilman to dinner, Dos Passos brought "a present to me of whiskey, me having a Storm-tossed for him, and ending by my drinking the Storm-tossed, which I wanted really, and his enveloping the whiskey, shyly admitting, 'When people bring a present there's usually a pretty good reason for it. I personally feel the need of a little Scotch' " (*Diaries*, 116).

Powell and Dos Passos shared an interest in people, that is, all people, not just those whose lives intersected with their own. Of particular interest was the common man; as Dos Passos wrote, "What right did we have to rate ourselves higher than successful businessmen or the corner grocer or the whitewings who swept the streets for that matter? It wasn't that I accepted their standards: it was that I felt that to challenge a man's notions you had to meet him on his own ground" (Dos Passos, 153). This attitude is echoed in Powell's novels, as she explored the lives of ordinary people. Powell was roundly criticized for not picking on people her own size. Of *The Locusts Have No King*, critic Diana Trilling wrote that the flaw of the novel

> lies . . . in the discrepancy between the power of mind revealed on virtually every page of her novel and the insignificance of the human beings upon whom she directs her excellent intelligence. . . . We are always, after all, only as big as the things we laugh at, and if we choose to mock some poor pub crawler or some silly little Southern tart trying to make her way in the big city, who are we to say that life owes us any better possibility for ourselves?[25]

Exactly, Powell would say.

Powell consistently voted a straight-party Republican ticket—a legacy of her Ohio upbringing. She was, however, essentially apolitical, more concerned with how people interact than with what they wear on their sleeves. Dos Passos became known as a radical in part because of publicity about his appearances in marches and rallies. Powell maintained that Dos Passos was not a radical and later tried to set the record straight, but she soon saw

> [the] hopelessness of explaining a person to someone who knows the Legend. Young Mr. L. who is doing thesis on Dos: Why He Turned Conservative. He always was. I tried to explain that Communist rallies were always advertising him when he wasn't even present, that he never led meetings, had a horror of organizations, etc. At end of interview young man says—"Then it was *after* Sacco-Vanzetti that he gave up leading Communist rallies?" (*Diaries*, 359)

Dos Passos evoked in Powell an openness and warmth that was not always evident in her public, or even private, discourse. Her letters to

him are honest, fresh, intellectual, witty. Her admiration for Dos Passos
shines in this brief passage: "Dos' *1919* is knocking people cold. He is
no longer a promising writer but as arrived as he can ever be—like
Lewis or Dreiser—and is scarcely older than I am" (*Diaries*, 45). The last
note betrays not envy, but rather a wistful awe of this great writer, with
whom she happens to be friends. When Dos Passos lost an eye in a
dreadful car accident that left his wife, Katy, dead, Powell wrote to him:

> I am thinking about you all the time and I find two things to be glad
> about. One, that you are a writer so that agony is of service to you, cruel
> as our work is—and another, that you have physical pain to dull the
> unbearable other kind. I am glad you aren't rich so you can concentrate
> on some hardiron thing like making money because physical pain and
> the need of money have often saved me from going crazy.[26]

Their friendship was based on pure affection and admiration for each
other. Powell wrote that Dos Passos was "one of the gentlest, sweetest,
finest characters the world has known" (*Diaries*, 69).

One common denominator for Powell and Dos Passos was a love of
Sara and Gerald Murphy. The Murphys had made it their business to
provide a respite for artistic luminaries, among them Dos Passos and
Powell. Heirs to the Mark Cross leather goods company, the Murphys
entertained Picasso and E. E. Cummings in southern France and played
croquet with Scott and Zelda Fitzgerald at the Hamptons. Gerald was,
in part, the model for Dick Diver in Fitzgerald's *Tender Is the Night*,
which was dedicated to the Murphys. Dos Passos described the Fitzger-
alds' adoration of the Murphys this way:

> The golden couple that he and Zelda dreamed of becoming actually
> existed. The Murphys were rich. They were goodlooking. They dressed
> brilliantly. They were canny about the arts. They had a knack of enter-
> taining. They had lovely children. They had reached the highest rung on
> mankind's ladder. Fortunatas incarnate. (Dos Passos, 170)

Powell described the Murphys as "superior, intelligent, superficially liberal, gay, resourceful people, but only when alone or with old friends of
known gaiety. They would never *impose* gaiety" (*Diaries*, 289). Similarly,
Dos Passos wrote of time spent at one of the Murphys' homes: "It was a
marvelous life. Fond as I was of Sara and of Gerald's conversation I
could stand it for about four days. It was like trying to live in heaven. I
had to get back down to earth" (Dos Passos, 168). Like Dos Passos,

Powell preferred to spend time with the Murphys when there were no other guests. During these weekends, Powell was often able to renew her energy for writing. On one weekend, she returned with the basis for her novel *The Wicked Pavilion* and wrote, "If this goes it will be due to Murphy weekend—early bed in strange, river atmosphere and without the dull callers" (*Diaries*, 289). One of those dull callers once wrote home that "We had a marvelous time in Haiti, especially after Dawn Powell got there. Dawn was darling—and much funnier always than Dorothy Parker ever imagined being."[27]

The Murphys' home was one of the few places that Powell and Parker converged. "Those who had met both 'Dottie' and Dawn sometimes expressed the wish that the two might hold a bout together, which they, however, carefully avoided," Josephson noted (Josephson, 20). The Murphys' home was not a place for bouts, and the eclectic nature of the Murphys' social circle allowed them to entertain Parker and Powell at the same dinner table. Powell records at least three such meetings in her diaries. An entry on 22 May 1942 simply notes "Lunch at 68, cocktails at Dos', blackout night (Murphy's) with Alan Campbell and Dorothy Parker" (*Diaries*, 200). In December of that year, Powell provided a glimpse of the banter that ensued when the two women met: "Dinner at Gerald Murphy's with Dorothy Parker. I told them about [John] Latouche's letter describing the lepers of the Congo and Parker thought it might be a good idea if Touche came back with an All-Leper revue called 'No Faces.' . . . She was delighted with this thought and pursued it to having Mark Cross put out a special Leper Leather bag to be opened with no fingers" (*Diaries*, 208). Powell wrote that Parker was the kind of "famous writer who is touted to fame by journalists, whose actual work is of no importance but rides on personal notoriety" (*Diaries*, 178). But, as she noted, a bad wizard doesn't necessarily make a bad person: "I used to have some good times with Dorothy Parker who gets too much credit for witty bitchery and not enough for completely reckless philanthropy—saving many people, really without a thought."[28]

Powell and Parker initially converged in the 1920s, perhaps without realizing it. It was on a rare trip to New York City in 1926 that Ernest Hemingway met both Powell and Parker for the first time, though in different places. During this extensive visit, in which he "met hells own amount of people,"[29] Hemingway rapped on Powell's window late one night to ask her to join him and some friends in drinking. She did. Powell and Hemingway enjoyed a long, and long-distance, friendship. One of Hemingway's biographers claims that "their long-term friendship may have been assured by the fact that they saw each other infrequently."[30] Powell admired Hemingway's exuberance but was puzzled by his refusal to write about America because, he said, "American life was dull. Nothing important ever happened" (Baker, 268). In her diaries, lamenting the lack of fellow writers dedicated to capturing contemporary manners, Powell wrote, "We have Hemingway, who writes of a fictional movie hero in Spain with the language neither Spanish nor English" (*Diaries,* 188). She was not terribly fond of his writing: "I tried once again to read *Farewell to Arms* and it seems as clumsily written as ever to me—wooden, like Walter Scott, difficult reading, pidgin English" (*Diaries,* 332).

After attending the Writers' Congress in 1937, Powell wrote to Dos Passos that Hemingway's speech was good, "If that's what you like and his sum total was that war was pretty nice and a lot better than sitting around a hot hall and writers ought to all go to war and get killed and if they didn't they were a big sissy."[31] Powell occasionally visited Hemingway at his Key West home and, in the early 1940s while the Hemingways were off covering the war, Powell had use of Hemingway's home in Cuba. When he was out of the country, Hemingway consistently asked his editor to provide him with Powell's current novels. Powell noted in her diary in 1944: "Letter from Hemingway very cheering. Said I was his favorite living writer" (*Diaries,* 226). Despite disagreeing with his philosophy of writing, Powell was fond of Hemingway, saying that he "spread excitement and glamour wherever he appeared" (*Diaries,* 471). Accordingly, as a chronicler of her times, Powell included Hemingway in her fiction in the guise of Andrew Callingham, a character who strides through several of her novels and is a central figure in absentia in *Turn, Magic Wheel.* Twenty years later—four years after Hemingway's death— she wrote: "[Morris] Philipson says I should do Hemingway memoir for a magazine but I feel presumptuous. This need not be really for I'm sure he would rather I write what little I know of him than his relatives" (*Diaries,* 470). Her loyalty to her friends was paramount.

The Domestic Carnage

"Domesticity crowds me," Powell wrote (*Diaries,* 51). Like many women, she was weighed down with the responsibility not only of producing work but also of caring for the house and her child. She lightened some of this burden by employing a housekeeper. Furthermore, after Jojo was moved to an institution, he required only intermittent hands-on care. Gousha made a sizable salary as an advertising executive, but he did not contribute regularly to Jojo's care or to domestic needs. Powell recorded her frustration with the demand on her sporadic income: "Tired to death but work out of sheer nervous desperation, weight of responsibility, necessity for making plans about Jojo this fall, making money for these plans. I can't see or think of anything else; Joe's concern over me, to the neglect of his child, makes me doubly responsible" (*Diaries*, 31). In one exasperated entry, she wrote:

> The domestic carnage of my life—fatigue and wearing down of hopes when no audience is around, the isolated life I am obliged to live, partly financial but also social shyness and the awkwardness of asking guests when Joe hates everyone and either gets plastered or makes a production of simple, friendly calls. Now I have manuscript back for revision and I realize I could revise forever but my frayed brain isn't doing what is needed for I've forced it and played it long after the original inspiration and joy had been beaten to death by boredom and isolated domesticity— Louise[32] and Joe, Joe and Louise, and my own boring self. (*Diaries*, 332)

Though Powell was devoted to Gousha, she frequently was frustrated by his heavy drinking and financial recklessness. Throughout their married life, Gousha and Powell were plagued by financial problems, due in part to Jojo's care and, perhaps in larger measure, to the inability of either to negotiate a budget. When given a large sum of money, Powell frequently disbursed it right away, much of it going to overdue bills and no small part of it going to others as loans and presents. The result was that Powell was nearly always broke. In 1940 she lamented this crumbling of the American dream:

> The one thing my own childhood taught me was that a child should be freed from the cloud of debts and indifference of parents. The sad end is that my own child is worse off than I ever was—with me hand-tied, and Joe ever romantic and elocutionary about ideals and not about reality. For years I have faced it that I could pay for myself and Jojo's care modestly and without debt, but with Joe's big salary nothing is ever paid but extravagances. What a waste of blood and spirit this has cost one little boy, innocent and undemanding! (*Diaries*, 179)

Still, it seems that her state would have been worse if she had given over the financial care of the household to Gousha. As she advised her sister:

Keep everything you have in your name and anything else you find, because nobody will be sorry for you when you whimper that your good mate has given it all to somebody else out of the goodness of his heart or liver. (Least of all will the mate be sorry. He will only be mad at you for not having hid some for HIS protection.)

After a lifetime of juggling this sort of thing my own mate finally INSISTS that I hang on to whatever comes in and shouts DON'T put anything in my account, keep everything in yours and for Godsake don't tell me about it. That's all that has ever saved us.[33]

Powell and Gousha were occasionally saved by the generosity of Powell's longtime friend Margaret De Silver.[34] Powell and De Silver were linked by the sad fact that they both had a child in an institution, where the two met. Born to a wealthy family and later married to a successful lawyer, De Silver had the means and desire to support liberal causes, including artists and writers. It was primarily through De Silver's largesse that Powell was able to travel to Paris in 1950—a vacation also marred by lack of money. Powell noted that "You can live very cheaply in Paris but it's no pleasure" (*Diaries*, 296). Most of her letters to Gousha during her Paris stay were punctuated by requests for money; it was not until the last week that she secured money for her return to America.

Not among the least of their problems was a dependence on alcohol. Both Joe and Dawn drank heavily, a habit that necessarily affected both their income and their ability to get along under the influence of a hangover. Powell had occasional dry spells, but Joe's drinking did not seem to abate until his final illness. Norman noted this habit:

[Dawn] drank gin, and it is extraordinary that she should have produced so much, and of such high quality, considering the number of tuns of gin she must have consumed in the years that I knew her. Like Joe's, her figure, in time, rounded out, while her tongue got sharper. But, unlike most literary lushes, she never attacked her friends. I see her two images in my mind—the warm, eager, pretty, and ambitious young woman from Ohio, and what she became. (Norman, 51–52)

The Goushas' financial woes came to a head in 1958, when they were literally put out on the street for nonpayment of rent on their Greenwich Village apartment.[35] Powell was dismayed at the immediate, large costs of storing her books and cat while she and Gousha sought temporary living quarters; not having a home was more expensive than having a home.

Throughout their marriage, Gousha and Powell had extramarital affairs. For decades, Powell was rumored to be lovers with Coburn Gilman, a professional barfly.[36] "I no longer remember when I first learned that Dawn had a lover," wrote Charles Norman.

> As they were so much together, for so many years, there must be many people who never knew that she had a husband. Her lover looked all his life like a combination country squire and man-about-town. He was the editor of a travel magazine, and it may be that it was under his tutelage that Dawn became such a steady drinker, since the only traveling he ever indulged in was a pub crawl. His name was Coburn Gilman. They grew stout together. (Norman, 53–54)

Powell's diaries suggest that Gilman was less of a lover and more of a source of amusement. Norman wrote that he "went into the Cedar Tavern—the original one, on University Place near 9th Street—and saw Joe Gousha in a booth. He was drinking a martini and reading the *World-Telegram* with a scowl. In another booth sat Dawn and Coby Gilman, glowing with gin and laughter" (Norman, 55). Powell remained married to Gousha, despite the difficulty of living with him, in large measure because of the faith that he had in her: "What a woman wants in a settled marriage is a kind of support that enables her to be herself and to get the most out of herself—sort of support Joe has in large part given me, assurance of my value" (*Diaries,* 416). After his death in 1962, she wrote:

> Someone asked me about the long marriage to Joe—42 years—and I reflected that he was the only person in the world I found it always a kick to run into on the street.
> As for his death, this is a curious thing to say but after 42 years of life together—much of it precarious and crushing—we have been through worse disasters together, and I'm sure Joe would feel the same way about me. (*Diaries,* 436)

Gousha died on 14 February 1962, an irony not lost on Powell, who noted on the third anniversary of his death: "Typical of that loving golden Leo lad to die on Valentine's Day" (*Diaries,* 468). For the next three and a half years, until her own death, Powell continued to mark critical sentimental anniversaries, including Joe's birthday and the anniversary of their first date; she bought roses to celebrate.

Creative Labor: Powell's Process and Product

"Every day I don't work means questioning the quality of what I have already done," Powell wrote (*Diaries*, 198). She worked constantly, not only on producing her 15 novels but also dramas—both originals and repairs of others' works—and the short stories, reviews, and articles that paid the bills. She wrote steadily in her diaries and corresponded frequently with family and friends. Occasionally, she made some quick, painful money in Hollywood, producing or rewriting scripts. Two of her own novels were adapted for the screen. For a brief time, she presented song analyses on a radio show.[37] Throughout all of this, she worked hard as a wife and mother. Powell's diaries are threaded with notes of frustration as she struggled to find the time to devote concentrated labor to her first love, the novel.

> One reason women (and some men) writers are kept back is that they spend their brains and heart on writing but their fighting ability they must use for others—to protect, advance, heal, feed, support. Whereas the complete egoist not only writes but fights every minute for his writing and his own professional advancement, losing no tears or blood on family or friends or even difficult lover. (*Diaries*, 373)

Powell was not a "complete egoist," admitting midway through her career that perhaps her greatest mistake "was the fear of vanity. I should have been more vain and shouted my merits to the skies. I have been outsmarted by my own peasant shrewdness and am not sure there is any chance of change" (*Diaries*, 276). It is extraordinary that Powell produced a novel every two years considering not only the constant juggle between home and work but also the tremendous volume of other work that she produced.

Throughout her life, Powell was compelled to produce short pieces to pay immediate bills. She wrote hundreds of reviews, scores of short stories, and several dramas, solo and in collaboration with others. The dramas were the least productive in terms of money and time, but they were close to Powell's heart. She poured her sweat into the theater for intense periods, then drew herself back, realizing that it was keeping her from writing novels. Powell strove to gather together the various fragments of her work life:

> I must get down to a more definite working plan. It would be excusable—my one novel and nothing else a year—if I had a fine time in all

my wasted time, or if I didn't have many ideas. But I have so many complete ideas ahead and so many unfinished plays, stories, etc., that my
confusion grows greater and greater every time I'm in the mood to work.
I ought to clear up a few of these things and my mind would be a little
better off. (*Diaries,* 49)

Although Powell finished many of these money making tasks fairly
quickly, they chiseled away at her time and concentration. Powell never
reached a point where she was not required to juggle several tasks at
once. A 1958 entry notes: "Jojo pale, gaunt, unsmiling, old—in M-5.
Must work to get him out. Hope to spend this week anti-domestically.
Do the dead life story, then the writing article. Collect stories and edit
for contract. Do piece on 'Live on $500 a Year' " (*Diaries,* 379). The
entry also underscores the continual concern for Jojo's welfare. When
Jojo was at home, he wholly absorbed Powell's time. Depending on
Powell's own mood and intensity, his presence had varied effects. At one
point, she wrote: "Definitely upsetting to have Jojo in house with his
legitimate demands for program, attention, etc. Novel continually van-
ishes in scattered thoughts" (*Diaries,* 105). At another time, Powell perceives the same disruption positively: "Good thing about intensiveness
of Jojo visit is that no conscious thought of novel is possible. Result—
subconscious suddenly has decided to return to [novel-in-progress]"
(*Diaries,* 293). Through all of the distractions, Powell continued to
work. It is clear from Powell's diaries that her novels were her priority,
but because these other works sustained Powell throughout her life, this
huge quantity of written material must be taken into account in assess-
ing her legacy.

Powell's first published works were short pieces. She wrote short stories in college, and when she first arrived in New York City, the writing
that she did was short pieces for newspapers. Very early in Powell's
career, her writing time was challenged by the effects of the city itself
and by the pull of procrastination. Her occasional visits to Ohio also dis-
tracted her from her work. She wrote to a college friend in 1919:

I came back [from Ohio] all charged up with new ideas, ambition and
could have written I'm sure if I'd stayed there another week. Get back
here and feel it all oozing away again because I can never get into that
complete detachment necessary for creation. If I have a free evening I
think "Ah, I will write." I sit down. I listen for a telephone call. I yearn
for somebody exciting to call up. I meditate. I decide I need new tooth-
paste—also that I'm hungry. I buy food. I see it is 10 o'clock. No one has

called me up. I'm mad. I go to bed huffy. Such is genius midst the thrills of the city . . ."[38]

In the 1920s, without a studio of her own, Powell often went to the New York Public Library at Fifth Avenue and Forty-second Street and wrote in the children's section because, she said, "They have those low little tables in there that are just the right height for me."[39] In a letter to her sister, Powell said that she wrote in pencil at the library during the day, "Then the next day I stay home and copy them on the typewriter. And like as not the next day I revise them."[40] Powell did not always have such a happy balance between longhand and typing. Sometimes she wrote longhand and had a typist transcribe her work. Most often, she could not afford to do this, and, as she notes, she frequently revised her work as she transcribed. She occasionally lashed herself for this revision, as if it were a fault and lost time, not having embraced the idea that much of writing is the act of rewriting.

> Have been typing direct last chapters. Should have done it before since this book shows the danger of loose large pages and pen—no sense of permanency or responsibility since typist will type it and then I will change it again. Great waste of sheer physical labor and expense and sprawling of mind. Never work this sloppily again. (*Diaries,* 266)

She blamed this process for a delay in producing a novel, as she wrote to her editor:

> I have been fearlessly attacking the latter part of my novel under the delusion that I could catch up on typing the handwritten original at the same time handwriting up to the glorious finale. Today I admit the two processes are paralyzing each other. I re-handwrite the typed parts and make trouble for myself, the enemy author. . . . I like what I'm doing right now in the handwritten department and my typewriter makes too much noise.[41]

In addition to testing the merits of writing longhand versus typing, Powell experimented with writing at different times of day: "New York. Writing nights steadily till two and three o'clock, and finding that I get more done by these uninterrupted midnight hours than a day of half-interrupted work" (*Diaries,* 42). The time of day and medium of writing corresponded with the mood of the novel that she was writing. While writing *Turn, Magic Wheel,* Powell noted: "I want this new novel to be delicate and cutting—nothing will cut New York but a diamond. Probably should do a night job on it as on *Tenth Moon*—it should not be a daylight book but intense and brilliant and fine like night thoughts" (*Diaries*, 84). Twenty years later, Powell was experimenting with writing longhand in the early morning: "On roof at 7 a.m. For some time, I have been enjoying early morning writing—the precious creative link between sleep and fiction without the increasingly unbeatable destructive interruption of the domestic voice. I do as much before 9 a.m. as I used to do struggling all day. Longhand is a help too" (*Diaries*, 350). At this time, she was working on her ill-fated *A Cage for Lovers,* and the "sleep link" probably helped her to re-create the Parisian scenes from her memory.

Powell treated her three-month trip to Paris much as she treated extended writing retreats at motels on the East Coast. Before she left for Paris, she noted various tasks to be done: "See Leo Lerman for *Mademoiselle* article. Type 'Broadway' article. Make will. Type birth affidavit—have Joe sign. Take certificate and Joe to 630 Fifth—have passport picture taken first" (*Diaries*, 293). She had little money in Paris, so she worked at small pieces of writing. In fact, she wrote a story titled "The Pilgrim" aboard the ship as it sailed to France. She wrote to Dos Passos:

> I wrote a very fine story about my cabin-mate on the boat—which the *New Yorker* said they would take except that they wanted revisions and since it was about Holy Year and pilgrims (my cabin-mate was a Boston pilgrim)—they wouldn't get my revisions in time to publish it as a timely piece [inked in margin: so no sale]. This depressed me as a sort of pointlessly jinxy thing.[42]

The trip abroad was rare for Powell, and by this point she had lost her youthful itch to travel overseas. She seemed to appreciate the Paris trip more for the break it afforded her than for the locale.

On occasion, Powell escaped the pressure of daily life at the homes of friends. Although Sara and Gerald Murphy occasionally drained Powell's energy, sometimes she found renewed strength in the break. Edmund Wilson's home in Talcottville also offered a refuge for Powell to write, read, and relax. Powell also rented motel rooms for weeks at a time so she could work. Most of Powell's escapes were to places where she could focus and concentrate on writing. Hollywood was an exception.

Powell went to Hollywood to work on movie scripts, of course, a process she described to John Dos Passos: "A very nice man named Lloyd Sheldon said 'Oh hello, Miss Powell, rewrite this shooting script.'

So I took it home and did it and he read it and said simply superb, take it right home and do it all over again, so I did. He added that it was so fine that I must foller him at once to the Stratosphere itself." Powell notes, too: "I haven't been so desolate since—well, let's see—since I was in Hollywood last.[43] Writing Hollywood scripts is a job that "makes you hate yourself," she said (Josephson, 28). During her time in Hollywood in 1932 and 1936, Powell recorded little in her diary, leaving her record instead in almost daily letters to Joe Gousha and frequent letters to friends, especially Dos Passos. It seems Powell was affected by homesickness as much as by the time away from her work. She insisted, too, that the climate of Hollywood was more conducive to lying about and sipping drinks than to actually working. One of the rare diary entries notes: "Now dallying with Paramount and Goldwyn on coast job— $1000 a week. Need a change for my mind. Too happy and contented— this is no good for my sort of writing" (*Diaries*, 126).

Because Powell so disliked Hollywood, she would not make extensive commitments to work there. In 1934 she noted: "Paramount wanted me to go to the coast again but I refused. Carol said it would pay $1500 a week—but money confuses me too much already" (*Diaries*, 90). Powell turned down several potentially lucrative jobs. Of particular note is her declining to work on *The Wizard of Oz* in 1936. She wrote to Dos Passos from Hollywood: "I am very distrait and I want to go on a choo-choo someplace. Would I be sorry should I do so—the immediate thing is a *Wizard of Oz* United Artists thinks would be darling for me to do— out there—."[44] Powell did occasionally toss Hollywood writing into her New York juggling act, reworking scripts for $1,000 a week without leaving New York City.

Powell had a higher tolerance for theater work, in which she immersed herself for a while before pulling back: "Plays are so much easier to write than novels. They count for more, too, and don't matter so much to you, the writer. If I could go away—some hotel in Asheville, Montreal, anyplace—I could work" (*Diaries*, 28). Unfortunately, Powell involved herself with the Group Theatre, a heavy-handed group of intellectuals who ensured that Powell's satire would be misunderstood, becoming a parody of itself. The Group Theatre, an offshoot of the Theatre Guild, staged *Big Night* in 1933; the Theatre Guild staged *Jig Saw* in 1934. Both were final additions to the season. One did not receive enough preproduction attention and the other received too much attention. Both were relative flops. Of *Big Night*, Malcolm Goldstein wrote:

[*Big Night*] had first come to Clurman's attention when it was submitted to the Guild; it too was a failure, and with a run of only seven performances the worst failure in the Group's history. A satiric account of a desperate salesman's last-ditch effort to succeed in business by offering his reluctant wife as bait to a client, it required the pacing of farce but was given an overintellectualized staging. After exploring the social implications of the play during several months of rehearsal, the company puzzled not only the audience but the author as well. J. Edward Bromberg, in the role of the lecherous client, insisted that his character's name be changed from Jones to Schwartz, offering the explanation that he felt better as Schwartz. As a result Powell was accused by acquaintances of writing an anti-Semitic play in which a Jewish businessman was exhibited as a drunken boor.[45]

Jig Saw was not so dismal a failure. Apparently having learned its lesson about overintellectualizing Powell's plays, the Guild did not alter the script substantially. The drama, a light farce about a mother and daughter vying for the same lover, lasted for 49 performances and received fair reviews. It was the only one of Powell's dramas to be published.[46]

Powell found an outlet in drama for her first forays into satire. The only novels she had published by the mid-1930s were the largely nonsatiric Ohio novels. In considering the satiric precursors to her dramas, she wrote:

> I was thinking of influences—of Marinetti's *Italian Futurist Manifesto* and somewhere the words "Consider yourself not as the observer of the picture but the center of it—take your angle from that." And it seemed to me all my plays followed that line. Now I think it is the key to great satire. In Petronius, John Donne, in Aristophones, Moliere and Restoration plays, the vitality of the satire is derived from the completeness of the picture—not one acting part or thought represents the norm, the audience, the critic or the author—there is, in a word, no *voice*, no pointer to the moral. In good satire, there is an absolute denial that there are people any different than those in this picture. The enjoyment of satire is that of nine-pins—seeing the ball strike truly and the pins go down. Audiences who can enjoy satire and at the same time recognize its imputations are limited, but there are millions who should be able to enjoy its surface entertainment. It should not be so bitter as to cancel its theatrical duty to an audience. (*Diaries*, 75)

The Group Theatre overintellectualized Powell's dramas so that the surface entertainment was lost. *Jig Saw* was Powell's final staged drama.

Powell's short stories are of mixed quality. A few are set pieces that appear in another form in her novels. Others are close character sketches. Some are plotted in classic O. Henry, zinger-at-the-end style. The short-story form did not provide a large enough canvas for Powell to exercise her form of satire. Although she had a sharp eye for detail, she preferred to provide the details throughout the course of a novel, rather than condensing them. Powell considered her short stories to be light. John Nerber thought differently in his review of *Sunday, Monday, and Always,* Powell's collection of short stories: "It is impossible to reduce these stories to plots, to apt descriptions. . . . Whether these stories are traditional or not, Miss Powell presents four-dimensional human beings, and with such penetration that their very gizzards show. . . ."[47]

Powell frequently dashed off her short stories, then sent them to her agent. One diary entry notes, "Wrote short story . . . 3300 words, in about four hours" (*Diaries,* 197). The swiftness with which she wrote these stories—contrasted with the longer labor of writing novels—suggests something of her attitude toward these pieces. Powell did not believe that the short story was a medium worth devoting her time to. She occasionally saw in them the germ of a drama or novel, but most often they were short set pieces that exposed a bit of human relationship. As such, many of her stories are quite inventive and biting. They suit the *New Yorker* style of story, which often begins and ends in some region outside the pages of the story.

Powell did feel strongly about some of the pieces that she wrote late in life because they, unlike the earlier, hurriedly written stories, were the results of a lifetime of learning. In particular, she was delighted to sell within a short time frame two pieces that were close to her heart: "The Elopers,"[48] a story about mothers meeting outside the state institution that houses their unbalanced children, and "What Are You Doing in My Dreams?"[49] a lovely, slightly mystical account of Powell's Ohio ghosts coming to picnic with her.

Another late publication is "Staten Island, I Love You,"[50] an ode to New York and to Joe Gousha. Published the month before she died, the six-page spread, replete with reproductions of oil paintings of Staten Island, is as much a tribute to Powell's strength as to Joe Gousha and New York City. Even in times of utter despair, Powell still worked. Her final comic novel, *The Golden Spur,* was written over a period of four years in which Powell experienced the greatest despair of her life: She nursed Joe Gousha for two horrible, arduous years as he died of cancer and then stood by Margaret De Silver as she died of cancer five months later. Powell herself was beset by illness, later diagnosed as cancer. Midway through her life, Powell wrote: "Wits are never happy people. Their anguish that has scraped their nerves and left them raw to every flicker of life . . . is the base of wit. . . . Wit is the cry of pain, the true word that pierces the heart" (Josephson, 28).

Lost Member of the Lost Generation

In 1963 *Esquire* magazine asked Powell to pose with "other members of the Lost Generation." Powell was as baffled by this request as were her friends, but she went along, in part because she "had failed them on an assignment and wanted to patch connection for future," she wrote to Dos Passos.

> The photograph was in fact a scream. I told them before I was not in Paris—they said this was the literary scene 20s and 30s. So there I am, rosy and overfed, squeezed between Carl Van Vechten and Glenway Wescott, Man Ray, Marcel Duchamp, (Gertrude and Alice couldn't make it), and a guard of Cowleys, Josephsons, Slater Brown, Virgil Thomson, Caresse Crosby and Kay Boyle.[51]

In the essay accompanying the two-page photograph, Malcolm Cowley wrote, "Dawn Powell looks as if she has just made one of her funny remarks, but as if the remark was dangerously true, so that she has to laugh hard to smooth things over. In the group at the table Dawn is the only one who didn't live in Paris at some time during the Twenties. When we got back to New York, we looked for her in the French café of the Hotel Lafayette, where the repatriates used to read the Paris papers at marble-topped tables."[52]

By 1963, alone and battling cancer, Powell wrote: "I must use these few remaining years to get my own mind free—not to have it harnessed at this late date to articles and popular magazines, as Twain, Lardner, etc., were harnessed and wasted so that they have a bulk of trash to show for their minds" (*Diaries*, 451–52). Powell kept working, publishing a novel that was nominated for the National Book Award, then working on a musical adaptation of it. Despite the difficulties of her life, she was able to make a living in a career of her choosing. She supported her husband and son. She nursed her husband until his death in 1962. Her friend Coby Gilman stayed sober so that he could nurse her as she died from cancer. After her death, Wilson wrote: "She was really an old-fashioned American woman not far from the pioneering civilization: strong-willed, stoical, plainspoken, not to be imposed upon. She was nearer the East than the West. I once talked to her about Ohio, which has produced so many talented writers and so many mediocre presidents. 'It's not a Middle Western state,' she said" (E. Wilson 1993, 489).

In the letter to Dos Passos about the *Esquire* group, Powell wrote, "I see Dwight MacDonald's beard wagging accusingly—'You weren't in that group'—and I will say, 'Look at the record, man. The camera doesn't lie'."[53]

For the record, Powell's legacy doesn't lie, either.

Chapter Two

"After a Night with the Dead": The Ohio Novels

In the Ohio books I was not interested in making up romances, but in archaeology and showing up people and places that are or have been familiar types, but were not acceptable to fiction, because of inner wars in their nature that make them confused human characters instead of standard fiction black and white types—good, bad, strong, weak. (*Diaries*, 151)

In Powell's consecutively published Ohio novels, she returned to the landscape of her youth, traveling from the rural Ohio of 1900 in *The Bride's House* (1929) into small towns in *She Walks in Beauty* (1928) and *The Tenth Moon / Come Back to Sorrento* (1932) and into the factory town in *Dance Night* (1930). In these early novels, she trod known land, remembered from her own past. In the final novel of this cycle, *The Story of a Country Boy* (1934), she moved into unknown territory: the burgeoning suburbs of the 1930s. Along the road, she refined her style and experimented with structure, stretching the form of the novel and decidedly refusing to be cast into a type of novelist. The Ohio novels are intriguing for their breadth of observation and array of characters. Conjured from Powell's childhood memories, the characters seem a bit removed from reality, as they move through a world that no longer exists.

Powell wrote that when she ran away from Ohio, "People and places froze into position and nothing I've seen or heard of them since makes any impression on that original picture" (*Best*, 446–47). The scene remains static in the novels as well, and the very point of Powell's narratives is that little happens in these small towns to promote change. Powell establishes the scene to define her characters; the plot is the working out of the characters' problems and dreams that arise as a result of being in this scene.

Because Powell's novels are set in small-town Ohio, critics were and are tempted to confine Powell's early work to the category of regionalism. Powell does tap into small-town life, but she does not create local color portraits detailing the mannerisms of a place and a people. "Coming as I do from many generations of small-town American people," Powell wrote, "I am basically interested in the problem of the provincial at home and in the world, in business, love and art. I would like to portray these Americans as vividly as Balzac did his French provincials at home and in Paris."[1] Each novel is distinctive, made so by the location of the characters within the small town. The problems faced by the sisters in *She Walks in Beauty* arise from their position on the "wrong side of the tracks." Connie Benjamin and Blaine Decker retreat to their "interior lives" in *The Tenth Moon* because they cannot realize their dreams in the small town. All of the characters are outsiders in these towns, reflecting Powell's own outsider feeling as she tumbled from relative to relative when she was growing up.

So, although these first novels were published in the wake of the "revolt from the village" that reached its peak in the 1920s with the publication of Sinclair Lewis's *Main Street* (1920) and *Babbitt* (1922), Powell's Ohio novels do not properly belong to this movement.[2] Powell's novels neither satirize nor idealize the small-town life. The setting is simply the place that Powell knows best. The characters reflect their environment, as they must, and their stories can take place only in a small town. Powell is not seeking to redeem America, to save it from encroaching urbanization, but rather to set down the stories of people's inner struggles.

The books that shaped the revolt—Masters's *Spoon River Anthology* (1915), Anderson's *Winesburg, Ohio* (1919), and Lewis's *Main Street* (1920)—reveal the tiny provincial minds of Middle America. For these writers, writes Anthony Hilfer,

> The village was synecdoche and metaphor. The village represented what Americans thought they were, what they sometimes pretended (to themselves as well as others) they wanted to be, and if the small town was typically American, the Midwestern small town was doubly typical. The basic civilization of America was middle class, a fact somewhat obscured in city novels that tended to treat the extremes of the very rich and the very poor to the exclusion of the middle. Even the East, dominated by its cities, usually granted the superior "Americanism" of the Middle West. Thus the Midwestern novelists of the teens and twenties could see their locale as a microcosm of the nation and, provincial bourgeoises that they were, of the world. But their view was critical. The town was the focus of what was in actuality an over-all attack on middle-class American civilization.[3]

The revolt from the village was losing power in the 1930s, but these novels of the 1920s cast a shadow that affected the reception of Powell's Midwestern novels. An unsigned review of *She Walks in Beauty* begins: "Here again we have youth in a small Ohio town portrayed in a meticulous and sympathetic fashion. As the blurb proudly intimates, it is a photographic picture of Middle Western life on the order of Sinclair Lewis and Sherwood Anderson, with an added dash of womanly sentimentality."[4] Another reviewer described the same novel as "unexpectedly pleasant and interesting to a reviewer who confesses a distaste for another story of a mid-western small town."[5] Yet another reviewer noted that "It is written in the Winslow-Suckow tradition."[6] This last reviewer, referring to the works of Thyra Samter Winslow and Ruth Suckow, came closest to the mark, as these works, too, focus more on capturing the lives of small-town people than on mythologizing, eulogizing, or satirizing the small town.[7]

Her mission, Powell wrote, "has always been to feed a historical necessity" (*Diaries,* 151). She was recording people and places before they utterly faded from memories. In recording these lives, she is kind to these Midwesterners. "I don't think satire is what I do," she once said. "I think it's realism. It's not making fun. It's just telling the truth."[8] Though they are not satire, the Ohio novels share with the satiric New York novels an inconclusiveness that reflects the sense of reality that informs both forms:[9] Reality does not allow for tidy endings.

In the Ohio novels, the plot is the playing out of the characters' responses to scene. As Eudora Welty wrote: "Place. . . has the most delicate control over character . . . by confining character, it defines it" (Welty, 122). Confined in the small towns, the characters frame their dreams accordingly. The most common plot in these novels revolves around plans for escape. A few characters succeed; most dwell on the plans without acting upon them. The inner movement of the characters is of more interest to Powell than the outer movement. The plots of these novels, though fairly simple, are complicated by the motives of the characters. The plot section will close with a consideration of structure and satire, as Powell moved toward the more complex structures of the New York novels.

Scene: "You are here! here! here!"

As Connie Benjamin swings on her porch at the opening of *The Tenth Moon,* she travels in her mind away from Dell River: "She swung slowly back and forth in the hammock, one foot under her, the other rhythmically touching the porch floor, it was swing, tap, swing, tap; one move-ment released her fancy, sent her soaring through years but the tapping of her slipper brought her back. You are here! here! here! it reminded her."[10] Throughout the Ohio novels, the scene is an insistent presence, confining the characters and refusing to be ignored, but never being embraced by the characters. The scene is more than a backdrop, but it does not dominate as in local color fiction. It is place exerting its "deli-cate control."

The small towns of these novels are similar to the towns Powell knew as a child. The attention to scene changes according to the characters' response to and interaction with the scene. In *She Walks in Beauty* and *The Bride's House,* once the defining exterior scene is established, the interior scenes dominate. In *Dance Night,* the characters move in metro-nomic pace with the factory town. In *The Tenth Moon,* the town is more a force than an entity. In nearly all of these novels, the scene is static and the characters act according to their given place in the scene. The excep-tion is *The Story of a Country Boy* in which Powell explores the effect of changing scene on Chris Bennett as he moves from the country to the town to the city and back again. All of the novels challenge the myth of simplicity in the small town, as described by Hilfer:

> The myth of the small town was based on a set of ideal antitheses to the city. The cold impersonality of the city contrasted with the "together-ness" of the town; the vice of the city with the innocence of the town; the complexity of the city with the simplicity of the town. The sociological cause of the myth is evident enough: the myth of the small town served as a mental escape from the complexities, insecurities, and continual changes of a society in rapid transition from a dominantly rural to a dom-inantly urban and industrial civilization. The myth was a symptom of immaturity; it was sentimental, escapist, and simple-minded. (Hilfer, 5)

For the most part, Powell's Ohio novels do not feed this myth. In *The Bride's House* and *The Tenth Moon,* the town appears idyllic, but the beauty is undercut by the tormented lives of the characters. Industry is a large part of life in *Dance Night*'s Lamptown; the only "mental escape" in this town is the dance night of the title.

The boardinghouse by the railroad track in Birchfield, the setting of *She Walks in Beauty,* is not unlike the boardinghouse of Powell's Aunt May in Shelby. Poised on the edge of everywhere, as trains head off to the great cities, the boardinghouse is a critical scene: situated away from "the paved respectability of Maple Avenue [in] . . . the tumbled South

End,"[11] on the "wrong side of the tracks," it defines the social status of Dorrie and Linda at their Aunt Jule's boardinghouse.

> Jule's was a huge old square house painted a dull charcoal by time and the B. & O. A narrow porch was thrust out in front like a sullen underlip. Over it a great oak leaned a protective elbow. Elderberry bushes obscured the side of the house, yet a row of garbage and ash cans always managed to peep triumphantly out of the foliage. The grass was always high and uneven in the front yard. . . . Up by the front steps a scraggy vine attempted to reach the porch railing but grew discouraged a few inches above the trellising and dropped a barren and exhausted shoot back to earth. (*Beauty*, 3–4)

Aunt Jule notes, "Some say Birchfield's nothing but a dirty little railroad town, but to my mind it's one of the prettiest little cities in Ohio. Ideal for a home. And such lovely people" (*Beauty*, 53). Aunt Jule is too kind to note the irony in this last line, which overlooks the continual gossip about the comings and goings at her house. Despite the uneasy relationship with the aristocracy of Birchfield, Jule is at home.

The railway that separates the house from the town is no mere single track: it is modeled after the Big Four Depot in Shelby, as recalled by John F. "Jack" Sherman:

> It was called the Big Four because the New York Central railway ran between Cleveland, Columbus, Cincinnati and St. Louis. It was a very busy railroad stop. Passengers got off the train there—there was no New York Central train stop downtown at Shelby. In order for passengers to get to downtown Shelby in those years, they had to order a horse-drawn carriage from the downtown livery service, or wait for an Interurban street car that stopped at the depot at specific times. Knowing all of this, Aunt May decided to have her home built in the near vicinity of the depot and serve meals, which she did very successfully. She was a superb cook, and became known for serving excellent meals. Her home was a haven for children and other family members in need of help, as well as lucky hoboes riding the rails of the hundreds of freight trains passing through Shelby.[12]

The track separating the house and the town is a world wide. Dorrie embraces this distance because it allows her to explore worlds without leaving home. Linda resents this gap and devotes her energy to leaping the chasm by wooing the son of Birchfield's most aristocratic family in order to establish her place on the right side of town.

As in *She Walks in Beauty,* the characters in *The Bride's House* and *The Tenth Moon* are removed from the townspeople. The primary scene of *The Bride's House* is geographically farther from town, so they are outside its social structure. Situated on a farm, the Truelove family has to hitch horse to buggy for the weekly ride to town. Viewed through the eyes of the three city children who arrive at the beginning of the novel, the "forest darkness" seems forbiddingly remote, "the trees were so black and what were those strange crackling noises?"

> "I'm afraid of the country," Lois' voice came finally. "I wish I was in Washington." . . .
>
> A keyhole of starlight appeared through the trees—the road was about to come out across the open fields. Way off on the hill beyond the frozen creek was the big farmhouse, a dark hulk pierced with pin-points of lamplight. The bays snorted happily and their heels flew high along the crackling highway, past snow-feathered hedges that defined Truelove fields. Now the house loomed enormous and radiant, spilling its light through fences into geometric patterns on the road.
>
> "Home," said George. [13]

The remoteness of the scene underscores the insularity of the Truelove family. They are sufficient unto themselves and do not require the approval of the town; they require only themselves.

In *The Tenth Moon,* the village itself is stuck in time, slightly removed from the real world.

> The town buildings in Dell River were old, few changes had been made for decades beyond the new wing on the schoolhouse for manual training and domestic sciences inaugurated a few years back. Occasionally a modern pink-stuccoed cottage popped out among the older shingled residences but not many, for the town's population had not grown since it was founded. A small foundry, a few garages, a candy factory, a sawmill and flour mill, these were practically the town's only industries unless you counted the enormous nurseries just outside the city limits, whose trading in irises was the only cogent reason for trains to stop here. (*Moon,* 14–15)[14]

Despite living in the midst of the residential area of town, Connie is psychologically distanced from the townspeople. Powell's chosen title *Come Back to Sorrento,* named for the song that Connie sang before the great Morini, serves well to indicate the pull of place, real or imagined, upon the characters—and upon Powell, who was pulled into the novel initially by her own remembrance of place. When the novel was published in 1932 as *The Tenth Moon,* Powell was dismayed: "How I hate the empty, silly, pointless title!" she wrote. "How I wish they would have allowed me to call it 'Come Back to Sorrento'; since one gets so little else for one's work, a title that pleases the writer seems such a little boon to ask" (*Diaries,* 47). In 1997, Steerforth Press reprinted the novel as *Come Back to Sorrento,* providing a new kind of life for the book, some 60 years after Powell first observed with some satisfaction:

> As soon as this new book came to life, my other one seemed too stiff. This one . . . laid in the little town, is known to me. I smell the town, with its bonfires of autumn leaves, the meadows far off with wild flowers in them. Every person is familiar to me. Perhaps this is what really wanted to be done all the time; these others had to be weeded out before I could get to this. (*Diaries,* 24)

Again, though, once the scene is set, the characters take over. Connie Benjamin resists the natural intimacy of the village and remains within her own garden.

> Everyone knew Mrs. Benjamin. They knew she was not snobbish,—she was far too gentle for that and in actual material possessions had less than her neighbors; her aloofness was not due to a sense of superiority but very likely to shyness. No one could blame a woman for natural reserve though often people speculated on how any human being could live fifteen years in one village without friends or confidantes. (*Moon,* 7–8)

Connie and Blaine Decker create distance between themselves and the townspeople with their affectations of speech, dress, and mannerisms.

In *Dance Night* the lives of the townspeople are integrated with the town. Morry and his mother live in the heart of the commercial strip of the town, over the Bon Ton Hat Shop, which Elsinore Abbott owns and operates. As a merchant, Elsinore interacts daily with the townspeople and with the rare visitors to the town. The central industry of Lamptown—perhaps based on Powell's hometown of Shelby with its Shelby Electric Company but merged with the toughness of nearby Mansfield—is the electric factory, which employs primarily female workers who fuel Elsinore's business. The factory sets the pace of the town with its insistent thrumming, which merges with the beat of the dance hall: "They didn't need an orchestra for Lamptown dances, Elsinore thought, holding her splitting head in her hands, the engines and the factory machines could keep two-four time."[15] Added to this undercurrent is the whistling of trains, taunting the townspeople with the promise of quieter, far-off lands. Toward the end of the novel, developers arrive to transform Lamptown, but the story predates the development boom found in *Main Street* and *Babbitt*. There is little social striation in the town—the store workers feel superior to the factory workers, but all are equally prisoners of the factory.

In *The Story of a Country Boy*, Chris Bennett moves from the farm in Bennetsville to the town of Aviland, then back to the farm. At the peak of his business career, he also makes forays into the cities. As Bennett moves to increasingly larger houses, his social status changes in the view of the townspeople, though he continues to perceive himself as a country boy. Under the influence of John Howard Lawson—a radical playwright and screenwriter—as informal editor, Powell created a story strongly defined by class distinctions, which are reflected primarily through scene. For a time, the Bennetts live in a modern apartment: "The rooms were equipped with door-beds, dining-tables that turned into beds, electric fireplaces, house telephones and apart from being rather small, dark, and scantily furnished, answered the provincial need for marvels to write home about" (*Boy*, 33).[16] After Bennett is promoted to general manager, the family moves to Aviland Heights, to a "spacious cobblestone house . . . [with] great space, huge rooms sliding into other huge rooms . . . [and a] windowed alcove which contained two huge leather club chairs and was Chris' particular retreat" (*Boy*, 87, 89–90). By the time Chris moves to Aviland Heights, he has nearly abandoned his roots. He still has asparagus and limas in a little patch, but they are tended by Deeney, his chauffeur-gardener-handyman. His "land" in the suburbs is not impressive to his boyhood friend El who reported back to Bennetsville residents that "Chris didn't have more than a couple of acres of land and that a very poor grade—sort of a sandy clay" (*Boy*, 16).

Bennett's penultimate move is the extravagant purchase of "a country place at the shore, a hundred-acre estate named 'Willow-Bridge' . . . [which] included a landscaped garden, golf course, caretaker's house, six-car garage with servants' quarters" (*Boy*, 227). Spending the summer at the estate, the Bennetts find that

> the great house with its rolling lawns and walled gardens never seemed *theirs*, nor was its possession any pleasure except when company came to admire or envy it, always declaring it was the finest estate in the whole

country. The baronial rooms, scantily furnished, did not really appeal to either Chris or Joy. You couldn't settle any place, somehow, you had to wander from room to room hunting in vain for some little cozy corner to welcome you. . . . After a few weeks Joy gave up trying to use each room in some way and spent her time upstairs in the bedroom and for that matter they ate in the kitchen except when company came, since the great oak-paneled dining-room was too majestic for the enjoyment of food. (*Boy*, 263)

Joy, having little to do around the house, continues with her addictions to Benedictine and bridge, developed in Aviland Heights, which "were doing for Joy what psycho-analysis does for more advanced women" (*Boy*, 221). Her compulsive card-playing is a motif for the "house of cards" in which the Bennetts live and that, inevitably, comes tumbling down.

The mobility of the Bennetts reflects a changing lifestyle not only for the Bennetts but also for Ohio. As Powell found on a trip to Ohio while writing the novel, the world that she remembered had utterly changed:

To Canton to see Phyllis. I am amazed at the change in the Midwest—it is exactly like Hollywood or Forest Hills. The radio, the war, the automobile have leveled off the entire country—the only different place is still New York (and that the bohemia of New York since Park Avenue is so much glorified Westchester which is so much enlarged Shelby or Galion).

There is not the anxious "striving" to be like society that used to characterize the Ohio little towns. Their possessions are more truly a gauge of their financial stations than the city person's possessions, which are merely a testimony to his glibness with creditors. (*Diaries*, 71–72)

This visit to Ohio radically changed Powell's view of scene in the novel. She realized that she could not put the Ohio that she remembered into near-current time. She wrote to Joe Gousha: "I am horrified and embarrassed to think how near I came to finishing that book without a check up on this country. It's so different at first I almost decided to chuck the novel out of sheer ignorance—but now I'm getting my bearings. . . ."[17]

After gathering her bearings, Powell completed the novel, then "moved out" of Ohio. Powell divided herself when writing the Ohio novels. By immersing herself in her recalled world, she removed herself from her current surroundings of Depression-era New York: "The Benjamin [novel (*The Tenth Moon*)], calling on my Ohio background as it does, offers an escape from modern New York desperation (too much a part of my own life for me to write about calmly) and a prison in another sense, shutting me off completely from my present life and interests" (*Diaries*, 25).

As one way of uniting her worlds, Powell found a place for the city in the Ohio books. In *The Tenth Moon*, Connie Benjamin runs away to New York with Tony the Daredevil to pursue their dreams. She soon finds herself pregnant and abandoned in Atlantic City. Her dream thwarted, she is left to the grim, grimy city:

> Day after day watching from behind the torn lace curtain in the Atlantic City hotel, watching for Tony to come back, the heavy ache of her own body, her heart a dull metronome of pain, ticking out the days till doom came . . . the days walking up and down the Board Walk, huddled in his discarded overcoat, her mind dulled to everything but the thundering of the waves. Who was she, why was she here, what was to happen to her, these things were lost in the rhythmic beat of the sea, but back in the dreary little room, waiting behind the lace curtains—. (*Moon*, 79–80)

Connie's negative experience of the real world reinforces her reluctance to leave Dell River. The city has only a cameo in this novel, as the far-off site of greater, unrealized dreams.

New York City is a hazy city of dreams in *She Walks in Beauty* also, though Dorrie's notion of big cities also encompasses "strange exotic places like South Bend, Dayton or even Louisville" (*Beauty*, 85). Dorrie does appreciate the enormous pull of New York City, and she "yearned to be from the East, so she could see that awe in people's eyes when she told them" (*Beauty*, 16). After listening to a boarder, Marie, tearfully recount her "mad dancing courtship" in New York City with the man who married her and brought her to Birchfield, Dorrie "thought she might write a poem about New York . . . —the city that made people so unhappy" (*Beauty*, 60–61). Dorrie, like the other townspeople, has no real idea of the city: "to Birchfield New York was as meaningless and remote as a billion dollars—Akron or even Mansfield meaning far more to them as a symbol of culture—still, New York was East, and, as East, Birchfield bowed to it" (*Beauty*, 44). The nearest "big city" is Columbus, Ohio, where two of Aunt Jule's children live, but Dorrie and Linda are merely baffled by their aunt's view of "those ghastly Birchfielders," whom she perceives as "bumpkins" (*Beauty*, 143). When her Aunt Laura invites Linda to come live in Columbus to find a husband, Linda declines; "she didn't want to leave Birchfield. She could not keep her still vigil over her lover if she were sixty miles away" (*Beauty*, 144).

Birchfield is the place of Linda's dreams. She has no desire to go to Columbus because her goal is to conquer the north end of Birchfield ("nice people didn't live in the south end" [*Beauty,* 163]), away from the boardinghouse with its unsavory reputation. Linda rejects her aunt's offer to visit Columbus in order to find a husband who is not a "Birchfield bumpkin."

> [Linda] had no desire to be impersonally envied by women all over the States for some brilliant match she might make. For her the definite envy of . . . Birchfield. Her triumph must be one of intensity rather than scope—a triumph over tiny Birchfield, the town that had known her degradation. She wanted to show them—but she wanted her triumph to be always before their eyes; she wanted to enjoy it the rest of her life—to satiate herself with their groveling respect. (*Beauty,* 145)

Linda embraces the social machinations of the town and sees it as her particular challenge to surmount the obstacles.

For one boarder, Esther Mason, "after seventeen years on a farm, Birchfield was Paris" and she was "drunk with love of the city" (*Beauty,* 48):

> Ah—the city!
> The haunting allure of Main Street at dark, with its dim street lamps and whirring automobiles. . . . Glimpses of a strange fair man at the wheel of a roadster passing by . . . men, knowing-eyed men, bending over pool tables in a blue fog of cigarette smoke . . . ragtime airs tinkling shrilly from some porch gramophone . . . creakings of vine-shaded porch swings . . . glowing of cigarette ends on hushed dark side streets . . . breath of stale beer and jangle of men's voices from corner saloons. . . .
> On hot summer nights one caught the sense-maddening odor of tobacco smoke and masculine sweat when one passed close by a man.
> Ah, the city! (*Beauty,* 48–49)[18]

Esther reveals that "the city" is not simply a place larger than one's town, but rather a place that provides the means to fulfill dreams. Even for Marie, who loves New York City, Birchfield becomes the city of dreams when she has a baby and settles into a house with her husband.

The city is also a far-off place in *The Bride's House.* Unlike the characters of *She Walks in Beauty,* though, Sophie Truelove actually makes her escape to the city, rather than just dreaming of it. The focal city in this novel is Washington, home of Lotta, aunt to Sophie Truelove and mother of the children sent to the Truelove farm. The city does not represent a place of dreams so much as an "other" place, far removed from the safe insularity of the farm. The city becomes a "safe" place for Sophie Truelove Hamilton to meet her lover, Jerome Gardiner, because it allows for anonymity.

In *Dance Night,* the city is a generic destination, the end of the line for any train leaving Lamptown. No particular city holds allure, but all of them offer the possibility of escape. Elsinore and Mrs. Pepper do free themselves of the town's constraints by going on "buying trips" to Cleveland where

> They went to matinees together . . . to see what new costume touches were in vogue, not so much for the Bon Ton clientele as for themselves, they worked hard for the Bon Ton but they lived for their "trips," the whistles of admiration, the whispers, "Gee—what a figure!" the perfect applause of a man stopping in his talk to stare attentively as they passed. (*Dance,* 283–84)

The city provides anonymity for the women and allows them to be flattered in a way that they are not at home. Unlike Esther in *She Walks in Beauty,* the older women are discreet and remain above the reproachful gossip of Lamptown.

The scenes of these novels, unlike the chaotic scenes of the New York novels, are ordered—maddeningly so. The static nature of the scene is what drives characters to their interior lives in an effort to escape the monotony of their surroundings. The monotony is alleviated when carnival arrives, quickening the pace and turning night to day with its colorful lights. The carnival force is disruptive enough to alter plot machinations. In their everyday scene, the characters develop their own methods of escape.

Character: The Problem of the Provincial

The central problem of the provincials in Powell's novels is that they are outsiders, made so by geography, social status, or personal choice. The characters' relationship to place—that is, whether they embrace their outsiderness or fight against it—largely determines their actions. Powell played against the notion of a typical provincial, writing that she was interested in "showing up people . . . that are or have been familiar types, but were not acceptable to fiction" (*Diaries,* 151).

Blaine Decker in *The Tenth Moon* is such a type. What sets Decker apart from the "artsy provincials" of other Midwestern novels—for instance, Erik Valborg in Lewis's *Main Street*—is that he is a central figure of the novel, not just an oddity. Further, several details indicate that he is a homosexual: his fastidiousness about clothes and his fondness for bits of lace, tapestry, and china; his close relationship with Starr Donnell, the novelist, with whom he traveled for a year before a rift forced them apart; and his reluctance to touch Connie, despite their close spiritual relationship. The homosexuality is not overt, but his eccentricities remove Decker even further from the sensibilities of the townspeople. With such a lead character, Powell is justly frustrated by this review of the novel:

> The final *Times* review of *Tenth Moon* made me realize how discouraged I am about my work—rigidly classified as "accurate photography" when a study of feeling (as this is) could not possibly be done by photography, nor could those people be so cheerfully listed as "small town types." (*Diaries,* 56–57)

Decker's spiritual companion is Connie Benjamin. Together, the two embrace their outsiderness and distance themselves through diction and mannerisms. Their affectations are employed not only in front of other people but also with each other, removing them to the world of their unrealized dreams: hers, to be a great singer—"I sang one day before Morini. . . . I might have gone into grand opera, perhaps"; his, to be a great pianist. When Decker arrives in town to be music teacher at the high school, he tells Connie, "I studied in Leipsic and Paris, you see. . . . I intended to be a concert pianist . . . however . . . " (*Moon,* 19–20). He asks Connie, "And you—you belong to Dell River?" "Indeed no—I'm a stranger here, too, Mr. Decker," she responds. "You see I am—or was a musician, also" (*Moon,* 20). And thus they set themselves apart from the scene and from the provincials, and they begin their imagined life.

> Connie's heart swelled with unknown excitement, for a moment she had the curious sensation of having invented this character for her evening fancies, it was almost too difficult to bring him from her ideal into her actual world. Now it was like meeting another exile in a strange land, a fellow countryman, and all the treasured experiences locked away from the blank gaze of the world could be freed for these familiar understanding eyes. (*Moon,* 20)

In this adventure into the minds of two alienated provincials, Powell taps into the emotional life of provincials who cannot or will not physically escape their scene, but who daily travel beyond reality into the

escape of dreams. Connie's story is the story of Willa Cather's Thea Kron-
borg in *The Song of the Lark* turned inside out. There are so few Thea
Kronborgs and so many Connie Benjamins. Powell's story honors those
who did not make the escape.

Powell recognizes that she is an exception in overcoming great odds
to pursue her dream; she does not berate those who do not have the
strength to do the same. In her 1915 diary, Powell wrote:

> Oh well. I must make myself strong for the knocks that are to come, for
> no matter what you tell me—"You've had enough knocks. You'll have
> happiness the rest of your life—" something in me says that life for me
> holds more knocks than joys. And the blows will leave me crushed,
> stunned, wild-eyed and ready to die, while the joys will make me deliri-
> ously, wildly, gloriously happy. ("1915 diary," 20 August)[19]

Powell understood the difficulty of overcoming the knocks. She
described *The Tenth Moon* as a purely cerebral activity, "the only thing
I've ever done completely on brain power" (*Diaries*, 45).

The initial reception of the novel was positive:

> John Farrar called up (as did Ann) to say this was a "literary gem," wor-
> thy of a Willa Cather, etc., and Coby says it's by far my best book. Odd I
> should feel so little emotion; the whole thing was a trick to save me los-
> ing more blood as I usually do in my novels. Though I think I did a fairly
> excellent study of certain characters, they are my adopted children—I do
> not find my own dear faults coming out in them, or my own ideas.
> (*Diaries*, 46)

In this mental exercise, Powell explored the minds of those would-be
artists who could not or would not sacrifice all and overcome obstacles
in order to achieve their dream—instead of just dreaming it. What she
calls "dear faults" in herself one might perceive as strengths. In the 1915
diary, she wrote:

> Here I am, eighteen years old—nothing especially striking about my
> appearance—not any more clever than the average, not especially fasci-
> nating, interesting or possessing "personality," poor as a church-mouse,
> and possessing only one virtue which I sometimes think is only a curse—
> ambition. The real me isn't anything but a lazy, good-natured, fun-
> loving girl with a taste for luxuries and perfectly content to be like every-
> body else of my class. But some energetic, discontented, aspiring little
> spark in me insists that I must go to college. The lazy me reminds itself

of the sacrifices—the self-denial—years of hard work—borrowed money—but by this time the energetic me has placed the L.M. in college and keeps digging at it and nagging, scolding and lashing so that poor L.M. is kept so busy working that she doesn't have time to ponder and wonder if it's worth the sacrifice. ("1915 diary," 4 July)

Sixteen years later, in writing the lives of Connie Benjamin and Blaine Decker, Powell articulated what might have happened if the Lazy Me had won out.

Of all the characters in Powell's Ohio novels, Chris Bennett in *The Story of a Country Boy* is the only primary character who comes close to the role of typical provincial. Powell was not content with this portrayal:

I want the man to be at heart a simple peasant, with an inborn passion for cattle, farmland, soil, stable smells, that is his only life. What has bothered me was doing an inarticulate type when my whole success is in emotions and sensitive grades. But he is not dumb—he is deeply moved by earth and sunsets and all the simple primitive things—alone in the woods, hunting on the marshes, etc. (*Diaries*, 49)

In the novel, Powell's vision is tempered by reality, and there is little evidence of honest emotion in Chris Bennett. He is not a lovable man, so one wonders at the unerring devotion and adoration of his wife, Joy, and their longtime friend Madeleine. He is, however, honest and sincere, and Powell sets up the contrast between his real world and his imagined world at the outset of the novel:

Before he opened his eyes each morning Chris heard the swallows swooping in and out of the eaves, he heard the rush of their wings, their tiny exclamations pricked the cathedral silence of the triple-lofted barn. Waking, there was his astonishment first over a silk coverlet, a glimpse of fluttering pink curtains, a hint of Joy's flower perfume and finally the disappointed recognition of his familiar bedroom, the translation of early morning swallows into Joy's love-birds in their silver cage, the hills and hedges of his dream shrank to a window-box of geraniums on the bedroom sill. Minutes were required for these morning changes, though they'd been going on for many years, and Chris was wont to sit on the edge of his bed with his hands over his eyes until he could see correctly, with the old farm tucked decently out of sight. For him always reality was not the rose bedroom but the rustic dream and he was perpetually amazed that others could not see the farm shining in his eyes like a guilty secret. (*Boy*, 3)

The fact is that Powell didn't know farm life that well; she knew small towns in Ohio. As Phil Stong noted in his review: "There is so much truth so delightfully managed in 'The Story of a Country Boy' that it seems almost malicious to remark that when Miss Powell is compelled to touch on matters of farm technique, she is not really the Old Pioneer Mother she pretends to be."[20] Powell felt a bit of this inadequacy as she was writing the novel, noting that "Chris will be a failure . . . unless I can be him as well as I could be Blaine Decker" (*Diaries,* 54). It is inconceivable how Powell thought she could effectively get into the head of an inarticulate, wholly rural, somewhat oafish man.

There are some stereotypical minor characters in these novels who fit the role of provincial: "the mentally man-obsessed old maid, the physically man-obsessed young trollop, the gibbering and decrepit philosopher, the small-time vaudeville group and the Main Street aristocrats."[21] Like Sinclair Lewis, Powell writes of the social striations within small-town life, but she is more concerned with the emotions of the characters as she works to convey the reality of those frequently dismissed as being "mere provincials." By telling the stories of these characters, Powell hoped to reveal the true depth, to move beyond caricature to emotion.

Plot: Action and Inaction

As a result of their confinement in place, these characters often act out of a desire to escape. The wished-for escape is sometimes a literal one—to travel to far cities and meet new people—but most often it is a mental escape—into books, music, or the imagination, anything to take the characters beyond the routine of daily life. Sometimes this escape is realized, as in the psychological escape of Connie Benjamin or Linda Birch's marriage and subsequent move to the north end of town. Powell's own urgency to escape, motivated by her unpleasant childhood, is transferred to her characters. She continually drew upon her strength to succeed in New York City, so that she wouldn't have to return to Ohio.[22] In her 1915 diary she wrote:

> I do hope I won't get so sick and tired and disgusted with [work] that I won't feel glad to go back to school. I have had so many unpleasantnesses in my life that I think a few more years or even a few more months would make me throw up the whole thing, get a job in the telephone office at home and sink into a rut—let college, ambition and future go hang. I wonder if I wouldn't be just as happy. ("1915 diary," 1 July)

These moments of despair, of nearly losing strength, lend compassion to Powell's portrayal of those characters who do not literally escape Ohio. She allows them the little escapes that she sought as a child: books, day-dreaming, writing, music. The characters do not all share Powell's bleak childhood—though there is more than a fair share of children with dead mothers and absent fathers—but they all have strong psychological motivations for their personal escape.

The plots of these novels revolve around inaction rather than action, with the exception, again, of *The Story of a Country Boy.* At the core of the inaction is a means of hoped-for escape that makes life bearable for the characters. Their desire is not a movement forward so much as a move-ment out of their current place. The ultimate means of escape differ in the novels, but some recurring features allow for some unity among the various narratives.

A "whistle way off"

Trains play a special role in the Ohio novels. Powell attached particular importance to them as a means of potential escape. In fact, when she finally did escape her stepmother's house, she did so by train, by means of an elaborate scheme concocted by her Aunt May and her sister Mabel:

> The morning after Mabel came I got up at 3 o'clock and planned. Mabel announced that she was going back to Cleveland on the 8 o'clock car and I was to take her down—board another car for Wellington and then change cars for Shelby. I wore my checkered suit over my white dress. I didn't dare wear a hat or my stepmother would guess something wrong. Mabel was so excited and I was praying and crying all in one breath. At Wellington Auntie May had arranged for a ticket for me to Shelby and so I had no trouble. ("1915 diary," 20 August)

Certainly, Shelby was not the destination that Powell had in mind in her daydreams. But the train trip to that small town was the first step toward Powell's eventual escape to New York City. She wrote much later in life:

> The best time to run away is September. . . . What you have to do is walk right on down the street, keeping your eyes straight ahead, pre-tending you're on your way to someplace a lot better.
>
> And that's the way it turns out, too; wherever you land is sure to be better than the place you left. (*Best,* 443)

Her characters share this need to be someplace better than where they are, and even the daydream of a train trip to a far-off land is better than living the reality of where they are.

Trains roar through *Dance Night,* taunting Morry and Jen with their bright beams leading to far-off places emblazoned on the sides of the cars. Jen confesses when she first meets Morry: "I like the trains going by, . . . I like it in my sleep when I hear them whistle way off. And I like it in my sleep when I hear the piano going downstairs and the men laughing" (*Dance,* 6–7). The trains, new to the ears of Jen, fresh from the orphanage, infiltrate her dreams:

> Trains whirred through the air, their whistles shrieking a red line through the sky behind them, they landed on Jen's bed without weight, vanished, and other trains, pop-eyed, roared toward her. Trains slid noiselessly across her eyelids, long transcontinental trains with diners, clubcars, observation cars. The people on these trains leaned out of their windows and held out their hands to Jen.
>
> "California, Hawaii, Denver, Quebec, Miami," they chanted, "oh you dear child, New Orleans, Chicago, Boston, Rocky Mountains, New York City." (*Dance,* 26–27)

For Morry, the trains have become part of his daily music. But he is not immune to their promise of a greater life.

> [When] the Chicago train thundered by . . . Morry and Jen watched it hungrily, they were on that train whizzing through Lamptown on their way to someplace, someplace wonderful, and looking a little pityingly out of their car window at a boy and girl sitting on the backsteps over a saloon. The train went ripping through further silence leaving only a humming in the air and a smoky message painted on the sky.
>
> Morry and Jen looked quickly at each other—this was the thing that had always bound them—. (*Dance,* 130)

At the end, Morry responds to the train's siren; he will travel to that promised faraway place.

The train in *The Story of a Country Boy* provides a curious escape for the Bennetts. Chris Bennett's return to Bennetsville should have been triumphant, a casting off of the town life that he reluctantly lived. But because of his fall from society, it is a forced return, and the train provides a slow, jolting return to the town of his youth. Because the novel is set in a time when the automobile was racing its way into the American heart—Chris Bennett, at the height of his career, owned four cars—and air travel was available to the moneyed, it is a bit startling to turn to the opening of the final chapter: "The train was incredibly slow. It meandered downstate like a lazy mule, pausing at every cross-corners, then jolting amiably on its way as if no one going in this direction could be really very anxious to get there" (*Boy,* 297). The lumbering train underscores the Bennetts' return to a much slower way of life in Bennetsville.

In *She Walks in Beauty,* the trains do not promise an escape so much as adventure. Dorrie would rush home from school because "You never could tell what fascinating strangers might have gotten off the afternoon train, and be sitting at that very moment in Jule's parlor" (*Beauty,* 95). The characters seem permanently committed to watch others come and go, while they themselves remain fixtures of immobility at the boardinghouse.

Escapes Within

Dorrie, positioned as she is at the apex of the Big Four, does not look to trains for escape but to her bookshelves. One evening, deliciously free of responsibility,

> Dorrie had collected half a dozen books from the bookcase, including "Wormwood," "Wedded and Parted," "Père Goriot," and of course her beloved Shelley. Lodgers were always leaving books, but they seldom left anything worth reading. Dorrie opened "Wormwood," and, shuddering, cast it aside. "Wedded and Parted" she dismissed after the first few paragraphs and the last page. "Père Goriot" interested her. Dorrie turned up the gas light above the dining table and prepared for a literary evening. She had her pencil and a few pages of Linda's notepaper in the Shelley, in case—as often happened—the inadequacy of other authors would inspire her own muse.
>
> Before settling down she inspected the pantry and found a great crock of sweet pickle, and another jar of her grandmother's best pickled watermelon rind. It looked like a very pleasant evening. (*Beauty,* 165)

In addition to others' writing, Dorrie finds escape in her own writing: poems shaped in an attic room in an old brown ledger much like the ones Powell wrote in as a child. Dorrie shows her writing to only one other person: Roger Wickley.

> Roger's hard brown fingers leafed page after page. The lines about the attic in starlight. . . . About Claire. . . . Now he put his hand over his gray absorbed eyes to study a difficult phrase. . . . Hill sonnets. . . .

Things about People. . . . Towns in Darkness. . . . Queer little verses about insects and tiny things, from her eight-year-old imaginings. . . . Formal twelve-year-old reflections on love. . . . Shy, adolescent yearnings for remote things, intimations of passion. . . .

A slight smile, an ironic thing, tugged at his mouth. He was going to protect this girl from the world about her! When the only world she had ever known was the enchanted lovely world of her own fancy! (*Beauty*, 227–28)[23]

Dorrie creates a world peopled with those she met at the boarding-house but viewed through a far lovelier light. Roger, who finds Aunt Jule's boardinghouse "enchanting," had not even begun to fathom the beauty that Dorrie found here. Dorrie's imagined world is far lovelier than her surroundings: "The thing that was in her,—that dark pool,— was beautiful to Roger" (*Beauty*, 228). Dorrie's escape parallels Powell's own adolescent retreat into the "dark pool," an image so central to Pow-ell's mission that it was an early working title for the novel.

Dance Night opens with a view of Morry reading Jules Verne's *Twenty Thousand Leagues Under the Sea*, a novel of great escapes. In his room, he "turned page after page until words again took living shapes and allowed him to enter the book" (*Dance*, 12). Thus removed, Morry is able to leave behind the sounds and smells of Lamptown and plunge into his escape. Later, Morry pores over architecture books in order to try to realize his dream of building great, beautiful, unique houses. He wants to create beauty where there is none. He wants to inject light into the ironically dim Lamptown. But he finds, like Carol Kennicott in Sin-clair Lewis's *Main Street*, that Lamptown folks just want to be like other folks; they don't want to live in houses that are different from other folks' houses. So his beautiful castles become behemoths on the fringe of town, unwanted and unappreciated—not unlike Morry himself, blessed with an eye for beauty, cursed with an oafish, oversized body. He cannot find a place where he fits in Lamptown, like his houses cannot find a place. So he must escape to a place that can appreciate his beauty. Like Kennicott, he will light out for more exciting horizons. If he follows Carol Kennicott's path, he will leave Jen behind, as Carol left behind her husband and children. And, perhaps, like Carol, he will return.[24]

The escapes do not have to be into something that a character per-forms particularly well. It is simply something that the character enjoys. In *The Bride's House*, Mary Cecily finds escape in music, "although she did not play the piano more than fairly well, nor did she know much of music. . . . When Sophie was only eleven, she had stood in the hall outside the parlor, puzzled and vaguely unhappy over the endless monotonous rhythm of Mary Cecily's playing. Presently the parlor door would open and a radiant, rapt Mary Cecily would emerge . . . " (*Bride's,* 80). Mary Cecily escapes wholly into the music, becoming "breathless, flushed, immersed" (*Bride's,* 212). Her escape enrages her husband—"When a woman gets so excited over a piano that she can't see her own husband . . . I tell you I won't have it" (*Bride's,* 212)—so he forbids her to play the piano. The loss of escape kills Mary Cecily. After days without the solace of creating music on the piano, she wanders to the brook with her son to listen to the "low purling octaves and arpeggios" of the water. Transfixed, Mary Cecily walks into the water and drowns, and she is finally utterly transformed by her escape.

Music provides another form of escape in these novels, in the shape of dance night—*Dance Night,* of course, revolves around this small-town phenomenon. *She Walks in Beauty* reveals the class distinctions inherent in this small-town event, as Linda yearned to go to the country-club dances, but "refused to mingle with the factory girls who went to Max's Saturday night dances" (*Beauty,* 20). Dorrie, in her direct manner, questions Linda's adherence to these socially imposed distinctions:

> "Why do they call it the Country Club? . . . They don't have any clubhouse, and they don't have it in the country. They have their parties in the Elks' Hall, just like Max's Saturday night dances. Almost the same people go, too, except that they pay a dollar instead of a quarter, and old Mr. Remer wears his dress suit. . . .
>
> "I don't see what difference the name makes when it's the same thing. . . . 'Course, they do take the cab to Club dances, and walk to Max's; and then they have punch. . . . But it seems to me they might as well call the Club dances Max's dances, and Max's dances the Club dances. See?" (*Beauty,* 24–25)

Linda, however, "refused to comfort herself with cynical reflections on the insignificance of the society that rejected her. The more cruelly society treated her, the more exalted it became in her eyes, and the more desirable became its favor" (*Beauty,* 25). When Linda does finally have the opportunity to go to a Country Club dance with the man of her dreams, she is the belle of the ball in her cousin's old yellow organdie.

Elsinore Abbott's life revolves around Thursday night's dance night as a means of escaping the psychologically abusive relationship with her husband. Elsinore lives in a fantasy world built upon a crush on Mr. Fischer, the dance instructor. As with Mary Cecily, Elsinore finally finds a more final form of escape. Rather than killing herself, though, Elsinore kills her husband, Charles. In the only violent death in Powell's novels, Elsinore shoots her husband with his own gun. The explosion of passion leaves Elsinore free, but also empty and cold; no longer in need of an escape, she loses focus.

Carnival Time

At times, a change in scene provides a temporary escape. The most notable change in the small towns of Ohio in the early twentieth century was the arrival of the carnival. It is carnival unlike that of modern New York City, conveyed in Powell's later narratives; in the city, the modern translation of carnival is played out in cafés and bars and is very nearly a part of daily life. In the Ohio towns, carnival is purer, closer to its roots as a disruptive force, riding into town but once a year, altering the mindset of the provincials. Powell conveys the disruptive, freeing effect of the annual fair when it arrives in Ashton in *The Bride's House:*

> Buggies and wagons lined the streets of the self-satisfied little town, flags flew, bands played parading down the street, Civil War veterans marched, and a group of youngsters bore a Loyal Temperance Legion banner and sang "Saloons, Saloons, Saloons must go!" But on the contrary saloons had sprung up over night to meet the county's annual thirst. A fragrant alcoholic haze flung over the town, and tented the entire Fair Grounds. Streets were giddy with laughter and the shrill voices and megaphoned speeches of visiting politicians. There were clusters of starched white and flying ribbons here and there, groups of rosy farm girls giggling and ogling each passing man. By nighttime the groups—with good luck—would be scattered, each girl giggling with an awkward young man in some tree-shaded buggy behind the Fair Grounds, hysterically sipping from a jug of corn whiskey and abandoning herself to private yearnings. The wretched little frame hotels, supported comfortably all year by half a dozen travelling salesmen, now bulged with guests, and window shades were drawn night and day, boasting of the iniquity of their bedrooms. Carnival gods rode over the city and sprinkled the orthodox with their confetti. (*Bride's,* 131–32)

At the fair, Lynn watches his betrothed, Sophie, turn again and again with Jerome in the dance pavilion, neither of them speaking a word: "Their feet moved in marvelous accord. They were part of the music, part of each other" (*Bride's,* 144). At the fair, Sophie and Jerome are free to waltz without fear of exposure, because everyone at the carnival is equally exposed. All action is free action because, as Mikhail Bakhtin notes,

> The laws, prohibitions, and restrictions that determine the structure and order of ordinary, that is noncarnival, life are suspended during carnival . . . All *distance* between people is suspended, and a special carnival category goes into effect: *free and familiar contact among people*. . . . People who in life are separated by impenetrable hierarchical barriers enter into free familiar contact on the carnival square.[25]

Thus, at carnival time, a married man and a betrothed woman may hold each other close. When they leave the fair/carnival, their love again becomes illicit. Sophie begins her return to her self as she and Lynn leave the carnival: "The gaiety had brought color to Sophie's cheeks. The blend of music, shrill shouts, the strident discords of the carrousel fed in her a hunger for vulgarity, though to herself she said, 'This is not for me but for people like Bessie. This is cheap' " (*Bride's,* 138–39). For a time, Sophie is "cheap" also.

In *She Walks in Beauty,* the "magical, beautiful carnival night!" (*Beauty,* 183) is also the scene of extramarital shenanigans. Esther is used to this activity but is freed even more by the wildness of the night:

> It was all spread out over the Fair Grounds down by the Birchfield River. You could hear the insane music of the carrousel from far up the street— hollow, soulless, strident. Then the creaking of the machine and the giggle of a farm girl astride a wooden camel. . . . Nearby the Ferris wheel revolved gracefully, and high up a lady squealed. Her man's callous conquering laugh echoed hers. . . . Strange, oddly dressed people—mostly rural—walked about, eating popcorn, gravely bearing grotesque dolls and balloons, staring at the side shows, mumbling innuendoes at the Living Statues before one tent, or casting hopeful glances at tittering groups of bareheaded town girls. (*Beauty,* 182)

Dorrie runs to a tent, then turns and finds "to her surprise Esther was nowhere to be seen. She looked anxiously around her. When she had run from that storm of confetti she must have lost her" (*Beauty,* 183–84). Esther appears next to a car with two men, and Dorrie, enchanted by the evening, goes riding "Fifty miles an hour—pretty good for the little boat" (*Beauty,* 184). Then the car stops and "Dorrie felt a wet tobaccoey mouth pressed on hers. A nausea of fear seized her. She pushed him back. Even in the darkness she could see Esther and the other man slip quietly off into the weedy fields" (*Beauty,* 185). Dorrie jumps from the car and runs: "The beat of her flying feet on the cement road and the menacing clop-clop of her pursuer's. Around them the air was full of echoes, echoes of carnival music, carnival laughter. . . . A drop of rain fell on her face. . . . Confetti." (*Beauty*, 187). Dorrie trips and her pursuer catches her—and walks her home. And all is well. The carnival atmosphere induced Dorrie to do something that she probably would not have done otherwise—riding in the car with strangers—but the carnival here does not have lasting effects on the protagonist.

In the crucial carnival scene of *The Tenth Moon*, a sword of flame divides Connie's real and imagined lives. Still glowing from the "sudden holy feeling of being divinely selected for great things" after singing before the great master Morini, Constance Greene walked across her grandfather's lawn and

> At the edge of the estate she heard sounds of a brass band. There was no night-life in the village so, curious, she walked down the lane to the town center. . . . the whole village was jeweled with colored lights, a carrousel and an illuminated ferris wheel glittered through the trees. A little shy, she kept in the shadow till she came to the Square where the crowd was collected, waiting for some special performance. As Connie looked around, she was jostled by a young man in a spangled tunic and white tights. "Look—there—that's Tony, the Daredevil! Look! there he goes!" She heard the whispers from the crowd about her and caught their excitement. She was glad when he turned back and smiled boldly at her. She pressed forward and saw him climb the torch-lit ladder to the balcony from which his wire stretched across to a warehouse roof on the other side of the brook. His smile had made his performance somehow her special responsibility, she blushed at the crowd's rapture. That would always be her picture of Tony,—that first glamorous impression, red torch-lights illuminating a hundred upturned faces, a band playing, and high up the glittering figure of a boy in spangled tights, dancing on a silver thread. When she thought of herself singing in some great concert hall later she could not untangle the dream of her own fabulous triumph from this triumph of Tony's. (*Moon*, 73–74)

The effect of carnival for Connie Greene is more profound than for Dorrie; it changes Connie's life utterly. After this point, she cannot differentiate between the life of the carnival, with its bright lights, and her own dull existence. When reality fails to live up to her imagined life, she retreats to the life begun during carnival. Connie's fate is not far removed from the effect on Sophie. The difference is that Sophie had feelings for Jerome before the carnival; the carnival simply freed her to act on those feelings without retribution.

Marriage: A False Escape

Sophie's carnival encounter occurred the night before her wedding. She had hastened the wedding date in the hope that marriage would provide an escape from her tortured thoughts: "She must marry Lynn quickly before this confusion in her brain drove her mad. If she were married to him she would not think of anyone else. She would not be alone in the night, tormented with a desire to see Jerome Gardiner again. She would belong all to Lynn and Jerome Gardiner would be only a dark, heavy-eyed ghost" (*Bride's,* 111–12). Marriage does not provide the hoped-for escape. Sophie thinks of Jerome even on her wedding day and continues to meet with him late at night. Eventually, she runs away to be with him.

Powell continually points out the falseness of marriage as an escape from loneliness. Her diaries chronicle a lifetime of trying to balance her work as a wife and her work as a writer. "There is certainly something the matter when I am forced to confess that for the past year I am bored almost to the screaming point. Mr. and Mrs. Jones visit Mr. and Mrs. Smith, Mr. and Mrs. Smith return the call, and the doughy, numbing routine of bourgeois matrimony continues—blah!" (*Diaries,* 51). Though Powell clearly loved her husband, there are indications that she had an early love affair with John Howard Lawson, and it is certain that she had a lifelong friendship with Coburn Gilman, though there is not clear evidence of a sexual relationship between the two. After Joe's death, Powell wrote:

> Old retired couples . . . are each other's prisoners, as Joe was mine and I was his. Lovers become prisoners, eventually needing each other against the world, protecting each other, kind to each other through necessity. The cage is too small but they must live in it and with it so after a while they control the quick word because such intimate necessity is close to murder. (*Diaries,* 433–34)

After a lifetime of marriage, Powell had developed a less-than-romantic view of the institution.

The Bride's House, in particular, focuses on the "caged" nature of marriage, as Sophie struggles to determine whether her place in "the bride's house" will bring an end to her desperate yearnings. She continually shifts between the certainty that marriage will quell her urgings and the cold knowledge that, as Mary Cecily sagely, softly offered: "Marriage doesn't make any difference" (*Bride's*, 85) . . . "Sophie knew and feared in her heart that what Mary Cecily had said was true . . . that even in Lynn's arms she would be desolate . . . that in the white house with the green shutters she would go on longing for unknown things" (*Bride's*, 86). After Sophie marries Lynn, she indeed finds that marriage does not provide solace. When her husband is gone at night, she flees the little white house to roam the frosty fields, dark except where "pierced by lights on far hills. She knew that each light meant a fireside, a dozing husband, a tranquil wife knitting beside him, children asleep upstairs under sloping eaves. She pitied and envied those women their serenity" (*Bride's*, 226). And, ultimately, for Sophie, marriage doesn't make a difference. She leaves Lynn, carrying his child, to go to Jerome Gardiner where "there was no calm or safety" (*Bride's*, 291). As she sits with Jerome, "twisting her wedding ring on her finger" (*Bride's*, 291), she wonders, "will there be others?" And later that night, in his arms, she "knew that he would hurt her as she had hurt Lynn, and that he would hold her forever because of his power to make her suffer. . . . A woman needed two lovers, one to comfort her for the torment the other caused her" (*Bride's*, 293–94).

Mary Cecily, who seems to all to be happily married, has a curious indifference about her husband.

> He was Husband. Mary Cecily had not the faintest curiosity about him except when her baby was born and he sat beside her white still bed with his granite shoulders shaking. Then a vague wonder stirred her, and she put her hand out curiously to touch him, as if perhaps there might be some reality in him after all.
>
> He did not exist in her world, and sometimes she was aware of his misery in being left out. (*Bride's*, 210)

Mary Cecily's "other love" is her music; when her husband forbids her to play the piano ever again, she submits: "She must not touch the piano, because music flung a towering wall between herself and her husband. Her fingers burned for the cool keys. She ached with the desire to pluck lovely sounds from the air with her two hands" (*Bride's*, 213).

The barbed courtship between Anna Stacey and George Truelove shows a vicious view of marriage. Anna Stacey is determined to rebuff George because his sister, Sophie, took the man she wanted. Anna Stacey "hated him. . . . But that was not saying she might not marry him" (*Bride's*, 173). For his part, George thought "a woman was for a

man's conquering, and there was little sport in following a girl who had
no desire to run" (*Bride's*, 174). They do finally marry, in the worst of
circumstances: They marry shortly after Mary Cecily's suicide, with the
misguided hope that Anna Stacey, "odd creature" that she is, could take
the place of the quiet, sweet Mary Cecily, who has died for love of her
music. After the very small ceremony in the spinster sisters' living room,
the newlyweds move into the Trueloves' house and "Sophie's own room
was given to the bride and groom, and the maple branches . . . heard a
man's conquering love-making, with a woman's whispered interpola-
tion—'I hate you, I hate you—I hate you!' " (*Bride's*, 219).

In *She Walks in Beauty*, Linda's life goal is to marry Courtney Stall
and live in the privileged lifestyle of Birchfield—on the right side of the
tracks. Various couples contrast Linda's ideal view of marriage. One
such couple is Lew and Esther Mason: "Lew was forty, and had been
dully surprised to find himself married to Mart Brown's daughter. He
had gone out to Mart's farm to buy a bay mare, but found the filly on
the market as well. She was tall, flashing-eyed, full-bosomed, well-
developed at seventeen, wild to be free, and thirsty for life" (*Beauty*,
13–14). Esther married Lew primarily to escape the farm, and she fills
her evenings with trysts with other men:

> Esther thought of [Lew] as a satisfactory enough husband. She would
> always love him for bringing her to the city. When she lay in a damp
> clump of weeds, in some boy's arms, she looked up at the lovely moon
> and was grateful to Lew for opening the gates to Paradise. When she sat
> on the schoolhouse steps long after midnight, pressed hotly against some
> man's moist breast, she thought of how much she owed to her husband.
> (*Beauty*, 48)

Lew responds to Esther's infidelity as he would respond to a horse that
has escaped the pen: "All she needed was a good beating and she'd be as
good as gold" (*Beauty*, 263). Rather than a beating, though, Esther is
caught philandering with Courtney Stall. In order to save the reputation
of the Stalls, Courtney agrees to marry Linda. Linda achieves her
longed-for escape by default.

In *Dance Night*, Elsinore blasts her way out of the trap of marriage.
Her various escapes were artlessly designed to provide her a release; she
never expected much from her marriage, it seems, but is nevertheless
trapped, because Charles is too jealous a man to ever let her go freely.
The only surprise is Elsinore's inability to recognize the lovelessness of
the marriage much earlier than she does.

It had never occurred to Elsinore, for ten years self-and-home-supporting, that Mr. Abbott's opinion deserved little attention. She accepted his husbandly domination without demanding any of its practical benefits. If Charles, home for a week from a three months' Southern tour, objected to a gown of hers or a new arrangement of furniture, things were quietly changed to his taste. In Elsinore's scheme a husband was always a husband. (*Dance*, 13)

With this philosophy, Elsinore's only means of escape are to kill either herself or her husband.

In all of the novels, Powell explores the escape mechanisms available to those lacking the inclination or strength to physically escape the bonds that hold them.

Shades of Wit

Powell's focus on the interior lives of these provincials does not allow for much humor. There are, however, moments of lightness in these novels that hint at Powell's droll side. The wit most often takes the form of subtle irony—as in the figure of Mrs. Pepper, the corset saleslady who is quite plump—and in the form of comic relief characters. Grandmother Truelove's interior monologues provide some humor as she juggles decades-old memories with present-day occurrences, weaving them into rationale that functions only for her. For instance, when her son notes that she hasn't eaten anything, his wife, Cecily, responds:

> "She never eats anything. . . . Never anything but biscuits and syrup."
> "Cecily, I do eat other things," said Grandmother Truelove haughtily. "It just happens that today I—I—"
> She forgot what she started to say. That happened at noon always when she was so drowsy. But she did remember that Cecily had said something to annoy her and that the dignified thing to do would be to proudly leave the table. (*Bride's*, 35)

Such sad amusement—rather than quick, biting wit—suits the pace of these novels.

The wit occasionally serves to soften particularly ruthless caricatures. For instance, in *The Bride's House*, the Anderson sisters with their "avid spinsters' eyes and sagging fish mouths" (*Bride's*, 47) devote themselves to the cause of prying into other people's business, then broadcasting their own version of the news. But in one ridiculous scene, Powell humanizes them by revealing their vulnerabilities. This glimpse is permitted when George Truelove arrives at their house to propose to Anna Stacey, the schoolteacher who is living with them. Because Miss Lucy answers the door wearing a "heavy green-veiled hat," George assumes they are going out. But, no, Miss Lucy says,

> "I have a hat on because I always wear a hat. With the garden to take care of, you're just running in and out all the time so we keep our hats on. It saves bother really."
>
> Sure enough Sara appeared behind her sister, her withered face framed in a similar hat. Anna Stacey could have told him that the two old maids wore their hats to breakfast, and even on winter days sat by the fire from morning to evening without removing them. It was not the garden but an experiment in dyes many years ago that had made the Andersons sensitive about their bare heads. There were still strange purple and green streaks in Lucy's scanty locks, and a variety of cerise, lavender and chocolate shades in Sara's that gave her sister complete nausea in those brief moments in the bedroom when they revealed their mutual eccentricities. Out of deference to each other they wore their hats. Natty felt tricorns with kimonos as they pared their nails in their bedroom. Velvet poke bonnets with calico aprons as they made a two-egg angel-cake in the kitchen. Venerable plumed Gainsboroughs as they milked the cows in the stable yard. Their storeroom was filled with hats for they had never thrown away any of their clothes from earliest girlhood. (*Bride's*, 176–77)

The absurdity of the hats reveals the eccentricities of these women, in addition to providing a glimpse of their daily routines as they plod along in a curiously formal intimacy, having known each other all their lives but not trusting even each other. In addition to shearing off the forbidding veneer of the sisters, the scene also relieves the reader before the ponderous scene between George and Anna Stacey.

The Story of a Country Boy is Powell's first satire, though she doesn't seem to have recognized it as such. The focus of her satire is not the provincial or the small town but the "revolt from the provinces" itself, in addition to a completely unwitting satire of proletarian works. As with Connie Benjamin, Christopher Bennett perceives himself as someone other than who he is. But unlike Connie, who lives in an imagined world where she is famous, Bennett clings to his humble rural roots despite his continual economic rise. This novel is characterized by its shifting voice, from third person to stream of consciousness, so that the path of Ben-

nett's "economic, social and moral decline" is clearer to the reader than
to Bennett. Powell explains this devolution: "My novels are based on the
fantastic designs made by real human beings earnestly laboring to mal-
adjust themselves to fate," she said. "My characters are not slaves to an
author's propaganda. I give them their heads. They furnish their own
nooses."[26]

Powell's initial concept of the story was to "write a novel about a boy
. . . who works himself up from class to class to factory head, then
unable to understand the strikers, explaining he's one of them—there
are no classes. Finally, ruin of success; prepared for great deeds, he could
not stand up to rich man's private life" (*Diaries,* 41). Very early on, Powell envisioned the protagonist to be "Morry grown up now, an official in
Lamptown factory, and still yearning for cities, to go away and see Jen,
their egos still fighting" (*Diaries,* 42). When Powell fleshed out the
story, the link to Morry was gone and Powell had developed a plan ripe
for 1930s interests:

> Decided to do next book about Charlie Miller—shy boy who only hopes
> to do his work in Handlebar Factory well, who works dutifully and is
> pushed up and up until he is general manager of big factory. Puts money
> in real estate—because he doesn't know how to buy luxuries beyond fine
> hotels, Miami, Hollywood, San Bernadino Hills, etc. Great empty house
> without pictures or books, lots of dogs and cats and good automobiles
> and good food.
>
> Then strike. Workers shoot at him as his car goes to work, call him
> lousy capitalist; he is horrified because by instinct and labor he is one of
> them, hurt by their lack of loyalty. They're all workers together, the rea-
> son he has a chauffeur is he's so damned nervous he can't drive, he has
> maids because of bad digestion caused by his wife's cooking.
>
> They hiss, and he goes back, the factory is weakened, he is so upset by
> accusations of his living on fat of land that he is flattered at dawning real-
> ization that he is one of those marvelous idle rich. He starts in furiously
> doing all those things—women, drinking, cars, New York—but he is
> simple peasant stock, he can't take it in his stride, he must either work or
> play. Canned from job, he drinks at home all day, uses his private golf
> course as a public one, uses house as tea-room, finally is back with old
> father saying, "No such thing as a man being worth more than $25 a
> week" and happily damning the damn capitalists once again. (*Diaries,* 43)

Powell's development of the plot was heavily influenced by John
Howard Lawson, a proletarian writer who encouraged Powell to nurture
the Marxist implications of Bennett's refusal to embrace his social rise:

Jack [Lawson] is thinking and talking so much more clearly and directly
than ever before owing, he says, to Trotsky and a study of Marxian theo-
ries applied to creative work. The business of thinking straight—what do
you want to prove and what type of protagonist will best prove your idea
and is the idea sound to begin with?

In trying to follow what Jack pointed out for clear thinking in my
new works planned, what do I want to prove in this "Farmer Boy" novel?
Answer: that a simple, clear person is forced to serve a cause distasteful
to him but because of his simplicity does not see where he changed from
proletarian to capitalist. I wish to show that these labels and classifica-
tions are external only, but that the external label slowly forces its way
inside if you are to be happy. Chris' tragedy is that he remained a bare-
footed farmer boy through his capitalist career—a friend of the work-
man, against capitalism always as he had been taught by his father and
did not know the mask was on him until the laborers hooted and stoned
his car in the street. (*Diaries,* 52)

The theory, clearly stated here, is not as evident in the execution of the
story. Rather than appearing to be a man of high morals, who prefers
simplicity over the trappings of capitalism, Bennett instead appears to be
a delusional, selfish, oafish man who cannot see why the factory workers
do not see him as their peer. He cannot see why they don't understand
his need for four cars. He is unable to conceive of why they interpret his
real-estate investments as greed. Bennett is blind to his absorption of the
wealth given to him and does not see the widening social chasm until he
is stoned by the workers. After this point, Bennett sets out not to rid
himself of his wealth in order to prove his allegiance to the workers but
rather to flaunt his wealth and drink his way into joblessness. Bennett is
unable to be either a proletarian hero or a capitalist. Instead, he is simply
a provincial who failed to make it in the big city.

The satire in this novel is not as effective as in the New York novels.
It is more Juvenalian, perhaps because Powell is aiming her pen at the
upper middle class, those who have more money than they can spend.
The biting, overwrought satire may reflect, also, Lawson's Marxist influence on the development of the novel. Powell's most effective satire, dis-
played in her New York novels, is aimed at the middle class, but conveyed indirectly.

Structure: Experiments in Form

Powell begins pushing the boundaries of conventional narrative structure in the Ohio novels. *She Walks in Beauty* skips like a rock across the

surface of a "dark pool" as Powell seemingly attempts a Midwestern version of Dos Passos's modernistic fragmentary composition, though Powell focuses on far fewer characters than Dos Passos does. With the exception of a few appealing juxtapositions, the resulting patchwork of *She Walks in Beauty* is more discordant than harmonious.[27] This method works well when Powell employs a Dickensian cliffhanger that stops the action at a critical moment. For instance, early in the novel, Ella, a "grotesque" who is wheelchair-bound and somewhat bitter, voices her opinion on the marriage between Lew and Esther Mason. She is, however, oblivious to the fact that a stranger in the room is, in fact, Esther Mason. After two pages of diatribe, Ella ponders, "Wonder what she looks like?"

> Esther Mason walked slowly over to the wheelchair, her hips swaying with insolent rhythm. She pulled the red hat leisurely over one eye and then rested one hand on her hip, her dark eyes scornfully on the cripple. "Have a look," she said. "I'm Mrs. Lew Mason." (*Beauty*, 19)

A review of *She Walks in Beauty* notes that "In spite of the genuine insight into small-town types, the story as a whole has just been 'set down,' not created; it has neither point, integration, nor form."[28] It is hard to find a pattern in the 11 chapters, which range from 6 to 47 pages long. Each chapter is further broken down into several segments of varying lengths with transitions that are alternately effective and jarring. The turnover at the boardinghouse serves as an endless source of vignettes, and the erratic structure reflects the erratic lifestyle.

The structure of *The Bride's House* is more controlled. The narrative is presented in a series of small segments, but the transitions between the segments are more effective and are reined into a more manageable frame of three chapters, the lengths of which do not vary tremendously—the first is 98 pages long, the second 133, and the final 61.

In *Dance Night's* bold structure, there are no chapter divisions. While writing the novel, Powell recorded that she felt that it was "damned huge and unwieldy" (*Diaries*, 14). The structure does parallel the largeness of the subject matter, but rather than being a "huge and unwieldy" read, the novel is very tight, as it is broken up into a series of vignettes—or melodies—held together by a thrumming bass note that is an omnipresent reminder of the trap that is the town. This novel evidences Powell's growth as a writer, as she apparently realized that the Midwest is not well suited to the improvisational jazz of

Dos Passos. The novel moves smoothly from melody to melody, marked by particularly harmonious transitions at some points, as a note echoes in the following segment. In this example, the action shifts from Mrs. Bauer's drawing room to the dancing lessons taking place two floors above her:

> "A temper, that Jen," said Mrs. Bauer, and counted four stitches under her breath.
>
> * * * *
>
> "One, two, three, FOUR, one, two, three, FOUR, one, two, three, FOUR," chanted Mr. Fischer, walking backwards, and the line of thirty wooden figures advanced toward him, one, two, three, steps, then kicked out a stiff left foot on the fourth count. (*Dance,* 57)

Powell's control is evident in the way that the movement of the language echoes the movement of the story as Powell guides the reader through the chapterless novel with prose occasionally interlaced with a song floating up from the dance hall that is the focus of action in the novel. The dance instructor's booming "one, two, three, FOUR" pulses throughout the novel, punctuating the metronomic pace of the town. It is a novel that one hears as much as one reads, as is apparent from the opening lines:

> What Morry heard above the Lamptown night noises was a woman's high voice rocking on mandolin notes far far away. This was like no music Morry had ever known, it was a song someone else remembered, perhaps his mother, when he was only a sensation in her blood, a slight quickening when she met Charles Abbott, a mere wish for love racing through her veins.
>
> The song bewildered Morry reading Jules Verne by gaslight, it unspiralled somewhere high above the Bon Ton Hat Shop, above Bauer's Chop House, over the Casino, and over Bill Delaney's Saloon and Billiard Parlor. It came from none of these places but from other worlds and then faded into a factory whistle, a fire engine bell, and a Salvation Army chorus down on Market Street. (*Dance,* 3)

In these opening lines, Powell tunes in the music of the town and introduces the primary character, Morry. In this passage, it is revealed that Morry is no stranger to this town, and that he is sensitive to changes in his environment: He can name the landmarks from which the sound does not come; he has an appetite for adventuresome literature; and he has something of an intimate relationship with his mother. What is revealed about the town is that beautiful sound is alien to it and that the town drowns out such lovely sounds with its own insistent whistles and bells. Underlying all of this is the sense of yearning conveyed by Morry's apprehension of the sound; it "bewilders" him and bewitches him, as he sits reading of escapes.

The end of *Dance Night* comes round to the beginning, placing Morry in the midst of the same sounds, under different circumstances. The ending is not conclusive, because it is not certain whether Morry will stay in Lamptown with Jen or leave the town—with or without Jen. But there is definitely closure, in accordance with the rhythm of the novel. The lack of chapters in *Dance Night* compels the reader to move onward, not looking back to the past, just as Morry and Jen and Elsinore continually press on, compelled by dreams of escaping into a brighter future.

The chapters in *The Tenth Moon* skip back and forth in time, allowing readers to pause occasionally to reconstruct a scene in their minds. This parallels the movement of Connie Benjamin and Blaine Decker as they continually reconstruct conversations and events, projecting themselves into a future conversation based on their past dreams. They are never wholly in the present. In a review of *The Tenth Moon,* Harold Stearns wrote that the book is "a fusing of the new stream-of-consciousness school and the directly realistic."[29] Powell wrote,

> This is definitely what I set out to do—to crash down new dimensions in character work, to make and know my people so that their past, present, future, wishes, regrets, dreams, and actualities were enclosed spirally in a conch-shell sort of growth, all braided simultaneously with time into one fused portrait which was not the image but the reality. (*Diaries,* 53)

Despite its forward and backward movement, the novel has a controlled feeling—paradoxically, the inexorable movement underscores the characters' lack of control over their fates. They are trapped in this movement. A larger force guides them to ends, even as they play at imagining a greater life for themselves. In the process of writing the novel, Powell wrote: "Wrote three pages on Decker. Daren't stop to think now of whether it's worth doing or not—too much tightrope balancing" (*Diaries,* 29). Powell noted in her diaries, "This new novel . . . runs along easily and solely by intuition, unlike the careful solid planning of *Dance Night*" (*Diaries,* 31).

After its completion, she mused, *"The Tenth Moon* is an excellent, lucidly written book—above the average, point for point, the only thing

I've ever done completely on brain power—a correct book—a work that can be measured with all the proper rulers" (*Diaries*, 47). Reviewers received this controlled specimen variously: Carl Van Doren said that it had "natural perfection of proportion and execution" (*Diaries*, 55). Powell herself called it "light lady writing" with "no margin of wonder in it, therefore not a vital living work" (*Diaries*, 47). More than a decade later, Powell reread *The Tenth Moon* and found a new appreciation for it:

> I looked over my journal for *Tenth Moon* but first I read the book. I seldom can read very far in my own works even if I don't recall them but to my amazement this particular book which I despised as a mere tour-de-force . . . I was actually absorbed in it and read it all the way through weeping and moved to my depths! The fact is that it is a beautiful book—the best writing I ever did and technically flawless, with the most delicate flowering of a relationship that grips interest far more than my dramatic plots such as *Country Boy*. I then examined my notes in my journal and found all the way through references to the pleasure of writing something that left my emotions absolutely uninvolved, a mere craftsmanship job, a literary joke—okay, critics, I won't give you a pound of flesh, I will cheat you. Result: a quivering book filled with pain and beauty. (*Diaries*, 214)

Powell nursed a purely intellectual interest in the development of the characters and let them shape the story, rather than plotting out the structure beforehand. She wrote early in the process, "I want to do the [novel] of the woman (or man) frustrated in the little town—crying out their greatness, their art, to jeering village multitudes" (*Diaries*, 24). After deciding to focus on both a woman and a man, Powell wrote: "I am curious about Mme. Benjamin, fascinated by Decker. The prospect of a long winter with them satisfies me utterly" (*Diaries*, 38). In shifting from *The Tenth Moon* to *The Story of a Country Boy*, Powell said of the latter: "This needs the same elaborate charting and constructive preparation that *Dance Night* did—unlike *Tenth Moon*" (*Diaries*, 49–50).

The Story of a Country Boy charts the rise and fall of a conflicted capitalist. But Powell's twist on the story subverts the conventional structure. She allows Bennett finally to achieve his dream of returning to the land, but she does not allow him to do it on his own terms: "what had for so many years seemed the fair reward for enduring the city now was the punishment for failing in the city" (*Boy*, 298). Bennett returns to the farm out of necessity, not by choice. Bennett achieved the American Dream, but when he was forced to embrace the dream and recognize that he was, in fact, a privileged member of society, he was unable to hold onto the dream. One of Powell's aims in this novel was to balance the inner life of Bennett with the outer symbols of his wealth: "I hope to combine here the objectiveness of *Dance Night* with the subjectiveness of *Tenth Moon*. I feel that I can break a little further through pages into life. I hope in this to have a new freedom, to be able to use my complete language" (*Diaries*, 66). Of considerable importance in the development of this novel is Powell's recognition that the Ohio of her youth had changed utterly. After her revelatory visit to Ohio, Powell changed the movement of the novel:

> One important key in this new novel: the *new* Ohio must be the keynote—the dizziness of speed through broad auto highways, hot dog stations, not the tranquil hayfields of my recollection. That was one problem with *Dance Night*—an arrested background. Backgrounds should be fluid to be alive. (*Diaries*, 54)

The shift in speed is marked in the novel by Bennett's wild, three-day driving-and-drinking binge, in which he devastates the countryside by tearing up fields with his car and defiling haystacks and barns. He is, in essence, destroying his real dream of returning to the country on his own terms, to tend and nurture the land.

In addition to altering the novel, the visit had an impact on Powell's perception of time past and present. After the visit, Powell embraced her present time and place, devoting her energies to the New York novel that had been simmering for four years. Although Powell herself occasionally had great longings for the country, she also had a great fear of having to return home to live. Perhaps out of fear of "failing in the city" herself, Powell returned to her New York novel *Turn, Magic Wheel*—which she had begun work on by 1930—and spun into her New York cycle.

In the Ohio novels, Powell moved from the long-ago, remembered past of her Ohio childhood to a time nearly contemporary with the year of publication. By shoring up the fragments of her past, she cleared the way to write of her own time and place. *The Story of a Country Boy* revealed to Powell that she no longer knew this place, this Ohio. It would be another 10 years before Powell returned to Ohio as a setting—and a world of change happened to her writing in between. For a decade, she embraced her new home, ready to write of New York City. Years later, she wrote in a short memoir: "Over the years, this one died and that one, but I never went back to funerals. So they're dead, so the past is dead, and Ohio is gone. All right. Today is here. New York is here. Why go back to the dead?" (*Best*, 446). Powell turned to the living.

Chapter Three
"Half of Me by Day": The New York Novels

"I am New York—this minute—now. I know more about it than any-one—not historically but momentarily. I must do a New York novel to be happy—one in the *Magic Wheel* series" (*Diaries,* 285). Powell, feeling fully a part of the city, began consciously writing in the genre of the city novel, with a sequential scheme for her work within this genre. Laid over this "city novel" genre is Powell's satiric penetration, which shows her characters in a super-real, comic light that illuminates them beyond the merely realistic. Thus two genres—the New York novel and satire— merge in this cycle of novels. Powell does not attempt to capture the spirit of the city in a single novel. Instead, she focuses on slices of the city in each novel, drawing upon the broadly accommodating form of Menippean satire, characterized by its seemingly random patterns of detail that ultimately reveal a complete picture. In *The Happy Island,* the chaotic Menippean elements wind through the novel so thoroughly that it sends the novel genre spinning away like a top. In the other novels, the two genres dip and part like dancers as Powell orchestrates the development of the idea.

To better appreciate Powell's vision, it is helpful to isolate first the elements of city fiction. Of the studies of city fiction—some few of which focus on New York City fiction—most are concerned with detail-ing particular haunts and residences of literary figures rather than with studying the structure of the fiction itself. Of the handful that deal with city fiction as genre, Joan Zlotnick's *Portrait of an American City: The Novelist's New York* (1982)[1] provides a chronological route of fiction set in and about New York City from colonial times to the early 1980s. In *The American City Novel* (1954),[2] Blanche Housman Gelfant arranges her discussion structurally according to the definition of the city novel, focusing on exemplary authors in each category.[3] Both Gelfant and Zlotnick identify three categories of city novels: "portrait novels" are "works about young men and women who come there in search of wealth or fame" (Zlotnick, 3); the curiously named "ecological novel," which Gelfant defines spatially—that is, a novel focusing on a particular neighborhood or area—and that Zlotnick defines socially as "novels written about particular groups of New Yorkers whose life styles are shaped by the environment in which they have been born and raised" (Zlotnick, 3); and the "synoptic novel" (Gelfant, 14), in which the city itself is the protagonist.[4]

Most of Powell's New York novels fall into what Gelfant dubbed the "ecological novel," but they differ from both Gelfant and Zlotnik's definitions because most of Powell's characters were not born and raised in New York. As the visiting provincial Jeff Abbott observes in *The Happy Island:*

> I expected to find New Yorkers different but not another race of mankind. Sure, I listened to 'em for a while, but it's not my language, not even my country they're talking about. Don't they speak anything but Stravinsky and Hollywood? Didn't anything ever happen to them but the opera and *Esquire*? Where did they get that way? Where the hell do they come from?[5]

"Iowa" his companion responds, "Iowa, Fall River, Terre Haute, places like that. I don't know their language, myself. I'm a New Yorker. We're rather simple here" (*Island*, 40–41). The characters who people the "social sets" that Powell satirizes are more "New York" than native New Yorkers, and the novels might be best termed "social-set" novels, rather than "ecological" novels, because the characters are not always restricted to one place in the city. In this type of novel, the characters have on their "public" faces most of the time, even in private.

From the outset of this cycle of novels, it is apparent that Powell is working outside clearly defined parameters of the city novel. Unlike the Ohio novels, which incorporated occasional modes of satire, in the New York novels her satiric vision permeates the structure of the writing, transforming it into something other than the traditional novel. The diversity and quick pace of the city throb as Powell echoes the pulse of her adopted city. Powell lived in New York City for a decade before embarking on her first "New York novel," and it was another six years before she completed the novel to her satisfaction.[6] This novel, *Turn, Magic Wheel* (1936), is presented in a series of fragments that reveal character, scene, and, finally, plot. In order to make the spirit of the city come alive, Powell shifts interior scenes rapidly and incorporates a variety of rhetorical forms, including the soliloquy and the symposium, to move in and around her characters. Powell's New York novels are engaging, in a way reflective of Menippean satire, which was developed in part for "the beguiling of a less-initiate audience."[7] The "lightly spun and seemingly frivolous or aimless plots" that Matthew Josephson noted in Powell's novels are also characteristic of Menippean satire, which is subtly biting beneath its smiling veneer. Readings of Powell's New York novels are enriched by an understanding of this eclectic genre.

Anatomy of Menippean Satire

Gore Vidal said that Powell "saw life with a bright Petronian neutrality, and every host at life's feast was a potential Trimalchio to be sent up."[8] Petronius's *Satyricon,* oft-cited by Powell as a favorite book, remains the classic example of Menippean satire. Although parts of the *Satyricon* have been lost, the remaining fragments of the narrative—a mixture of prose and verse—detail the adventures of a young man and his acquaintance as they expose the follies and vices of ancient Rome. Trimalchio presides over an incredibly lush, decadent banquet in which he reveals not only an amazing appetite but also a perverse pleasure in causing discomfort to his guests as the price of admission.[9] Dustin Griffin notes:

> Trimalchio's feast serves as a metaphor for Petronius's satire, and Trimalchio a figure for the satirist. What is the feast but a display of ingenuity and wit, a series of tricks, from the *trompe l'oeil* dog painted on the entrance wall to the culinary cleverness that disguises cooks as hunters and pastries as pigs or eggs? By means of a series of bizarre surprises and reversals, Trimalchio stimulates the jaded palates of his guests and compels their admiration. So too Petronius himself, in a narrative satire constructed like a series of separate courses, startles and astonishes, keeps his readers off balance, makes them wonder what is coming next. . . . Dining with Trimalchio, or reading Petronius, does not gratify simple hunger or satisfy our basic needs, physical or ethical. . . . For readers the whole process is a little dizzying: we're glad to be invited, the fare is extraordinary, but it's all a bit too much, and we're finally glad to escape.[10]

Powell's presentations can also be dizzying. Her "Trimalchios" range from publishing magnate Henry Luce and writer Clare Booth Luce to art patron Peggy Guggenheim and writer Ernest Hemingway. The feasting patrons are the middle-class circles of friends who gather around such figures, hoping for a beam of fame to illuminate them, if briefly.

In the twentieth century, Menippean satire is most often found in the form of a novel. Analyzing satiric novels is a difficult task, as Griffin explains:

Satire in fiction is said to be detectable in a certain flattening of character toward caricature, a stylizing of action toward the emblematic, a reductive sharpening of narrative tone toward ridicule, and what Mikhail Bakhtin would call "monological" discourse. The problem with such accounts is that the satire so identified is finally not very interesting, not very good. At most it induces easy laughter. A better account of the subject would show that satire typically complicates narrative fiction. (Griffin, 4)

Griffin's comments summarize criticism of Powell's novels. As Northrop Frye notes, "It is the anatomy in particular that has baffled critics, and there is hardly any fiction writer deeply influenced by it who has not been accused of disorderly conduct."[11] This "disorderly conduct" refers to both the organization of the narrative and a certain civil disobedience that results from satire's necessary focus on the present or the very recent past. Frye's observation quite aptly sums up both Powell's vision and form.

A clear characteristic of Menippean satire is its focus on present action. Powell embraced this focus, writing that "The query—why did you write this or that?—is almost always answered in my case by a sense of historical duty to get a picture of a fleeting way of life. . . . Usually the urge comes when the special scene is fading—the new one hasn't been formed yet but is waiting in the wings. Swan Songs are my specialty" (*Diaries*, 452). Bakhtin discusses a complication of this focus in the interplay of satire—as a "serio-comical" genre—and the living present:

The first characteristic of all genres of the serio-comical is their new relationship to reality: their subject or—what is more important—their starting point for understanding, evaluating and shaping reality, is the living *present*, often even the very day. . . . the subject of *serious* (to be sure, at the same time comical) representation is presented without any epic or tragic distance, presented not in the absolute past of myth and legend but on the plane of the present day, in a zone of immediate and even crudely familiar contact with living contemporaries. (Bakhtin, 108)

So the author is simultaneously living in the present and viewing it in a serio-comical manner, then translating this view to prose in whatever form best expresses that view. That form is rarely a linear journey from beginning, through climax, to the end, because such defining points are usually apparent only from the distance of the future. The shaping present has no endpoints. This necessarily makes it difficult to place the Menippean genre within the traditional parameters of the novel.

To complicate the issue further, Menippean satire is highly experimental. Therefore, a reader may come to appreciate a certain form, only to find that the author's next novel is radically different, requiring a different kind of reading. Eugene Kirk acknowledges that, "There was never 'one kind' of Menippean satire, not even in the writings of Menippus himself—for Menippus parodied broadly the different ancient forms of learned discourse. Contaminations, fusions, and separations of form attend most of the history of Menippean satire, as the age and its occasions might happen to require" (Kirk, xiv).[12] In his attempt to confine the genre, Frye wrote that the Menippean satire deals less with people as such than with attitudes:

> Pedants, bigots, cranks, parvenus, virtuosi, enthusiasts, rapacious and incompetent professional men of all kinds, are handled in terms of their occupational approach to life as distinct from their social behavior. The Menippean satire thus resembles the confession in its ability to handle abstract ideas and theories, and differs from the novel in its characterization, which is stylized rather than naturalistic, and presents people as mouthpieces of the ideas they represent. (Frye, 309)[13]

Powell's satire also deals "less with people as such than with mental attitudes"—her focus was the spirit of a time and place. Her narratives were anatomies, to use Frye's term, of the middle class.

Powell's anatomies of New York life, revealed as they were through the language, called for a special form that both reveals and conceals the truth—an ambivalent game of hide-and-seek where the reader laughs aloud at a character's foolishness, then recognizes the familiar in the gesture. Understanding Menippean satire helps in reading Powell's novels, because it explains the lack of plot and closure. Before embarking, Bakhtin offers a warning:

> The application of such terms as "epic," "tragedy," "idyll" to modern literature has become generally accepted and customary, and we are not in the least confused when *War and Peace* is called an epic, *Boris Godunov* a tragedy, "Old-World Landowners" an idyll. But the generic term "menippea" is not customary (especially in our literary scholarship), and therefore its application to works of modern literature . . . may seem somewhat strange and strained. (Bakhtin, 178 n. 10)

Strange and strained though it may be, the term goes far to explain Powell's structure and vision. The Menippean characteristics should help elucidate the text, not confine it.

Additional help in understanding Powell's satires is provided by Alvin Kernan in his study of satire, *The Cankered Muse* (1959). Kernan's extended definition of satire first divides, then rejoins, satiric texts into the elements of scene, satirist, and plot. The distilled version of his theory asserts that

> no matter what the mode of presentation, the elements of satire . . . remain fairly constant. The scene is always crowded, disorderly, grotesque; the satirist, in those satires where he appears, is always indignant, dedicated to truth, pessimistic, and caught in a series of unpleasant contradictions incumbent on practicing his trade; the plot always takes the pattern of purpose followed by passion, but fails to develop beyond this point. For purposes of discussion I have treated scene, plot, and satirist as distinct from one another, while in any given satire where all are present they interact and reinforce one another to form a composite whole.[14]

Kernan's theory proves to be a valuable definition, precisely because it is broad enough to allow application to a variety of genres.[15] Bakhtin fleshes out the notion of chaotic scene by incorporating the tradition of carnival:

> Carnival itself . . . is not, of course, a literary phenomenon. It is *syncretic pageantry* of a ritualistic sort. As a form it is very complex and varied, giving rise, on a general carnivalistic base, to diverse variants and nuances depending upon the epoch, the people, the individual festivity. Carnival has worked out an entire language of symbolic concretely sensuous forms—from large and complex mass actions to individual carnivalistic gestures. . . . Carnival is a pageant without footlights and without a division into performers and spectators. In carnival everyone is an active participant, everyone communes in the carnival act. Carnival is not contemplated and, strictly speaking, not even performed; its participants *live* in it, they live by its laws as long as those laws are in effect; that is, they live a *carnivalistic life*. Because carnivalistic life is life drawn out of its *usual* rut, it is to some extent "life turned inside out," "the reverse side of the world." (Bakhtin, 122).

The carnivalization provides a reason for the disorderly and grotesque scene, out of which emerges the chronicler of the scene: the satirist. The satirist's ability to understand the scene has a great impact on his ability to perform his role as satirist. The person who has been a part of the carnival is best able to understand it—but he must also be able to remove himself from the scene and dissemble it in his mind in order to present it. Bakhtin also provides key events in the menippea—such as the crowning and decrowning of the "carnival king," or, in modern terms, the rise and fall of a public figure—which allow for a clearer understanding of the plot, or movement, of the narrative.

The Scene: New York City

New York City is both the setting and focus of these works, but they are not "synoptic" novels in the way that Dos Passos's novels are. Dos Passos was striving to reveal the whole city through a series of fragmented glimpses into characters' lives. Powell's novels are not nearly as cubist in structure. Powell was primarily interested in the interplay of character and city, showing how each shapes the other, much as she did in the Ohio novels. She reminded herself, "Never forget geography. New York is heroine. Make the city live, so that reader walking about town thinks—here is the Fifth Avenue hotel, where so and so came" (*Diaries,* 305). Powell's sense of reality does not translate into a slavish devotion to realism but rather to a necessity to capture those images that help to convey the spirit of the city.

Grounded in the events of Powell's living present, the novels provide a vivid portrait of the lifestyle of New York in a given time. In these novels, Powell does with mid-twentieth-century New York what Edith Wharton did with the same city a few decades earlier: She captures a people moving about their own lives in the surprisingly small world of New York City. Throughout Powell's novels, the city is a presence, shaping the actions of the characters and showing how little control they really have over destiny, the magic wheel that hurtles them forward. One of Powell's aims was to chronicle her age, to create a novel of manners for the twentieth century:

> In the last century, Thackeray, Dickens, Edith Wharton, James, all wrote of their own times and we have reliable records. Now we have only the escapists, who write of happenings a hundred or three hundred years ago. . . . When someone wishes to write of this age—as I do and have done— critics shy off—the public shies off. "Where's our Story Book?" they cry. "Where are our Story Book People?" This is obviously an age that Can't Take It. (*Diaries,* 188)

Powell was not an escapist. She faced her adopted city head-on and presented its people as she saw them, but with an edge, as if they were backlighted, bringing them into even sharper focus. Bakhtin observed this same near-obsession with the city in Dostoevsky's "Petersburg Visions in Verse and Prose" (1861), in which

> Dostoevsky recalls the unique and vivid carnival sense of life experienced
> by him at the very beginning of his career as a writer. This was above all
> a special sense of Petersburg, with all its sharp social contrasts, as "a fan-
> tastic magical daydream," as "dream," as something standing on the
> boundary between reality and fantastic invention. . . . the sources of this
> tradition go back to the ancient menippea (Varro, Lucian). Building on
> this sense of the city and the city crowd, Dostoevsky proceeds to give a
> sharply carnivalized picture of the emergence of his own first literary pro-
> ject. (Bakhtin, 160–61)

Powell shared with Dostoevsky this passion for a city: "There is really one city for everyone just as there is one major love. New York is my city because I have an investment I can always draw on—a bottomless investment . . . of building up an *idea* of New York—so no matter what happens here I have the rock of my dreams of it that nothing can destroy" (*Diaries*, 326). Dostoevsky's passion was born from youthful experience of the city; Powell's passion continued into middle age. She wrote to John Hall Wheelock in 1950:

> I feel compelled to do my own favorite city the service the old letter-writers
> did for their times. I know New York very well and am still exploring it—
> walking around the waters edge from Battery to Throgs Neck, under its
> bridges and God knows in and out of dozens of levels of society.[16]

Again, it is the interplay of city and people, converging and conveyed in language, that most interests Powell.

Turn, Magic Wheel (1936), Powell's first true New York novel,[17] was the product of six years of struggle, as Powell developed the ability to capture New York City's quickness and light without appearing to be a wide-eyed provincial experiencing the big city. During the time that *Turn, Magic Wheel* was maturing, Powell completed two Ohio novels— *The Tenth Moon* and *The Story of a Country Boy*—and honed her style and structure, moving closer to one that would encompass the pace of New York. More important, she absorbed more of New York City and was able to write of it with more confidence. As she worked occasionally on the novel that became *Turn, Magic Wheel,* she would set it aside, writing, "That New York novel sounded so strained and unnatural as I started it. I could see I was a fish out of water" (*Diaries*, 26) and "I'd go plugging on at the nurse novel only I dread doing . . . shallow, phony, pretentious writing with tricks" (*Diaries*, 26–27).

Powell's notes written during the creation of *Turn, Magic Wheel* make clear that she was consciously creating a narrative in which New York itself was a primary figure: "[the novel] should be full of delicate sharp outlines of New York of today—the sharp detail as seen by one who sees it seldom but then with desperate longing. The Empire State—Coney Island—the Ambassador or Waldorf—the pattern of New York" (*Diaries*, 61–62). She described this novel as "a thoroughly New York book with the beauty and sheer thrill of New York running through it, in contrast to the imprisoned life it is possible to live here" (*Diaries*, 80). Powell succeeded in evoking the city in such passages as this one that describes the view from the Empire State Building:[18]

> They walked out on the terrace and eighty-six stories below them the city night spread out in a garden of golden lights; trucks, trains, ferryboats crawled soundlessly in and out of the island puzzle. . . . New York twinkled far off into Van Cortland Park, spangled skyscrapers piled up softly against the darkness, tinseled parks were neatly boxed and ribboned with gold like Christmas presents waiting to be opened. Sounds of traffic dissolved in distance, all clangor sifted through space into a whispering silence, it held a secret, and when letters flamed triumphantly in the sky you felt, ah, that was the secret, this at last was it, this special telegram to God—Sunshine Biscuits. On and off it went, Eat Sunshine Biscuits, the message of the city.[19]

In a less electric moment, the city parallels the dismal mood of Dennis Orphen as he performs the quintessentially New York task of making coffee on the hot plate in his bathroom:

> The winter sun pulled aside a grimy negligée of clouds, a bit consumptive, this Manhattan sun, giving nothing but a pallid glow to windowpanes and a sickly fever to bare streets in summer, perpetual slush in winter. Instead of giving it went about its own racket of drawing life and color from city streets as it drew rainfall from mountain streams. (*Wheel*, 50)

The reminder that this same sun that wanly illuminates the Manhattan streets shines also over rural areas is a conjunctive note for Powell, figuratively pulling together her two worlds of New York and Ohio. *Turn, Magic Wheel* is filled with the sights, sounds, and smells of New York City as a whole. In later New York novels, Powell focuses on specific neighborhoods and locales, moving closer to the Menippean structure, which calls for scenes other than large portraits and intimate sketches. The Menippean satire needs an arena that allows for a number of people who move in and out of the limelight, sometimes at the center, sometimes at the fringes. Bakhtin called such a scene the "carnival square."

In Bakhtin's carnival, the carnival square is the most important scene. Here one finds the "crowded, disorderly, grotesque" elements of the scene that Kernan describes. The parallels for the carnival square in Powell's world include Washington Square, "Rubberleg Square" ("so called for the high percentage of weak-kneed pedestrians"[20]) various bars and cafés, late-night parties, and dinner parties. In these public arenas, slippery with liquor, the playing field is leveled. People cannot assume authority based on class; wit wins praise regardless of the social status of the wag. Bakhtin writes:

> The main arena for carnival acts was the square and the streets adjoining it. To be sure, carnival also invaded the home; in essence it was limited in time only and not in space; carnival knows neither stage nor footlights. But the central arena could only be the square, for by its very idea carnival *belongs to the whole people,* it is *universal, everyone* must participate in its familiar contact. The public square was the symbol of communal performance. The carnival square—the square of carnival acts—acquired an additional symbolic overtone that broadened and deepened it. . . . Other places of action as well (provided they are realistically motivated by the plot, of course) can, if they become meeting- and contact-points for heterogeneous people—streets, taverns, roads, bathhouses, decks of ships, and so on—take on this additional carnival-square significance. (Bakhtin, 128)

One such carnival square can be found in *The Locusts Have No King,* where some seemingly peripheral action takes place in the network of late-night bars described in the chapter "moonlight on Rubberleg Square":

> The real night does not begin on Rubberleg Square till stroke of twelve, the moment after all decisions have been made and abandoned. The reformed citizens who have cautiously stayed home reading four-dollar books that instruct as well as entertain, and have even gone to bed because tomorrow is a big day at the office, suddenly rear up in their sheets, throw on their clothes once more, and dash out for one night-cap to ward off wagon-pride. . . . Here on Rubberleg Square, the four dark streets suddenly come to life with running feet. "BAR," in red or blue

neon lights, glows in any direction as if it was all one will-o'-the-wisp, same bar, same Bill, Hank, Jim, Al pushing Same-Agains across the same counter. The whisper of light love is in the air; plain women brushing past are beautiful in veils of heavy bedroom perfume; men's eyes darting through the mist are ruthless hunters; hands touch accidentally, shoulders brush, smiles are smuggled in the dark to shadowy strangers. On Eighth Street the Russian shops, Chinese shops, Mexican Craft shops, Antique Jewelry, Basketweave, Chess, Rare Print and Rare Book Shops all darken simultaneously and life begins. (*Locusts,* 57–58)

The concreteness of this passage evokes smells, sights, sounds of a city stirring to life under the moonlight. There is no reminder here that the same moon shines over gently snoring Middle America; this is wholly of New York City. And it is here, in the public arena, that the "Four Pillars of Rubberleg Square" gossip about the protagonists of the novel, cutting them down to size, insisting that "Everybody's got to come from someplace, I don't care how big they are. They can't always have been up there in those top brackets. It ain't the way of the world. And in the long run you'll find everybody's only human" (*Locusts,* 62). Here, the merely human ensure that those on pedestals are knocked down. In this way, the carnival square provides an arena for linking characters of all classes.

Other scenes help transform a character's view of himself or of the world. This may involve what Bakhtin would call "experimental fantasticality," that is "observation from some unusual point of view . . . which results in a radical change in the scale of the observed phenomena of life" (Bakhtin, 116). The surreal madhouse scene in *A Time to Be Born,* which initially seems a gratuitous station stop for Julian's train, offers the opportunity for radical change.

Looking out Julian could see no village behind the lonely station at all, but a great building that stretched interminably across the sky, lit up brilliantly for the night.

"State Insane Asylum," some one in the corridor murmured.

As the train screamed by figures appeared in every barred doorway, shadows were at every iron window, every aperture of the Asylum was lined with the desolate prisoners. There they stood or crouched, hour after hour at doors or windows, like wild pets, knowing that this is the door and that the train whistle means escape, and some day the door will open to let them out as to let them in. In their torch-lit mad minds the train blazing and screaming past them in the night was no more real than the other images that shrieked through their minds, and when at bedtime the light would be dimmed for sleep, what did it matter, what peace was there in that silence for sleep? Darkness, four-footed, monstrous, blinked tiger-eyed in their minds, never sleeping, and at daylight the souls would wake to yesterday's torment, no pity or peace, no truce for them; the pursuit would continue, the demons yowling after their exhausted prey, tearing the shreds of poor brains to shake out one more wild cry of pain. This was the picture the passenger could see in the second's pause at the institution, this was the picture on his eye-balls, on the window-panes, tattooed on the backs of people sitting ahead, so that the Catskills sleeping in the soft June rain, the winding brooks, the arching trees, dozing village churches, silvery river, the whole quiet countryside for miles and miles around all cried of murder.[21]

Rather than being open to understanding this strange world, Julian responds to this glimpse into insanity with his characteristic insensitivity: "People let themselves go . . . People have no control, that's all. Unless, of course, it's genuinely pathological. As a rule, though, people give in to it too easily" (*Born,* 313), and a heartbeat later, Julian has opportunistically transformed the experience into potential capitalistic gain: "Remind me to get an article on that . . . for the Sunday magazine" (*Born,* 313). He then dismisses the asylum with a curt "No excuse for anyone losing their grip."[22] The irony of Julian's attitude surfaces in the next paragraph, where it is revealed that at that very moment, Julian's first wife was being taken to the sanitarium "obsessed with the desire to kill Julian" (*Born,* 313). The scene in this novel does not allow for transformation because Julian is incapable of relinquishing control over anything held dear to him, especially his prejudices.

In *The Wicked Pavilion,* the madhouse scene does cause transformation, as Jerry Dulaine awakens from a lost night into the nightmare that is Bellevue:

The electric light in the middle of the ceiling sent a steady unrelenting warning and it was this, more than the rhythmic moaning sound, that finally opened Jerry's eyes. What she saw was a dream, she knew, and closed her eyes again, reaching out an arm to the light she knew was by her bed but which somehow was not there now so she slowly opened her eyes once more. . . . this bulb in the ceiling? . . . The funny-looking windows with no curtains—dungeonlike windows—yes, with bars. (*Pavilion,* 109)

Jerry slowly comes to identify her environment and, in the process, she can no longer identify herself. Stripped of her clothes and jewelry, she is left alone with a fragmented recollection of the previous night:

> The band was booming out "Rose of Washington Square," the grizzled
> chorus boys in straw hats were shuffling-off to Buffalo, arms around each
> other's shoulders, the Lido Ladies, old variety hoofers and stompers and
> ripe young strippers, were prancing off the stage, the mission derelicts
> were peering in the windows at the uptown slummers whooping it up
> inside, the cops were getting their handouts at the bar—this was the real
> New York, the real people, the good people, the bitter salt of the earth.
> None of the phoniness of Fifty-Second Street, or the fancy spots. (*Pavil-
> ion,* 111)

The carnival square of the Lido Bowery had such an effective class-
leveling effect that, during the ensuing raid, police mistook Jerry, reefer
in hand, for a prostitute and hauled her to Bellevue. Here, clad in a
vomity sheet, Jerry discovers that her words have no power, because she
has lost evidence of her middle-classness. When she is finally permitted,
with the other women, to go to the washroom, her "murderous rage
changed to the humblest gratitude for this privilege" (*Pavilion,* 115): "It
was amazing how quickly the human mind adjusted, she thought, for
she felt more bound to these women than to any other group she'd ever
known" (*Pavilion,* 115). The women, made peers in the washroom, read
Jerry's body for signs of her class: Her nail polish, styled hair, and clean,
smooth hands reveal that she is not of their class in the outside world.
But as Jerry, still clad only in a sheet, observes to the doctor who interviews her:

> "Oh we're all guilty, I know that, . . . I know now that you become
> guilty and you feel guilty as soon as someone treats you as guilty. The
> only innocent ones are the accusers so all of you try to accuse the other
> person before you're found out yourself. You know it will make him
> guilty." (*Pavilion,* 122)

Finally, someone acts on Jerry's earlier insistent urging to call Collier
McGrew, who arranges for Jerry's release. Weeping, she leaves, after dis-
tributing the contents of her purse—compact, comb, lipstick, perfume—to the women who have no Collier McGrew on the Board of
Trustees of the hospital to bail them out.

> Jerry followed the attendant down the corridors and out, thinking of the
> doctor's advice to stick to her own class and with the people she knew,
> and she thought these were the people she knew, this was her class.
>   A chauffeur in livery was standing in the office waiting for her. (*Pavil-
> ion,* 125)

Jerry does not pause to appreciate the irony of this juxtaposition.

Powell felt that this chapter was key in presenting the transforming power of place. Only by experiencing inhumanity can one truly understand its nature.

> Finished the Bellevue scene and curiously enough feel this is major, since it entered into original scheme for novel, which was to show the medieval evil of the time and place and the way something evil happening unfairly to you makes you feel and act guilty. But this experience is tremendous because only this way do you *understand*—and from then you know mercy and pity for the falsely accused, the unfairly punished, just as you understand the marvel of others' good fortune in *not* being subjected to such misfortunes. (*Diaries,* 324)

The relationship of the character to those in the madhouse—removed as Julian is or immersed as Jerry is—reveals the level of humanity of the character. This level of humanity is, in Powell's works, usually inversely proportional to the level of success of the character. Although Julian is quite successful in business, he is physically impotent and emotionally sterile. Jerry is a dramatic failure at everything she puts her hand to, but after her revelation, she is rewarded with good fortune. After giving up all hope of being able to snag McGrew with wily tricks, Jerry is set up in an apartment by McGrew, who also establishes credit lines for her and gives her a job (he doesn't marry her, but, after all, it's a modern romance).

Removed as it is from reality, the madhouse can also be seen as a parodying image of the city itself. Compared to the rest of the world, New York City is a madhouse, peopled with inmates forced to adhere to the rules of the various cages in which they are imprisoned. Powell's novels highlight both the cages and those caged.

The Satirist

The satirist's function is to comment upon the madhouse and its inmates. This comment may be somewhat obtrusive, or it may be quite subtle. In the cycle of New York novels, the satirist has different forms. In *Turn, Magic Wheel,* Dennis Orphen is intimately involved with the turning of the plot, but he manages to maintain the objectivity of a detached individual. In later novels, Orphen reappears in quieter roles, intimating the destiny of characters but not acting directly upon them. In *The Locusts Have No King,* Frederick Olliver as satirist is also pivotal in the action, but unlike Dennis Orphen, Olliver is uncomfortable in his role as all-knowing observer, primarily because he lacks the ego and self-assurance of Orphen. Olliver resists the role, but rather than being allowed to shirk his duties, he merely shifts from the role of Everyman as Observer, like Dennis Orphen, to self-parodying double, as he is forced to recognize the contrast between the academic world in which he has lived and the real world. In *The Happy Island* and *A Time to Be Born,* accidental satirists provide parodying contrast to the protagonist, so that the protagonist's actions are thrown into relief, highlighting their ridiculous nature. The provincials who play these roles are often unwitting, functioning as satirists without ever being aware of it. The primary categories of satirist that Powell presents are the wise, or knowing, satirist and the accidental satirist.

Streetwise and Raffish: The Wise Satirist

Dennis Orphen shuffles into *Turn, Magic Wheel* muttering to himself, "Some fine day I'll have to pay . . . you can't sacrifice everything in life to curiosity" (*Wheel,* 3), thus beginning a 10-page soliloquy in which he debates with himself the merits of sacrificing one's morals for art. This "dialogic approach to oneself," Bakhtin wrote, "breaks down the outer shell of the self's image, that shell which exists for other people, determining the external assessment of a person (in the eyes of others) and dimming the purity of self-consciousness" (Bakhtin, 120). By immediately stripping himself in front of the reader, Orphen gains the reader's trust; he is Everyman, not afraid to show his "dark side," as Kernan calls it. Orphen reveals this side only to himself and the reader, not to the other characters in the narrative. In the process, he fulfills Bakhtin's conception of the hero:

> He has no firm socially typical or individually characterological qualities out of which a stable image of his character, type, or temperament might be composed. Such a definitive image would weigh down the adventure plot, limit the adventure possibilities. To the adventure hero anything can happen, he can become anything. (Bakhtin, 102)

Dennis *becomes* primarily through his novels; he lives through the people he observes, creating a life for them.

Orphen does acknowledge his lack of firm "individually characterological qualities" as he passes by a window during his strolling soliloquy:

In the mirror of a street weighing machine he saw how thin, narrow-chested, unimpressive he looked, unlikely seducer of Fortune. . . it struck him that he had a Passport face, one that could be placed on anybody's papers and not be entirely wrong; such a face could justifiably sweep through the world passionately examining other faces but exempt from the curious second glance itself. (*Wheel*, 8–9)

This lack of identifying characteristics might depress another human, but for the writer, it is a suit of armor that allows him to observe unobserved. Dennis Orphen demonstrates that he is able to wear his alienation well—he proclaims his solitude in his surname: Orphen / orphan.[23] Orphen is, in fact, an orphan. As such, he conveys, if not anonymity itself, a perception of anonymity that allows for heightened powers of observation. In the process of developing the novel, Powell herself developed a kind of anonymity in Orphen. Initially, the central character of the novel was a woman, Lila. But Powell found her voice best expressed through a male protagonist. Orphen was thus born and Lila was dismissed entirely. This shift—perhaps influenced by her choice of a male protagonist in *The Story of a Country Boy* (1934)—freed Powell's pen: "How much sharper and better to have the central figure a man rather than a woman—a man in whom my own prejudices and ideas can be easily placed, whereas few women's minds (certainly not Effie's or Corinne's) flit as irresponsibly as that" (*Diaries*, 96).

In Dennis Orphen, one finds Powell's alter ego voicing many of the same sentiments about writing and people that Powell expressed in her diaries. For instance, in one entry, Powell muses:

Curiosity is a rare gift, particularly when combined with acute observation, understanding or perception—not mere nosiness of the baffled ignorant who are only curious because it is different from their limited views. I am always surprised at how rare it is; I can be with an intelligent friend and overhear a curious conversation and the person with me has not heard or seen the episode—not because it is none of his business, but because the concerns of strangers do not concern him. He is not interested in life. (*Diaries*, 430)

This passage, written some 25 years after *Turn, Magic Wheel*, echoes the sentiments of Orphen in his opening soliloquy, though Orphen articulates the more eloquent version:

Face it, then, curiosity was the basis for the compulsion to write, this burning obsession to know and tell the things other people are knowing.

Unbearable not to know the answers. Behind those blank faces on the subway, *what?* . . . On paper you can fill in the answers, be these persons, transfer your own pain into theirs, remember what they remember, long for what they desire. Spread out in type, detail added to detail, invention added to fact, the figure whole emerges; invisibly you creep inside, you are at last the Stranger. (*Wheel*, 5)

Powell was quite fond of this "half-sentimental, half no-good guy" (*Diaries*, 414) who echoed her own thoughts. More than 20 years after writing *Turn, Magic Wheel*, she noted: "Dennis Orphen in *Wheel* I like, but the fact is I like raffish characters and might as well make them heroes" (*Diaries*, 383). As the satirist, Dennis Orphen is not simultaneously disinterested and involved in the way that Nick Carraway is in *The Great Gatsby*, because Orphen has an additional layer of complexity: Orphen is the teller of the story of the wife of Andrew Callingham, a Hemingway-esque character who strides through several of Powell's novels. So, Orphen is the storyteller of a storyteller. This immensely self-parodying role requires an enormous ego tempered by self-effacing wit. This is Orphen.

Powell was so fond of Dennis Orphen that he appears in later novels, where he has subtler roles. He takes a sabbatical from *The Happy Island,* but returns as the friend of Ken Saunders in *A Time to Be Born.* Here, Dennis is not so much the all-knowing satirist, though his presence calls to mind this role, as he is nearly a parodying double. He must abandon the solitary stance that he had in *Turn, Magic Wheel* to function as part of a couple in order to fulfill his destiny. Dennis, along with his lover Corinne, helps to show what Amanda's life would be like if she left her husband for Ken: Ken, like Dennis, would be living in the Village, and Amanda, like Corinne, would be penniless, spending her time watching Ken to make sure he doesn't pick up other women.

The Locusts Have No King contains a brief notice that Dennis Orphen has published some books, but he doesn't actually make an appearance. Apparently, he was present in Powell's mind, though, for she wrote to an editor, "in *The Locusts Have No King* I believe Denny was drinking much too much. In the present book [*The Wicked Pavilion*] it seems he's too drunk to even get into it, what a pity."[24] "Denny" does shuffle into *The Wicked Pavilion* long enough to write a few pages of reflections:

There was nothing unusual about that New York winter of 1948 for the unusual was now the usual. Elderly ladies died of starvation in shabby hotels leaving boxes full of rags and hundred-dollar bills; bands of chil-

dren robbed and raped through the city streets, lovers could find no
beds, hamburgers were forty cents at lunch counters, truck drivers
demanded double wages to properly educate their young in the starving
high-class professions; aged spinsters, brides and mothers were shot by
demented youths, frightened girls screamed for help in the night while
police, in pairs for safety's sake, pinned tickets on parked automobiles.
Citizens harassed by Internal Revenue hounds jumped out of windows
for want of forty dollars, families on relief bought bigger television sets to
match the new time-bought furniture. (*Pavilion,* 4)

After writing this cynical reflection, it is little wonder that Dennis
Orphen then slinks off to his hotel room "where he sat for a while star-
ing at the empty page in the typewriter until he decided it was time to
get drunk" (*Pavilion,* 3). He then apparently nurses his hangover until
the end of the novel, where he resurfaces. Through Orphen, Powell
expresses her worldview—of the police force, the welfare system,
income tax—without the overt didacticism of authorial commentary.
He fulfills the role of satirist without having to accept the responsibility
for his moral judgments. Further, Orphen can be poetic, as in this passage toward the close of the introduction:

there were many who were bewildered by the moral mechanics of the age
just as there are those who can never learn a game no matter how long
they've been obliged to play it or how many times they've read the rules
and paid the forfeits. If this is the way the world is turning around, they
say, then by all means let it stop turning, let us get off the cosmic Ferris
wheel into space. Allow us the boon of standing still till the vertigo
passes, give us a respite to gather together the scraps of what was once
us—the old longings for what? for whom? that gave us our wings and
the chart for our tomorrows. (*Pavilion,* 6)

In this role as guest satirist, Orphen can write large in a way that Powell
as author cannot without distracting the reader. The "cosmic Ferris
wheel" reminds the reader of his larger role in *Turn, Magic Wheel* and
lends poignancy to his query, "what is the prize and is it the prize they
really want? What became of Beauty, where went Love? There must be
havens where they may be at least remembered" (*Pavilion,* 6). Powell
could not deliver such lines directly and hope to keep her reader, and a
character couldn't believably speak the lines, unless it was very late at
night in a smoky Village room under the influence of mind-altering sub-
stances. But, through Orphen, Powell may muse; he is Powell's poet.

In *The Locusts Have No King,* Frederick also enters the action muttering, but rather than embarking on a soliloquy, he eavesdrops on various
bits of dialogue emerging from the haze of Rubberleg Square. Frederick
Olliver is, in many ways, the quintessential modern hero, conflicted
within. After seven years of self-imposed exile, researching and writing
his book on the seventeenth century, he emerges into a world that he no
longer understands. To further confuse the scene, he enters into the
night of New York City and finds that "Wherever he went that night
people insisted on confiding in him. Perhaps some fear of his fellow-men
gleamed in the young man's intense blue eyes that made them want to
reassure him that they, too, were unarmed" (*Locusts,* 1). Powell evokes
the White Rabbit in *Alice in Wonderland,* to underscore Frederick's
dreamlike state in this alien land, as he hops from bar to bar, evading
conversations: " 'I'm sorry, I'm late,' Frederick apologized and hastened
into the street again, darting in and out of the cafés of Rubberleg
Square" (*Locusts,* 3) in search of taxi fare from his roommate, Murray.[25]

Frederick evidences characteristics of the novelistic hero and the
satirist. As the hero, he ought to fit the character of the city novel hero
as described by Gelfant:

> the prototype for the hero is the self-divided man. Dissociation is a
> pathological symptom which results from, and reflects, a larger social
> disorder. The dissociated person has not found a way to integrate motive
> and act and so to organize his life's activities towards a continuous and
> progressive fulfillment of his desires. In contrast to inhibition, which
> implies coercive pressures from an organized society, dissociation arises
> mainly because of a lack of social unanimity: the community has failed to
> provide a cohesive tradition that can guide the individual in his choice of
> goals and moral alternatives. Dissociation is also distinguishable from
> frustration. One experiences frustration when he is prevented from
> attaining his goal; but one is dissociated when he cannot even clearly
> define what his goal is. (Gelfant, 21–22)

Frederick cannot define his goal, but he is somehow not absorbed
enough to fill this heavily introspective role. He has much in common
with T. S. Eliot's J. Alfred Prufrock, as Frederick asserts to himself, "He
wanted to be spectator, that was all, not actor; if possible, he wanted a
glass wall between him and other human beings . . . It made him
uncomfortable when the actors addressed him, as if Myrna Loy should
suddenly reach out of a moving picture to shake his hand" (*Locusts,* 9).
Like Dennis Orphen, Frederick has an unassuming visage; unlike Den-

nis, he does not reveal this himself, lacking the self-reflection of Dennis. Instead, it is left to a bar patron to observe: "Hi, fella. I like you. You're all right. You know what it's all about. Got a poker face but I can tell you catch" (*Locusts*, 4). Like Dostoevsky's "Ridiculous Man," Olliver has "clear traces of the *ambivalent*—serio-comical—image of the 'wise fool' and 'tragic clown' of carnivalized literature" (Bakhtin, 150). Frederick's ambivalence plays out in his love life—torn between Lyle, charming, intelligent, and married, and Dodo, the "pooh-on-you" girl—as well as in his professional life, where he is caught between the fruit of seven years' unpublishable labor on the Renaissance, augmented by lectures at the League for Cultural Foundations and essays in the *Swan Quarterly*, and the editorship of the popular comic *Haw:* "It disgusted him that he could handle *Haw*, which he hated, with belligerent efficiency, but was powerless to promote his own work" (*Locusts*, 151–52). He is successful at what he despises and cannot make a living doing what he loves.

As a hero, Frederick's ambivalence is disconcerting. As a satirist, Frederick is intriguing, as he moves in and out of the role, not sure whether to believe in himself or make fun of himself. It becomes clear that Powell is satirizing the work that Frederick initially held dear—the League and *Swan* work—and as the novel progresses, the author wrestles with the satirist to make him come round to satirize the same things that she is satirizing. In this way, Frederick Olliver eventually hones the cynical edge that brings him closer to Dennis Orphen's abilities as satirist.

As Provincial: The "Accidental" Satirist

Of Powell's novels, Edmund Wilson wrote that "[Powell's] real theme is the provincial in New York who has come on from the Middle West and acclimated himself (or herself) to the city and made himself a permanent place there, without ever, however, losing his fascinated sense of an alien and anarchic society" (E. Wilson 1962, 234). Wilson's comment has cast a long shadow, as many contemporary reviewers rely on it to sum up Powell's work. In fact, only two of the novels discussed in this chapter focus on this theme.[26] And in these novels—*The Happy Island* and *A Time to Be Born*—a provincial, newly arrived in the city, serves as parodying double to the protagonist, whom the visiting provincial knew in the Midwest. In this less overt role, the satirist ridicules the protagonist simply through his own actions and questions; after all, this satirist knew the protagonist well before she achieved fame. These native Midwesterners came to New York to escape or to realize a dream or both. The successful characters have usually squelched their humble Midwestern roots in order to gain fame and, in the process, they have sacrificed their morality and lost a part of themselves. Powell's aim is to point up this loss of morality, but with a sly grin. She maintained that she was a "permanent visitor" in New York, and her Midwestern protagonists have that same sense of impermanence. They are lashed onward by the certainty that if they fail, they must go home, a fate certainly worse than death; in *The Happy Island*, Dol quite literally goes home over his dead body. Powell's Midwestern characters are not wide-eyed buffoons in the big city but rather people who function quite well there, without ever losing their sense of where they came from.

In *The Happy Island*, New York is seen initially through the eyes of a young man and an old man. The young man fixes his eyes on the window "as if this keyhole view of the city must be permanently recorded" (*Island*, 4). Unwilling temporary partners in this doorway to the city, the pair present the two alternatives of the city: hope or failure. The older man, Van Deusen, asks the other: "Are you here for a visit or just to make your fortune? . . . I've come here a dozen times to make my fortune" (*Island*, 5). The young man, Jefferson Abbott, is intent upon achieving fame. Unlike many of his fellow provincials, Jeff Abbott has every intention of returning to Ohio when he has accomplished his mission. His position in the opening chapter, and his clearly anxious visage, would indicate that he is the protagonist. As it happens, he is more spectator than actor, and, by novel standards, he would be considered a minor character, someone who reminds Pru of her past and creates a brief love interest. By satiric standards, he assumes a critical role, which becomes apparent almost immediately when he refuses to believe that the Prudence Bly whom he knows from Silver City could be the famed nightclub singer whom Van raptures over.[27] Ignoring the coincidence of two women named Prudence Bly, surely nobody from his hometown would have her name in lights.

When Jeff is not present on the stage of the narrative, he is implicit in Pru's obsessing over him. When Pru first sees Jeff again, "Even before she recognized him for Jeff Abbott, she had the queer flash of self-identification, as if this man were a part of her, as if her name were on him" (*Island*, 78). Thus, Pru lays claim to him as her double. Among Jeff's first thoughts, spoken aloud, is, "I liked you better ugly" (*Island*, 79). Pru, who thrives on praise and adoration, perversely is drawn to this creature from her hated past, who utters not praise, but mockery. He is certainly the most righteous of Powell's satirists, fulfilling best Kernan's perception that "[the satirist] sees the world as a battlefield between a definite, clearly understood good, which he represents, and an equally clear-cut evil. No ambiguities, no doubts about himself, no sense of mystery trouble him, and he retains always his monolithic certainty" (Kernan, 21–22). Jeff continues to speak his mind as he pursues his mission, stated bluntly: "All I want is to write what I want to write in the place I want to be" (*Island,* 84). Here, Jeff acts as Powell's mouthpiece, voicing her own goals.

In fact, Powell did have an investment in Jeff, clear in her grumblings about the novel-in-process: "The position of Jefferson in relation to the group shows him weakening, giving in to them rather than firmly holding out as I intended. He needn't be so slapped down or such a complete ass—more Steinbeck than Odets" (*Diaries,* 143). As Powell's double, he plays out the role of playwright, Powell's initial aim in New York. As Jeff witnesses the failure of his opening night, he "suddenly wondered what he was doing here; his part was over, he had served his purpose" (*Island,* 124). But, reminded by his producer that "It's a gift when you can make 'em mad," Jeff stands taller: "He felt free now and he could breathe. He was alone facing Times Square; and now it was his city, it knew his whip, it recognized a new rider" (*Island,* 125). Rather than being discouraged by the reviews, he is encouraged, as he reveals in a letter informing Dol that he is leaving his house:

> I find the playwright's necessity is neither to pacify nor please but to refurbish the mind, houseclean it, shake it up ready to meet problems, and not to feed complacencies. If the truth makes the critics squirm, O.K.; if it satisfies them, O.K., too. Those are secondary results. The primary obligation is emotional reconstruction. So, feeling this way, I didn't want your pity for my having a flop. For me it was a success. It's shown me that I know what arteries to cut, where to operate. With the world the way it is, that's about the only kind of success I can expect for a while—a few good people who know what I'm after and respect it and the critics stirred up for better or worse. And in your eyes it looks like failure. Your house and your crowd are organized for success, and I don't fit in. I don't want to. I hope I never shall. (*Island,* 128)

The quiveringly self-assured tone of the letter reflects Powell's own view of critical response to her works. After the astounding failure of her play *Big Night,* produced by the Group Theatre in 1933, Powell noted:

Most people are furious at me for not lying down and screaming so they can forgive me and have a friendly pleasure in seeing the punishment sink in—the Olympian privilege of providing big-hearted consolation. Failing in this—I persist in regarding the whole thing as near a success as I've ever had—they decide to take digs. (*Diaries, 64*)

As with Dennis Orphen, Powell finds in Jefferson Abbott a voice for her own beliefs.

Even more than Dennis Orphen, though, Jefferson Abbott fulfills the role of the model satirist, according to Kernan's extended definition:

the satirist alternates endlessly between his purpose and the passion which brings it on. His characteristic purpose is to cleanse society of its impurities, to heal its sicknesses; and his tools are crude ones . . . He employs irony, sarcasm, caricature, and even plain vituperation with great vigor, determined to beat the sots into reason or cut away the infected parts of society; but the job is always too much for him. . . . His feelings of futility lead him . . . to the belief that he simply needs to apply the lash more vigorously. . . . This constant movement without change forms the basis of satire. (Kernan, 33)

Jefferson continues to stride purposefully through the narrative, resistant to the trappings of success: "it seemed neither failure nor success could alter Jeff's concept of himself or his work. He belonged to that baffling group of confident writers who need no applause" (*Island,* 144). He is committed to achieving his goal in New York.

Part of Jeff's purpose in the novel is to point out Prudence Bly's shallow nature. He does this best by ignoring her advances:

I don't want to see Prudence, . . . this Prudence of yours isn't the one I knew. What happens to people here? Does a person have to cut his guts out and hand 'em to the town on a silver platter to pay for having his picture in the paper? Prudence! I can't even talk to her any more except through that stone front of hers. (*Island,* 145–46)

Indeed, Prudence Bly has become a prototypical claw-your-way-to-the-top provincial-turned-New-York-star. More than for her ephemeral fame, though, she is known for her caustic wit.

Prudence Bly was not a person so much as a conspiracy. . . . In her [her social set] dimly felt they had a valuable machine gun, a weapon against society, their private egos were avenged by her destructive wit, they crowed over her ability to mow down large and small potatoes with a barbed word, for among the fallen was sure to be a rival or, better still, a friend. . . . Prudence slew with a neat epithet, crippled with a too true word, then, seeing her devastation about her and her enemies growing, grew frightened of revenges, backed desperately, and eventually found the white flag of Sentimentality as her salvation. (*Island,* 49–51)

Prudence herself struggles to find her identity as she merges with her public image:

In the ten years of her fame the printed word about her had come to be the woman, and even her private thoughts had now a publicity angle. . . . for the life of her she could not find the time or place where the little girl from Ohio, the ambitious, industrious little village girl, merged into the *Evening Journal's* Prudence Bly, the *Town and Country* Bly. . . . Prudence wondered if one could permanently become the third person singular, lose oneself, be nothing but one's name in a society column, one's photograph in *Vogue.* (*Island,* 49)[28]

The potentially emergent moments are lost on Pru, though, as she turns to embrace her "happy island," pushing such thoughts back. Jeff, like a good, inactive satirist, does not act to effect plot movement. And in the absence of action, Prudence shifts roles with Jeff, becoming his parodying double in his own land.

After eight months, Jeff is ready to leave New York despite the protests of Dol, who notes

You've had your production, your promise of a second one, an assurance of a foothold in the theatre, and you've learned your own power. But you're going back to live on that little place you've bought without the faintest notion of ever having been away from it. You've never tasted New York, even. . . . you might just as well have been in Silver City all this time, you have absolutely refused to take what New York has to give. (*Island,* 244)

Jeff goes home. And against all odds, Prudence, in a moment of extreme ennui, casts aside her (admittedly fading) fame to join Jeff, telling her friend Anna: "I want to find out what I'm like—inside, you know—and the only way is with a man I'm crazy about, someone I feel is really great, you know, instead of just a plain ham like me" (*Island,* 276).

The person Pru finds in Silver City is "Tracks," the adolescent girl who kissed Jeff Abbott behind the station all those years ago; "You'd have thought they would have forgotten that Tracks episode, but villages never forgot" (*Island,* 283). Of course, Pru is incapable of embracing the provincial life. Rather than caricaturing Pru's ineptitude, though, Powell gives her character strength, while toppling the noble scaffolding of Jeff's rhetoric and converting him to a whiny, petulant, demanding "husband" (the two never actually marry). The next-to-last chapter is monologue that establishes Prudence as primary satirist, casting her current rustic life in a charming anecdote to be told on the Riviera in 20 years—"make it fifteen." In the course of the creation, Pru comes to realize that "Some people aren't complete away from their city as a musician is nothing without his violin. So New York was my instrument, or I was its" (*Island,* 289). The staccato taps of Pru's heels across the linoleum of the country kitchen mock Jeff's quiet rustic dreams, and it becomes clear that she cannot live there.

Away from New York City, Pru's slick elegance seems merely tawdry, and Jeff's noble simplicity becomes typically provincial parochialism. In reflecting each other, they distort their best traits, as in a fun-house mirror. At least one reviewer, William Soskin, appreciated this neat twist:

> I admire Miss Powell for the fine way she takes the only good man, the only virtuous man, the only idealist in the book and reduces him to a priggishness and stuffiness far worse than the frivolous futility of the rest of the characters. You've got to be able to take such wholehearted disillusion with some laughter, otherwise you can't stand it.[29]

It is clear that the relationship cannot survive this power shift. The novel ends because it must; Pru is now in control of her destiny, with no mocking figure from her past casting a shadow over her glittering future. Had Powell given in to the happy ending, Jeff's parodying would have persuaded Pru of the debauchery of her ways and the two would have lived happily ever after. The closing chapter, with Pru back among her peers in New York, provides the final satiric twist.

The accidental satirist in *A Time to Be Born* is even less obtrusive than Jefferson Abbott. Vicky Haven has come to New York to get over a bad love affair in Lakewood. The great writer Amanda Keeler Evans, a very thinly disguised Clare Booth Luce, has her husband provide a job for Vicky. The two women are a study in contrasts: Amanda is outgoing and confident; Vicky is shy and unassuming. Through the course of their relationship, the two trade characteristics, and Vicky becomes stronger while Amanda weakens, though only temporarily. The moment of crisis that solidifies the exchange of characteristics is when

Amanda discovers that she is pregnant, but does not know where to have an abortion. Desperate and appalled, she approaches Vicky: "Here I am—all the money in the world—thirty-two years old—and as help-less as some farm girl in trouble. Not a soul to help me—no one I dare ask!" (*Born,* 286). After casting Vicky out of her life, Amanda is forced to go to her for help. Vicky balances her wounded pride with the specta-cle before her:

> The sight of Amanda in hysterics, strange and terrifying as it was, only left her numb. Some persons were suited only to triumph and they existed only in a blaze of glory; in descent they were not the same people, and must find new personalities for themselves. They needed their daily transfusions of victory for their blood and brain, and without this they had no corpuscles for defense, no philosophy for defeat. So Amanda, bro-ken with her little misfortune, was not Amanda to Vicky, but the curi-ously awful spectacle of a statue in fragments. (*Born,* 287–88)

This moment parallels what Bakhtin calls the "ritual act of decrowning":

> Under this ritual act of decrowning a king lies the very core of the carni-val sense of the world—*the pathos of shifts and changes, of death and renewal.* . . . Crowning/decrowning is a dualistic ambivalent ritual, expressing the inevitability and at the same time the creative power of the shift-and-renewal, the *joyful relativity* of all structure and order, of all authority and all (hierarchical) position. (Bakhtin, 124)

Vicky procures the name of an abortionist (Powell delights in revealing the worldly side of women who appear to be decidedly provincial to the core) and accompanies Amanda to the doctor. In the role shift, both women are empowered. Briefly, Amanda is humbled and allows Vicky to care for her; Vicky allows herself to take charge.

Generally, Vicky's satiric voice is rather gentle and unobtrusive. The strongest satiric voice belongs to the narrator in the opening chapter. In this classic Apology, Powell admits to working against tradition, but defends this act. She recognizes that a novel that focuses on the merely quotidian is out of place in a time when the world is focused on the demands of war:

> This was a time when writers dared not write of Vicky Haven or of sim-ple young women like her. They wrote with shut eyes and deaf ears of other days, wise days they boasted, of horse-and-buggy men and covered-wagon Cinderellas; they glorified the necessities of their ancestors who

had laid ground for the present confusion; they made ignorance shine as native wit, the barrenness of other years and other simpler men was made a talent, their austerity and the bold compulsions of their avarice a glorious virtue. In the Gold Rush to the past they left no record of the present. Drowning men, they remembered words their grandmothers told them, forgot today and tomorrow in the drug of memories. A curtain of stars and stripes was hung over today and tomorrow and over the awful lessons of other days. It was a sucker age, an age for any propaganda, any cause, any lie, any gadget, and scorning this susceptibility chroniclers sang the stubborn cynicism of past heroes who would not believe the earth was round. It was an age of explosions, hurricanes, wrecks, strikes, lies, corruption, and unbridled female exploitation. Unable to find reason for this madness people looked to historical figures and ancient events for the pat answers. Amanda Keeler's *Such Is the Legend* swept the bookstores as if this sword-and-lace romance could comfort a public about to be bombed. Such fabulous profits from this confection piled up for the pretty author that her random thoughts on economics and military strategy became automatically incontrovertible. Broadcasting companies read her income tax figures and at once begged her to prophesy the future of France. (*Born*, 3–4)

there are little people who cannot ride the wars or if they do are only humble coach passengers, not the leaders or the float-riders; there are the little people who can only think that they are hungry, they haven't eaten, they have no money, they have lost their babies, their loves, their homes. . . . These little people had no news value and therein was their crime. In their little wars there were no promotions, no parades, no dress uniforms, no regimental dances—no radio speeches, no interviews, no splendid conferences. What unimportant people they were, certainly, in this important age! (*Born*, 5)

These lengthy excerpts, mere slices of the introduction, eloquently define the target of the satire and defend Powell's reasons for writing it.[30] The escapist novels that proliferated during this time taunted Powell with their high sales volume. She was, admittedly, a bit jealous of Luce's immense popularity, but she was honestly appalled at Luce's being called upon to comment on matters of state based solely, it seemed, on the strength of her work as a Broadway satirist and social wit. This novel is Powell's chance to bite back. The target of the satire is larger than Luce, though. It also encompasses war profiteers, including Henry Luce, who owned *Time* and *Life* magazines;[31] contemporary literary trends, which look backward rather than to the present for material; and the general mood that overlooks average people in favor of heroes and politicians. By modeling the Apology after Ecclesiastes, Powell places herself on the side of the angels. She is the defender of Everyman (and woman) and will tell the story of how Americans go about living their self-interested lives in the face of global upheaval.

Running beneath these varied elements is the unifying thread of the persistent present in the voice of the anonymous satirist: "Somewhere in the midst of the satiric scene or standing before it directing our attention to instances of folly and vulgarity and shaping our responses with his language, we . . . find a satirist" (Kernan, 14). The strength of the voice in this Apology, the eloquence and perceptiveness of the passages, further underscores Powell's power of conviction. One almost wishes to hear more of the voice of the narrator or of Dennis Orphen when he is removed from the scene and musing aloud. The role of the satirist in Menippean satire, however, is limited, as Kernan notes: "in formal satire the satirist is stressed and dominates the scene, while in Menippean satire the scene is stressed and absorbs the satirist, to some degree or altogether" (Kernan, 15). The scene and the language of others dominate the satire. The author-as-satirist is allowed only to arrange the language in a way that best conveys the narrative.

Plot: New York Carnival

In writing about her contemporary world, Powell was dealing with unresolved issues unfolding in the present time, their outcome as yet unknown. To orchestrate actions leading to a resolution, Powell would have to know the outcome of the present; this, of course, is not possible. The narrative itself is the playing out of the idea to the extent that Powell can take it. Bakhtin calls this "carnival," a place "for working out, in a concretely sensuous, half-real and half-play-acted form, a new mode of interrelationship between individuals, counterposed to the all-powerful socio-hierarchical relationships of noncarnival life" (Bakhtin, 123). This is what Powell means when she says that her characters have taken over the job of writing the novel. The action is guided by "thoughts experienced and played out in the form of life itself" (Bakhtin, 123). Frye provides a parallel, less playful, summary of this idea:

> At its most concentrated the Menippean satire presents us with a vision of the world in terms of a single intellectual pattern. The intellectual structure built up from the story makes for violent dislocations in the customary logic of narrative, though the appearance of carelessness that

results reflects only the carelessness of the reader or his tendency to judge by a novel-centered conception of fiction. (Frye, 310)

The nature of satire itself helps to explain why Powell's works were criticized for lack of plot. Kernan summarizes the effect of the plot in satire:

> If we take plot to mean, as it ordinarily does, "what happens," or to put it in a more useful way, a series of events which constitute a change, then the most striking quality of satire is the absence of plot. We seem at the conclusion of satire to be always at very nearly the same point where we began. The scenery and the faces may have changed outwardly, but fundamentally, we are looking at the same world, and the same fools, and the same satirist we met at the opening of the work. (Kernan, 30)

The infiltration of satire into the narrative necessarily disrupts the pattern of storytelling, as Griffin explains:

> The narrative satirist tells a story in order to mock, to expose, to subvert. The story is only a vehicle; it may be interrupted at will; it may be broken into episodes; it may be extended ad libitum or broken off . . . "in the middle." Since satirists are not normally interested in narrative wholeness, in character consistency, in drawing that Jamesian circle by which a particular set of human relations appears to be bounded, they will feel no obligation to provide narrative closure. But in fact . . . narrative satire is in this respect typical of all satire, no matter what form it takes. (Griffin, 97–98)

Both Kernan and Griffin highlight two aspects of the satire that differ from the novel: the movement of the narrative, guided by the plot in terms of action in the novel, and closure.

Powell distances herself from the text by presenting information as the characters themselves encounter it, rather than through an omniscient narrator who fills in gaps in communication. Powell's alienation from the text is consistent with a thematic characteristic of New York novels. The city forces characters to strike out on their own. Even when the novel focuses on a specific milieu of interwoven relationships, individuals quickly learn that they cannot rely on the acquaintances within their circles. Characters sever ties with families—most do this willingly—in order to strike out in the rootless city. Gelfant describes this as an underlying theme in city fiction:

Twentieth-century life has thrust upon the modern artist certain obses-
sive concerns—to name some, a concern over man's aloneness and alienation, over the collapse of his community and the breakdown of tradition, the ineffectuality of love and religion, the impact of mechanization,
the materialism of modern life, and the conflict between artist and society. (Gelfant, 21)

Powell's characters embrace this alienation because they know that the
alternative is to return home, admitting defeat; this fear urges them
onward.

Powell's New York novels were occasionally criticized as being form-
less and inconclusive. Judged by novel standards, the narratives do lack
cohesiveness. But judged by the form of Menippean satire, they move in
a way that mirrors the haphazard sequence of real life. In Bakhtin's
terms, "everyday life is drawn into the carnivalized action of the plot"
(Bakhtin, 158). Carnival has no plot, only movement, revolving around
the characters' dialogic relationships to the idea. Kernan discusses this
movement more concretely:

The normal "plot" of satire would then appear to be a stasis in which the
two opposing forces, the satirist on one hand and the fools on the other,
are locked in their respective attitudes without any possibility of either
dialectical movement or the simple triumph of good over evil. Whatever
movement there is, is not plot in the true sense of change but mere
intensification of the unpleasant situation with which satire opens. It is
here that one of the basic differences between satire and the other major
literary genres, tragedy and comedy, becomes evident, for in both the latter kinds the developing plot is very close to being the absolute heart of
the form. (Kernan, 31–32)

In the menippea, the "absolute heart of the form" is "the adventures of
an idea or a truth in the world," as Bakhtin calls it (Bakhtin, 115). In
following the adventure of the idea, normal plot is not paramount in the
text. The point is not to *go* someplace, but to *be* someplace, experiencing
the adventure. Bakhtin explains this movement:

Plot . . . is absolutely devoid of any sort of finalizing functions. Its goal is
to place a person in various situations that expose and provoke him, to
bring people together and make them collide in conflict—in such a way,
however, that they do not remain within this area of plot-related contact
but exceed its bounds. The real connections begin when the ordinary plot
ends, having fulfilled its service function. (Bakhtin, 276–77)

Powell is concerned with the movement of ideas. So, rather than consider how a character moves from one place to the next, it is best to consider how ideas move in the narrative. As Bakhtin wrote, the menippea is really about "the adventures of an idea or a truth in the world." In Powell's novels, information may be revealed through a character musing aloud or to himself (soliloquy); through café conversations (a scattering of dialogue or overheard comments); through party chats (which may be similar to café conversations, but usually heightened by frivolity, or more organized, like a symposium); or other forms of social communication. Perceived this way, the fragmented nature of the text can be seen as an arrangement of the polyphony of voices that make up the narrative. In Powell's novels, the adventures unfold in various rhetorical forms, as is typical of Menippean satire:

> Characteristic for the menippea is a wide use of inserted genres: novellas, letters, oratorical speeches, symposia, and so on; also characteristic is a mixing of prose and poetic speech. . . . The presence of inserted genres reinforces the multi-styled and multi-toned nature of the menippea; what is coalescing here is a new relationship to the word as the material of literature, a relationship characteristic for the entire dialogic line of development in artistic prose. (Bakhtin, 118)

Through café conversations, party chats, or other forms of social rhetoric, the plot unfolds. Perceived this way, the fragmented nature of the text can be seen as an arrangement of the polyphony of voices that make up the narrative. The role of the author, then, is less the teller of a tale than the arranger of language.

Powell orchestrates the various types of rhetoric in her narratives. In *Turn, Magic Wheel,* the genres include both written and spoken genres: newspaper notices and excerpts from books, as well as soliloquies and dialogues, rendered in various dialects. *The Wicked Pavilion* is constructed primarily with spoken forms and draws more upon classical forms, including the diatribe and the symposium, and it weaves the forms together carefully. *The Happy Island* uses spoken forms almost exclusively, and presents them without setup or follow-through. *The Locusts Have No King* and *A Time to Be Born* also exhibit a variety of rhetorical forms, but they are not as prominent as in the other three novels.

Powell characterized *Turn, Magic Wheel* as "a novel of no plot but of mood, feeling, atmosphere, even glamour, seen but never attained. This should be done in shaded fleeting photographic shots with the basic reality of the book [Effie's] heartache—not a neurotic ache but a real one" (*Diaries,* 80). The narrative is presented in these "fleeting shots," frequently linked by wry transitions. Dennis Orphen's opening soliloquy, discussed above, is the first indication of the layers of Powell's satire, as her satirist strolls about telling the story of a storyteller, within the story that is Powell's own narrative. A chapter titled ". . . announcement in Publishers' Weekly . . . " is contained on a single page and it is just what its title says it is:

<blockquote>
Out Thursday, April 11
THE HUNTER'S WIFE
by Dennis Orphen

What they say. . . .
"Fine" . . . Louis Bromfield
"Significant" . . . Hugh Walpole
"Timely" . . . J. B. Priestley

Statement on the first page of
The Hunter's Wife:
"All the characters in this novel are highly fictitious"
(*Wheel,* 131)
</blockquote>

This brief "chapter" is playful on its face, and it manages to zing publishers with the blurbs, terse to the point of inanity. The final line is ironic, as Powell's novel is entirely about the effect of *The Hunter's Wife* on its real-life basis, Effie Callingham; the central struggle of the protagonist is the moral dilemma of mining his relationship for writing material. Implicit in the whole blurb is a parody of all contemporary novels, Powell's included. The complexity of the satire echoes in a way that more direct and fuller prose could not convey without flattening the effect. A bit later in the novel, the chapter resonates further when Powell—indulging in the form of satire described by Frye as "ridicule of *philosophus gloriosus*" (Frye, 309)—includes a very funny send-up of the publishing industry. In it, the great MacTweed, pedantic publisher, pronounces to his partner, And Company, "I doubt if Walter Scott is any good. I doubt if H. G. Wells is any good. I doubt if any author's any good. As a matter of fact, Johnson, I look forward to the day when all our books will be written by blurb writers." (*Wheel,* 119)

Implicit throughout *Turn, Magic Wheel* is a defense of contemporary American writing—that is, writing that portrays America. Powell takes stabs at the expatriates through the character of Andrew Callingham— a barely disguised Ernest Hemingway. Callingham—"a big hairy roaring sort of guy" who wears a shooting outfit while he writes his famously best-selling novels—returns to America amid a flurry of publicity. One article noting his return to the United States—in part to visit the dying Wife Number Two—opens:

> If Andrew Callingham were a less modest artist, as indeed all great men are truly modest, he would have reason to crow over his native land this morning. It was America's indifference to his genius eighteen years ago that sent him roaming the world, from China Seas to the Mediterranean until, decorated with literary prizes and an international reputation as one of our greatest living authors, he returned yesterday to these soils.
> . . .
> Asked what he thought of the work of the newer generation of American writers, Wolfe, Caldwell, and Faulkner, he answered that unquestionably they had something. He was equally spontaneous in praise of Dos Passos, Hemingway, Lewis, and Ellen Glasgow. (*Wheel,* 256)

Powell is clearly having fun granting faint praise to Hemingway from her own satiric portrait of Hemingway, as she tumbles him in with wildly diverse writers.

Turn, Magic Wheel is set closer to contemporary time than any of Powell's previous novels. In 1934 Powell wrote, "This novel, conceived in essence six years ago, planned, replanned, main characters shifted and plot changed. Manner, too, changed—inasmuch as all literary manners have changed, mine particularly" (*Diaries,* 102).

> In my last two books [*Turn, Magic Wheel* and *The Happy Island*] I have not deviated from my original purpose—the Provincial Out of Place, or the Provincial Attacking a Cosmopolitan Problem. My moral is always present, though never in black and white or concerned with criticisms of my characters' activities. In *The Happy Island* it is a picture of people ordinarily envied as Glamorous Idlers and showing up—not their immorality, which is always fun—but the niggling, bickering meanness of their life—not the great gorgeous Cecil B. DeMille idea of corruption, a pagan rout that any imaginative person would like to get into, but a story of miserly, piddling souls without one great, generous glittering vice to their name. (*Diaries,* 151)

The Happy Island is the pinnacle of Powell's language play. The novel is initially rather disorienting, but that is the point because "the happy island" is itself a disorienting place. Because of the narrative's focus on Prudence Bly, it would seem that it fails at an attempt to be a portrait novel, which focuses on the story of a person seeking fame in the great city. But Powell collapses the portrait of Prudence's rise to fame into a single six-page chapter ironically titled ". . . not for publication . . . ," which neatly reveals the saga of Smalltown Girl singing her way into the smoky bosom of the Big City's embrace. The narrative then rapidly shifts to a portrait of "Liberty Night":

> Thursday, for over a decade—ever since everyone had been analyzed at least—was Husband's-Night-With-the-Boys or Girls, Wife's-Night-Out-With-Gay-but-Trusted-Old-Suitor. . . . All over the city, as soon as the cocktail whistle blew, the freed husbands wandered, wearing their freedom like a dead uncle's overcoat, standing on corners wondering what grisly form their fun would take, staring at posters before burlesque houses, knowing it was the same show as last Thursday, the same Georgia Peaches, the same Southern Rose, sometimes wondering morbidly what the little wife did with these Thursday nights he had fought to have, for pride in liberty collapsed on going home to an empty house— who the deuce said she was to have a fling, too?—fun in smug secret was lost in frantic curiosity over what the little woman was up to. (*Island*, 26)

This breathless passage rushes forward to nowhere in particular, like the characters themselves, reflecting the "well-known tendency of satire to pass rapidly from one subject to another without lingering . . . on any single fool or particular piece of foolishness. . . . this quality . . . has earned satire the reputation of being fragmentary" (Kernan, 35). The entire narrative scurries from one form of discourse to another, as Powell arranges various genres and language forms so that knowledge unfolds as characters discover it, rather than relying on the narrator to provide information unknown to the characters.

The form and content of *The Happy Island* unite in a happy marriage. Like a mirror ball spinning over the rollicking island, the novel illuminates shards of life, each chapter, or bit of glass, giving way to the next without space between as the ball continues spinning regardless of the crisis or incongruity that it disclosed. The ball comes full circle, back to reflect the gay, rollicking island. The mirrored fragments vary, as is typical in Menippean satire.

This is apparent from the first chapter: The reader becomes curious about the recalcitrant young man befriended by the voluble Van Deusen, but he leaves the bus before revealing much about himself. The reader must rely on the same item that Van discovers—a dropped telegram: "It was addressed to Jefferson Abbott, Silver City, Ohio, and was signed by one of Manhattan's rising young producers. CASTING COMPLETE THIRD ACT NEEDS REWRITING COME IMMEDIATELY B.HYMAN" (*Island,* 7). This slip of paper immediately indicates that the reader will come by knowledge as it is discovered by or revealed to the other characters. One fragment, titled "Five-Cent Alibi," is a series of one-way conversations as various husbands try to establish their whereabouts the night before:

> "Rhinelander 9326? . . . Mr. Estabrook please. . . . Neal Fellows speaking. . . . Steve? . . . Steve, old man, you put me up last night. . . . I say, you put me up last night in case you should ever be asked. Let's see—we had dinner at—oh, say the Harvard Club, that lets out women, doesn't it, and they do have a dining room, don't they? . . . Yes, we had a nice dinner there. . . . Thanks, Steve. How's Prudence. Seen her lately? . . . Good. Don't mention this to her, she might spill it around Anna, you know the girls. . . . Yes, let's see—as a matter of fact you're putting me up tonight, too. . . . No, of course, I won't come in really. . . . But let's get together sometime soon. Lunch or something. . . . Thanks, old fellow." (*Island,* 32–33)

Here, the reader learns no more than an eavesdropping passerby might hear; the reader is not privy to the other side of the conversation. By incorporating these bits of discourse, overheard and picked up, Powell pieces together rhetoric in a fragmentary way that reflects the way that people usually obtain information.

Powell initially conceived of *The Happy Island* as a story of the social set of homosexuals. "The bachelors of New York in the Satyricon style," Powell wrote. "Do in swift fierce style of a race descending on the enemy" (*Diaries,* 119). Powell's satiric look at this group is almost purely fun; there is little malice in her jabs. The focus on homosexuals and the rampant drinking and eating in the novel do indeed echo Petronius's *Satyricon.*

Not surprisingly, Gelfant does not include a discussion of homosexuality in her 1954 book. Zlotnick does talk about homosexuality, but only in terms of the sordid portrayal in such novels as Charles Wright's *The Messenger,* John Retchy's *City of Night,* and James Leo Helihy's *Midnight Cowboy.* In these novels, the "homosexual subculture" is viewed as "the ranks of drifters, hustlers, bums, and perverts who hang out, waste time, and try to score in the Times Square area" (Zlotnick, 209). Powell's exploration of the "fairy world," as she called it, takes place not in Times Square but in Washington Square and other, more upwardly

mobile, neighborhoods in New York City. Because of their class,
wealth, and (re)location in New York, these men were able to embrace
their lifestyle wholly. New York City is important to these men because
it accepts the homosexual lifestyle; their provincial hometowns would
not. The untimely death of Dol points up the ignoble beginnings of his
life, as his aunts arrive to claim his body—his wish "that he should like
his ashes scattered around Caruso's monument was regarded as sheer
nonsense, cremation was granted only to his notes and life work"
(*Island*, 232)—and return him to the Midwestern soil from which he
sprang.

Powell's portrayal of homosexuals living a relatively happy, somewhat
privileged life is certainly singular in fiction of the 1930s. That Powell
would portray homosexuals in their homes and in the café society that
they adored is astounding. That she refused to moralize about their
lifestyle is more astounding. Most amazing is the refusal of contemporary critics to even mention the pervasive homosexuality in the novel.
Edith H. Walton does say in her review that "Above all—and in great
numbers—there are bevies of 'Doubtful Men,' together with quite a few
others whose status is not even questionable."[32] Walton's commentary
ends there.

Perhaps the most astute criticism of *The Happy Island* noted: "As a
picture of a certain section of New York life this book is a huge success.
As a novel it doesn't come off."[33] Indeed, it does not. It defies the novel
structure and embraces the carnivalistic Menippean form in its "picture
of a certain section of New York."

Powell also focuses on a certain section of New York City in *The
Wicked Pavilion,* as she explained:

> the focal point of the story is a place I call the Café Julien, a French café
> off Washington Square—I combined the Lafayette and the Brevoort so as
> not to step on toes. Both of these hotels have been torn down in the last
> five or six years and with their going a very special way of life went—
> frankly, I think the way of life was going before the building went. For
> writers, artists and people who work alone all day, this particular café life
> was almost a necessity. . . . This special kind of retreat has vanished and
> that's why I wanted to recreate it in fiction before it was completely for-
> gotten.[34]

The narrative observes café-sitters and then follows them to their work
and home. Some characters have or develop surprising links to each
other, but the only thing that binds all of the characters is the café. The

narrative displays Menippean elements, but it is tighter than the fragmented *Happy Island,* with each chapter fleshing out the scene, as the point of view shifts from one character to the next.

For instance, in the chapter "a young man against the city," Rick Prescott sits in the Café Julien, his reminiscing interrupted only by the insistent paging of "McGrew." Fed up with the lack of calls for himself, Prescott finally accepts a call for McGrew. Seventy pages later, it is revealed that the caller was Jerry Dulaine, who invited Prescott to her house. The chapter ends, leaving Rick Prescott standing at the threshold knocking on the door. The next chapter moves backward in time to tell of Prescott's journey between accepting the phone call and arriving at Jerry Dulaine's. Both Prescott and Dulaine are despondent over love and go out to have "one good time before we die" (*Pavilion,* 108). In the next chapter, Jerry Dulaine reveals the details of the "good time" as she recalls events in a haphazard manner, working through the haze of hangover in Bellevue. As Powell wrote:

> I thought in this book I would let the characters create each other—that is, you, as reader, get to know them not by what I tell you so much as by what other characters say about them. They're made up of gossip, you might say. It happens that way in life. There are certain persons you feel you know all about, yet you've never met them and perhaps never will. . . . the lives of strangers weave through our thoughts through gossip and hearsay and become part of our experience. The people in *The Wicked Pavilion* exchange confidences about each other, gossip about other friends until you—as their unseen guest—know them and have your own opinion about them before they enter. The advantage these fiction friends have over real friends is that if you take a dislike to them you can slam the book shut—and how often you've wished you could do that to even the dearest of friends.[35]

In addition to these forms of daily interaction, Powell includes rhetorical forms characteristic of Menippean satire.

Powell arranges rhetorical elements more formally in *The Wicked Pavilion* than in *The Happy Island,* drawing upon such genres as the diatribe, the soliloquy, and the symposium, which "are all akin to one another in the external and *inner dialogicality* of their approach to human life and human thought" (Bakhtin, 120). A notable scene in *The Wicked Pavilion* is the gathering at Cynthia Earle's studio: "It isn't a party, really, it's a sort of symposium of what old friends of Marius remember about him, speeches, letters—" (*Pavilion,* 219). Bakhtin explains:

The symposium is a banquet dialogue, already in existence during the
epoch of the Socratic dialogue . . . but receiving its full and diverse development only in subsequent epochs. Dialogic banquet discourse possessed
special privileges . . . : the right to a certain license, ease and familiarity,
to a certain frankness, to eccentricity, ambivalence; that is the combina-
tion in one discourse of praise and abuse, of the serious and the comic.
The symposium is by nature a purely carnivalistic genre. (Bakhtin, 120)

In *The Wicked Pavilion,* Okie describes the plan for the symposium on
Marius: ". . . a few of us hit on the idea of making a Long Playing record
of spontaneous reminiscences of Marius, tributes to him as man and as
artist, the sort of thing that pops in your head just sitting around like
this. We have Mrs. Earle's tape recorder and it will catch everything
that's said. . . . what a thrill we'll have afterwards with the playback!"
(*Pavilion,* 227). The participants of the symposium are delighted with
the notion of partaking in it, more for their own glory than for Marius's:

What a perfectly marvelous way of paying tribute to Marius, people
exclaimed, filling their glasses to pave the way for spontaneity. Older
guests smiled as they recalled old Marius anecdotes they would narrate,
and they could not help feeling relieved at the chance to shine in
reflected spotlight, so to say, knowing that if the master himself had been
present, they would not have a chance to open their mouths. (*Pavilion,*
227)

The humor is derived from the playback of the tape. The symposium
was designed to reveal information about Marius. Instead, it reveals
information about the speakers:

In the first playback private whispers and asides had come booming out
drowning proper speeches and a dozen quarrels had started because
someone waiting to hear his own pretty speech heard instead malicious
remarks about himself made at the same time. Almost everyone had
stalked out either wounded to the quick or eager to report the fiasco.
(*Pavilion,* 231)

The chapter is arranged with excerpts of the tape interspersed with the
listeners' comments about the tape. The listeners, of course, can manip-
ulate the playback, with buttons to play, stop, fast-forward, or rewind as
they react to the predicted effect of the symposium. The resulting chaos
is typical of the menippea: "Very characteristic for the menippea are
scandal scenes, eccentric behavior, inappropriate speeches and perfor-

mances, that is, all sorts of violations of the generally accepted and customary course of events and the established norms of behavior and etiquette, including manners of speech" (Bakhtin, 117). Frequently, these elements are arranged in sharp juxtaposition, because "the menippea loves to play with abrupt transitions and shifts, ups and downs, rises and falls, unexpected comings together of distant and disunited things, mésalliances of all sorts" (Bakhtin, 118). It is from these mésalliances that humor emerges.

Another rhetorical form included in *The Wicked Pavilion* is the diatribe, performed by Elsie after Jerry Dulaine's failed dinner party. Like the symposium on Marius, the diatribe here is a type of postmortem. Part of the humor derives from the fact that a formal argument form is utilized for a relatively trivial event. The dinner party itself parallels Trimalchio's feast in Petronius's *Satyricon*. Both events were orchestrated to show up the talents of the central figure: Trimalchio in *Satyricon* and Jerry Dulaine in Powell's narrative. The dinner fails to fulfill its function in *The Wicked Pavilion* because Jerry's prize guest, Collier McGrew—the man for whom all the other guests came—does not show up:

> the dinner was over, and at eleven o'clock the two ladies, deserted, knew they had failed. Jerry had known it was a flop for hours but Elsie refused to admit it till the last guest had fled. Then she decided to be philosophical about it, for she feasted on catastrophe, and there had been so many subtle angles to the evening's failure that she anticipated a whole season of warming over tidbits, souping and hashing. She enjoyed her power as secret entrepreneur of a grand comedy. . . . Her young friend's gloom gave her the opportunity for a few cheerful words on errors in strategy. She felt there might be consolation in analyzing the whole situation, now that the show was over. (*Pavilion*, 86–87)

The diatribe, a one-sided argument, is amusing rather than harsh here because it lacks the element of vitriol usually present in a diatribe. Elsie delights in the postmortem: " 'I know you wish I'd go home,' Elsie said, kicking off her slippers and stretching out her long bony legs in their stockinged feet to the fender, . . . 'Right now, I feel like a little cozy post-mortem. A party that's a flop is more fun to talk over than a good party' " (*Pavilion*, 89). In the death of the party, Elsie finds conversational life, a contradiction characteristic of Menippean satire: "All the images of carnival are dualistic; they unite within themselves both poles of change and crisis: birth and death (the image of pregnant death), blessing and curse (benedictory carnival curses which call simultaneously for death and rebirth), praise and abuse, youth and old age, stupidity and wisdom" (Bakhtin, 126). These dualistic notions, especially birth and death, pervade the narrative.

A principal character in *The Wicked Pavilion* is dead—almost. The artist Marius is thought to be dead, and as it turns out, he is enjoying much more fame than he did when he was alive, so he stays "dead." The reader does not know he is alive until it is revealed by the two men who have also been making a living off Marius's death: Ben Forrester and Dalzell Sloane, who used to be Marius's close friends, find that they can make quite a bit of money from forging Marius's works. Marius serves, in part, as a motif for Powell's larger mission of conducting a postmortem on the café lifestyle.

The dualistic image of birth and death is also apparent in *A Time to Be Born,* Powell's clearest satiric portrait of an individual. The narrative fulfills Bakhtin's "last characteristic of the menippea: its concerns with current and topical issues. This is, in its own way, the 'journalistic' genre of antiquity, acutely echoing the ideological issues of the day" (Bakhtin, 118). An element of the dualistic nature of satire is also apparent in the crowning and decrowning of the central character: "This central ritual act of the menippea is a dualistic ambivalent ritual. . . . Under [which] lies the very core of the carnival sense of the world—the pathos of shifts and changes, of death and renewal" (Bakhtin, 124). The figure elevated, and subsequently humbled, is Amanda Keeler Evans, who "at thirty . . . had all the beauty, fame and wit that money could buy, and she had another advantage over her rivals, that whereas they were sometimes in doubt of their aims, she knew exactly what she wanted from life, which was, in a word, everything" (*Born,* 24). Of Powell's compulsion to satirize Luce, Gore Vidal wrote:

> Dawn herself had enjoyed almost no success from her novels and plays; then along comes what she regards as a dilettante beauty who takes Broadway—and all the other ways save the strait and narrow—by the proverbial storm. . . . Like everyone else, Dawn takes it for granted that Amanda doesn't bother to do her own writing. . . . Dawn also reflects another generally held theory about Clare: that a woman so attractive to men must be, at heart, cold and calculating and . . . yes, the ultimate putdown in sexist times, frigid.[36]

Amanda is all of these things—cold, calculating, frigid—in the satire. But Powell saves the narrative from becoming a vehicle to express the "merely personal . . . hatred" that Frye warns against by putting

Amanda in the context of a world on the brink of war. The enormity of the backdrop simultaneously reduces Amanda's importance and minimizes Powell's wrath, born of both envy and outrage. Without the strength of Julian's press behind her, Amanda's power fades as quickly as newspaper ink washing into the sewers.

Satires are not strictly without action. Bakhtin notes that ancient carnival included ritual actions:

> The primary carnival act is the *mock crowning and subsequent decrowning of the carnival king.* . . . Under this ritual act of decrowning a king lies the very core of the carnival sense of the world—*the pathos of shifts and changes, of death and renewal.* We emphasize again: this is not an abstract thought but a living sense of the world. (Bakhtin, 124)

The "carnival king" is what Frye called the object of attack. In Powell's novels, this ritual usually plays out in the "decrowning" of the target of her satire. The decrowning may be effected by the target herself or by other characters, but in Powell's works, the "decrowning" is usually the result of words—perhaps malicious gossip or scathing reviews. When the novel opens, Amanda Keeler Evans has already been crowned as queen of the publishing industry. The narrative is the unfolding of her fall. Her demise becomes apparent when she finds that she is no longer able to fulfill the requirement of writing about worldly affairs. Amanda's descent is nearly complete with her abortion; she reaches bottom with her self-effected decrowning when she publishes the "true story" of Amanda Keeler Evans, baring her humble roots for all to see.

The birth in death motif continues in *The Locusts Have No King,* of which Powell wrote: "This novel . . . should show the breakdown of a love affair and its reconstruction as new, after its seeming destruction has broken each person into his and her basic cells. Patches of love left. Now it is a work of art—a mosaic" (*Diaries,* 252). The narrative also focuses on a single individual, Frederick Olliver, but he is not well known, as Amanda Keeler Evans is. Frederick must portray a worldview as he carries out a mission of Menippean satire: "Carnivalization . . . makes it possible to extend the narrow scene of a personal life in one specific limited epoch to a maximally universal *mystery play scene,* applicable to all humanity" (Bakhtin, 177). The novel is structured along "threshold scenes":

> These scenes, usually taking place in drawing rooms, are of course considerably more complex, more motley, more full of carnivalized contrasts,

abrupt mésalliances and eccentricities, fundamental crownings and decrownings, but their inner essence is analogous: the "rotten cords" of the official and personal lie are snapped (or at least weakened for the moment), and human souls are laid bare, either terrible souls as in the nether world, or else bright and pure ones. People appear for a moment outside the usual conditions of their lives, on the carnival square or in the nether world, and there opens up another—more genuine—sense of themselves and of their relationships to one another. (Bakhtin, 145)

Frederick stands at the brink of several thresholds as he tries to decide between two jobs and two lovers. Frederick must decide between pursuing what he loves, though it is elusive, or embracing what he has, though he doesn't love it. Gelfant describes this conflict more conventionally in terms of theme:

The modern experience of alienation and aloneness is thus related to a breakdown of tradition and community nowhere so striking and definitive as in the city. The materialistic temper of the age, as well as the mechanistic basis of our modern way of life, is also most intensely expressed in the city. And the tempo and tensions of the twentieth-century world of speed and hectic amusement are revealed in the rhythms and pace of big city life. In the same way that the city epitomizes the twentieth century, city fiction focalizes the main themes of twentieth-century literature. (Gelfant, 21)

The larger parallel to Frederick's conflict is a world on the threshold of doom, seemingly secure in peacetime but facing the threat of the cold war's atomic bomb. The novel's ending is ambivalent:

Frederick was idly fiddling with the bedside radio and there was a sputtering of words and confused noises.

"It's the Bikini test—the atom bomb the elevator man's wife is afraid of," Frederick said.

"When you hear the words—'What goes here' that will be the signal—" said the faraway voice, and suddenly Frederick was filled with fear, too. He went over to Lyle and held her tightly. In a world of destruction one must hold fast to whatever fragments of love are left, for sometimes a mosaic can be more beautiful than an unbroken pattern. (*Locusts,* 286)

Frederick's choice is clear, but the surety of its lasting is not at all certain in the face of an uncertain world. The novel has ended, as it eventually must, but the story cannot close.

The Story Must End

"The carnival sense of the world . . . knows no period, and is, in fact, hostile to any sort of *conclusive conclusions:* all endings are merely new beginnings; carnival images are reborn again and again" (Bakhtin, 165). The ending of *The Locusts Have No King* is bleak because of the horror of the reborn image. The nonendings of Powell's other New York novels are not as bleak, in part because of characters that cross from one novel to the next. In a narrative with little action, closure is problematic. As Griffin notes:

> Satirists must stop speaking, and their satire must end. But how can they accomplish this so as to satisfy their own psychological needs, as they have represented them, and the aesthetic or formal needs of their readers for closure? Given the special decorum of satire—an aroused or a merely chatty speaker, a virtually unlimited subject matter—endings present a problem that satirists have historically had difficulty solving. (Griffin, 96)

Powell encountered this criticism, as she noted in her diary: "Malcolm [Cowley] said I never ended my novels properly; they simply stopped. This could be true. The fault, I'm sure, is not in the end but in the structure earlier in the book, which should be so built to indicate the plausibility of the ending" (*Diaries*, 309). It is curious that Powell recognizes the critical link between the structure of the narrative and the ending, but, judging them by the standards of the novel, she perceives them as flaws.

Powell's sense of purpose and consciousness of tradition may be deduced from her diaries, in which she asserted that "The only record of a civilization is satire—Petronius, Aristophanes, Flaubert. These are so valuable that they are timeless" (*Diaries*, 215). Powell had the support of generations of satirists, most notably Balzac, who combined satire with a novel of manners, just as Powell was doing. "What influences a story writer most is the kind of stories he first thrilled to—and he is likely to put his own characters through *Sara Crewe* (my favorite) or *Graustark* or *Alice Adams,* situations completely removed from his own life or experience" (*Diaries*, 436). Powell consistently cited among her favorite books Petronius's *Satyricon*. It seems probable that she was influenced by the satires she had read, even if she did not consciously adopt the form. Powell's forays into literature invariably served to affirm her own motives. In 1943 she discovered a Flaubert work and wrote:

Reading for the first time a fine book (Flaubert's *Sentimental Education*) I
am again impressed by the importance of satire as social history and my
theory that what reviewers call satire is "whimsy" and what they call
realism is romanticism. But *Sentimental Education* gives a completely
invaluable record of Paris, its face and its soul, its manners and its talk of
1840, and no realistic novel of the period remains. The best sellers, no
doubt, were the freak books—as now (war in Spain, fun in Johannes-
burg, Civil War) but these are worthless journalism for posterity. (*Diaries*,
215)

Powell was aware of working within a tradition of satire, and Menippean
influences are apparent. Taken as a whole, her New York novels create a
mosaic, and in a way none of them ever ends. They continue into one
another.

The final chapter of *Turn, Magic Wheel* leads one to believe that
Orphen will finally honor Effie and give her the respect that she
deserves. The bond with Effie was "stronger than any love he had ever
known" (*Wheel*, 280), but in the final paragraph, he pulls Corinne out of
the rain and into the shelter of his home. This underscores the novel's
resolution that it is acceptable to exploit one's friends in the name of art,
freeing Powell to continue in her own mission of satirizing her beloved
city and those in it.

Though *A Time to Be Born* can be read in isolation, it is enriched by
the knowledge of key players from *Turn, Magic Wheel*—Dennis Orphen,
Corinne Barrow, and Andrew Callingham—as they have their brief
stroll on stage. They provide depth and allow the reader to share with
Powell some understanding of how these characters live in her mind.
Rather than being incidental characters who have crept in illicitly, they
help elucidate the seemingly inconclusive outcome for Amanda Keeler
Evans. Dennis shows up in a bar placating Corinne, whose husband has
left her. A link is established between Corinne and Amanda, when
Corinne provides the name of an abortionist so that Amanda can take
care of her problem. Amanda's life then follows the same path as Cor-
rine's; she is dumped by her husband. Amanda's career will not survive
without Julian's publishing backing. The one possible hope for the
future in this world on the brink of war is the baby; this, Amanda will-
fully destroys, as she destroys all hope for her future by running after
Callingham, a man who respects only himself. When Callingham strides
in from *Turn, Magic Wheel,* more blusterous than ever, he is still juggling
his women, and there is no reason to believe that Amanda's sacrifice will
pay off. Amanda appreciates Callingham's talent and hopes that an

alliance with him will further stoke her own creativity; but she pursues him primarily as a conquest, hunting him down in Africa. She apparently misfires: in the end, Callingham marries his dancer.

The repeated characters, which Powell claimed to include for amusement, greatly influence the cumulative effect of Powell's sharply detailed impressions of various social groups. By having characters stroll from social set to social set—as Powell herself did—she levels the playing fields, erasing the lines that striate the middle class into several layers. The city plays a critical role in this leveling, as its various venues—especially the café scene—are available to people with enough money or credit to join in a toast to the town. Dennis, Powell's favorite café-sitter, gets the last word in *The Wicked Pavilion.* This is fitting, since the novel is in part a funeral dirge for Powell's beloved Lafayette: "The Café Julien was gone and a reign was over. Those who had been bound by it fell apart like straws when the baling cord is cut and remembered each other's name and face as part of a dream that would never come back" (*Pavilion,* 306). Powell does her best to hold her characters together: "What I wanted to do in [*The Wicked Pavilion*] especially was to make the characters live so that their lives could extend beyond the limits of the book—and I may have succeeded too well for my own peace of mind."[37] If the characters lived beyond *The Wicked Pavilion,* it was only in Powell's mind. Her final New York novel, *The Golden Spur,* has only the ghosts of these characters. Before that, though, she grappled with the rather more real ghosts of her childhood.

Chapter Four

"At the Crossroads": The Autobiographical Novel(s)

In 1944, midway through her career and after developing a following with her sharply satiric, fast-paced New York novels, Powell published *My Home is Far Away,* a novel devoid of satire set in slow-moving early twentieth-century Ohio. Reviewers and editors, somewhat startled, seemed to view it as an aberration. Powell's editor, after receiving the first part of the manuscript, "called to say she 'liked the new book very much.' Maybe after the second part was finished she could tell more— 'and then the first part could be cut.' " (*Diaries,* 223). And Diana Trilling noted with some dismay, "The scarcity of satiric fiction in this country is something this department has often lamented. . . . even Dawn Powell, with [*My Home Is Far Away*], deserted satire entirely in favor of sentimental childhood reminiscence" (Trilling, 611).

But the novel is not so much of a departure as it appears. Powell's previous two novels led logically to this point. In *Angels on Toast* (1940), Powell explored the lives of businessmen on the road and at their occasional trips home, in an apparent effort to understand the motivations for her father's love of the traveling life, which led him to spend more time away from his family than with them. Despite the rollicking narrative, there is an underlying bitterness that reveals Powell's frustration with her father's neglect of his family. And at the end of Powell's decidedly New York novel *A Time to Be Born* (1942), Amanda Keeler—whose childhood bears remarkable resemblance to Powell's—stuns her reading public by exposing her low Midwestern past: "I CAME FROM ACROSS THE TRACKS" screams the headline, in one of her cosmopolitan husband's publications, no less. Powell does the same in *My Home Is Far Away,* laying bare the raw truth of her "bastardized life" as she called it (*Diaries,* 211), in an effort to explain both herself and the insistent compulsion driving her most ambitious female characters, who fear that failure might force them to return home. Powell's novel shows the horror of that fate.

In *My Home Is Far Away,* Powell portrays her Ohio childhood in a chillingly realistic way, unlike the lighter portrayals in her earlier Ohio novels, particularly *She Walks in Beauty.* Strengthened by the experimentation with structure and language in the New York novels, Powell's writing is free of the sentimentality that occasionally blurred the earlier novels. Clearly defined characters replace caricatures, and a consistent voice guides the story, rather than a wavering omniscient narrator. Most important, the novel allowed Powell to exorcise finally her Midwestern ghosts and go on with her life. When she finished it, she wrote:

> After long despondency over novel, my own future, past and present, I veered . . . and felt myself again. . . . I suddenly felt as if at last the wind had stopped blowing against me and the intense fear I've felt not only of Fate but of all life and people. I have spent most of my life being an adolescent cringing with painful inferiorities based on others' opinions of me—and leaping out of them with bravado. (*Diaries,* 230–31)

By admitting that her home is indeed far away, she apparently settled more easily into her role as permanent visitor, both in Ohio and New York.

The scene of the novel is, of course, Ohio, but it encompasses a broader swath of that state than her earlier novels did. The characters and plot have a closer relationship than in any of her novels; the plot is, in fact, the development of character.

Scene: Home Is Far Away

The novel had been simmering since 1935, when Powell visited Canton, Ohio, after suffering a sharp bout of homesickness that may have added depth to the emotional impact of the visit: "I have been lately as near homesick as I have ever been . . . Every time in my life when I have no solution for present problems I escape to the past and new clear-cut pictures emerge" (*Diaries,* 101). During the visit, which brought memories of her childhood flooding back as she reminisced with her sisters, Powell outlined a possible story:

> The story of three sisters meeting for the first time in three years for a trip—the invocation of their childhood, their joint recollections recreating the stepmother, building up their families, their memories, their so different lives, . . . they carry with them the rubber stamp, the indelible

impression of their childhood, their family reunions—put together the unfinished fragments of each till the fiend herself emerges whole. The stepmother, the sudden terror of attics, a glimpse of each one's life. (*Diaries,* 104)[1]

The novel came to a boil six years later, when Powell found herself quite literally in a fevered state over the material: "Unfortunately my fever brought back so many childhood memories with such brilliant clarity that it seems almost imperative to write a novel about that—the three sisters, the stepmother, Papa. . . . Wrote a start from 3 to 5 a.m. in bed with temperature" (*Diaries,* 189–90). Powell found a bizarre solace in this return to her past, as she dredged up the wreck of her childhood and mentally traveled through Ohio towns, from Shelby to Mansfield to Cleveland and back again.

The static scenes in the earlier Ohio novels provided a consistent background against which Powell could focus on character development. In *Dance Night,* characters move in pace with the industrial town, fighting the insistent rhythm of the pervasive factory noise. The pastoral Dell Village of *The Tenth Moon* provides an idyllic background to the characters' dream lives. The farm of *The Bride's House* allows seclusion. In *She Walks in Beauty* the small town is sharply divided by the B&O railroad, removing the main characters from the town. Powell could comfortably draw these backgrounds because she had known them all as she tumbled up. But after writing *The Story of a Country Boy,* Powell realized the limitations of "an arrested background. Backgrounds should be fluid to be alive" (*Diaries,* 77). The background in *My Home Is Far Away* is certainly fluid, distressingly so, underscoring the chaotic, rootless nature of the girls' upbringing. Even in London Junction, the girls' hometown for the longest cumulative time, they live in three different houses. The effect of the numerous homes in which they live is that it becomes apparent that the home of the title is far away in part because there is no single, specific physical place to call home. Home becomes a faraway notion of what home could have been, should have been.

Here Powell refuses the easiness of clear delineation found in *She Walks In Beauty,* where the railroad track uncompromisingly divides the girls from the townspeople. While writing *My Home Is Far Away,* Powell noted: "Very important to avoid the usual cliché, wrong side of tracks stuff of which only adults—and not many of them—are conscious. Not the real trouble here anyway" (*Diaries,* 229). The real trouble here is "the daily chilling misery of being unwanted, in the way" (*Diaries,* 186) as the sisters are shuffled between relatives and later as they suffer under a harsh regime in their stepmother's house.

Initially, the girls are not aware that this nomadic life is unusual, because it is the only life they know. Powell captures the movement without any cadence of pity: "This is not a Booth Tarkington midwestern family or a wrong-side-of-the-tracks family," she wrote to her editor, "but a family of floaters whose philosophy and experience is far different from the conventional family at home or at war with a secure environment; the philosophy inevitably becomes unprovincial, cynical, individualistic."[2] Recall the guidance of Eudora Welty in chapter 2: "Place. . . has the most delicate control over character . . . by confining character, it defines it" (Welty, 122). In the earlier Ohio novels, characters, confined in the small towns, frame their dreams accordingly. In this novel, there is no confinement, so there is no definement. The girls come into themselves as a tumbleweed grows by gathering bits to itself. There is no need for escape, until the end, because they are constantly on the move. And the outer movement nearly overwhelms inner movement.

In the beginning of the novel, their mother, Daisy, is the force that holds the girls together as they move from their beloved Peach Street house to a town 30 miles away to live in one half of a duplex. The children are not entirely content, because their father, in his fantastically improbable way, has promised to buy the largest house in town for the family and "Often the children walked past the Furness mansion on Main Boulevard and pretended they lived there just as their father had promised. . . . This was their real home, because their father had said so, and any other place was only marking time" (*Home*, 24–25). When their mother dies, the girls lose their center physically and emotionally.

They are shuffled from relative to reluctant relative, moving first to their grandmother's boardinghouse on Hodge Street in Cleveland, until their grandmother is overwhelmed and asks their father to take them back; "They didn't know where they were going till they got on the train, but they were glad to be with Papa again" (*Home*, 124). They find themselves at the London Junction Hotel where "the kitchen help . . . provided spontaneous entertainment and occasional discipline for the children" (*Home*, 129). Their father's neglect of the rent forces a retreat, and they find themselves at a relative's farm in Elmville where "the girls missed the careless freedom of the hotel, and country games seemed silly after the grown-up pleasures of London Junction" (*Home*, 140). Realizing that they are not wanted at the farm anyway, the girls go to Aunt Lois's house in London Junction.

Here they find that they "missed their old liberty, but their new life seemed to be a step upward in respectability, besides being luxurious beyond their wildest imaginations" (*Home,* 144). The luxury is short-lived, however, because their father has a falling-out with their aunt and they move to a boardinghouse in Lesterville. Of all their homes, the house in Lesterville is most bewildering to them: "The truth was that they didn't know how to go about playing in Lesterville. In Cleveland the Hodge Street district had been a little village in itself, but Lester-ville, in bursting from village into busy, industrial town, was too big for one center and too small for several centers" (*Home,* 163). Finally, their aunt arrives to reclaim them, and shortly after they move into a house with their father when he remarries.

The family—together again and increased by a stepmother and step-sister—moves into the very house that their father promised to buy their mother, but here they are farther away from home than ever before in their lives. In this house, the girls face the final betrayal in what they had seen as their "real home." Initially, "It was like a dream to walk home from school straight up the Furness front walk" (*Home,* 188). But their fortunes quickly change: "After a while Mrs. Willard ruled that they were to use the back alley and back door, because they tracked up the new broadloom carpet" (*Home,* 188). After "the glamour of their new life slowly sifted down to its disagreeable reality" (*Home,* 198), the girls began plans to escape the horror of home.

Throughout the rapid shuffling of scenes, the sisters move through shifting relationships with each other, from an amiable sibling rivalry in their first home with their mother, to a growing dependency on each other, to an ultimate splitting away. Emotions evolve inversely to the physical movement; for instance, when they shift rapidly from place to place, they find themselves growing closer together; and when they are finally together under one roof, they begin to split apart.

Plot: The Shaping of Character

The plot of *My Home Is Far Away* does not differ largely from the story of Powell's childhood related in chapter 1. Powell found herself shaping the novel along the lines of her own recollection, recording episodes as they developed. She was a bit uncertain of this progression: "Since it is episodic rather than plotted, I am not sure of it at all; since it is senti-mental, I am not sure it is not simply an elderly softening of the brain" (*Diaries,* 216). She persisted in this development, though, and the result is a novel that, contrasted with the earlier Ohio novels, is both more original and more controlled. The novel is, in some ways, a retelling of *She Walks in Beauty,* without the jarring shifts between anecdotes that result in a crazy quilt effect in that novel. *My Home Is Far Away* follows a more traditional pattern, structured in three roughly equivalent parts that describe first, the girls' life with their mother, then their erratic journey among various reluctant caregivers, and finally, their tortured life with their stepmother. The episodes that reveal their evolving moods are somewhat fragmented, but this dual evolution of plot and mood was successful in one reviewer's eyes: "Something like a miracle of illusion is presented by Dawn Powell, as she fills *My Home Is Far Away* with the starkness of particularly frustrated childhood and at the same time wraps it all in the haze of nostalgia."[3]

Perhaps more than in any other of Powell's novels, plot and character are integrally linked. Powell hashed out this idea in her diary:

> my book . . . seems vague and bare, and this sort of thing ought to have sharper characterizations to tie it together since there is no plot. I must not lose sight of my original plan—i.e., to let the story grow up as the children themselves do—let their perceptions grow more acute through their experiences, finding themselves different from each other and being amazed. The slow formation of character and tastes—the total difference between Lena and Marcia and Fuffy,[4] yet all open to some heredity and environment. (*Diaries,* 217)

Powell's freedom to let the characters shape the plot was won from her work with the New York novels, in which the way the plot unfolds is more important than the plot itself, and readers come by knowledge as it is discovered by or revealed to other characters. In this novel, the unfolding of the plot is equivalent to the unfolding of character, and readers come to know the characters as they come to know themselves. There is not the patchwork of remembered or invented scenes that clutters *She Walks in Beauty* or the obstacle course of events in her first novel, *Whither,* that causes Zoe to stumble finally onto her fate without a logical movement toward her destination.

Powell's aim was to capture this world from a child's point of view, and it is natural that Powell's fictional counterpart, Marcia, provides the primary viewpoint, revealing the world as she comes to know it. The novel's third-person view is not omniscient, as in *She Walks in Beauty.* "Technically it is from Dickens, particularly David Copperfield," Powell wrote.

At the beginning, it is written as for a child—words, images, etc., are on the table level of their eyes; everyone is good to the three sisters, their pleasures are simple, their parents good. As they grow, the manner of writing changes—the knowledge of cruelty, divorce, disillusionment, betrayal—the anguish of adolescence, of not being wanted, of struggle for survival. (*Diaries*, 211)

Though the novel is largely autobiographical, Powell moderated the factual knowledge by endowing Marcia with greater strength than Powell herself had as a child. As a result, Powell is not moving along an entirely known path because Marcia's different character allows her a life separate from Powell's memories. Powell acknowledged this masking and found strength in it:

A writer . . . needs . . . disguises. Since telling the truth is merely a version of events anyway and nobody else's "truth," the essential thing is to convey similar effects, similar emotions and in my own case arrive at artistic truth by artistic means, instead of handicapping myself by withholding some facts and enlarging or distorting others. Better to fictionalize all—more pleasure and more freedom. Deciding this, I believe I can achieve much more interesting and worthwhile effects. (*Diaries*, 222)

And so the novel opens, conveying this world as Marcia sees it, and her view is, quite naturally, egocentric:

Marcia was five years old now, fifteen months younger than Lena, but she was half an inch taller because she took after the Willards instead of the Reeds. It was an understood thing that Lena was the pretty one, with her yellow curls and rosy cheeks, but Marcia was proud of having bigger feet so she got new shoes first, and the fact that she could hold her breath longer. (*Home*, 22)

The first sentences here show Marcia making sense of the inequities of her little world through fragments probably overheard by older relatives; readers can hear the echo of a grandmother or aunt assigning familial features to each child. Marcia accepts her lot and asserts her own strengths. She is an exceptionally strong-minded child and perceives herself as an adult trapped in a child's body. Childhood was an ordeal that must be survived; adults were creatures to be tolerated; the world was a place to be observed until one was old enough to change it. And the world, from this child's point of view, can seem pretty ridiculous.

> Marcia could remember everything that ever happened, almost from her first tooth. She could remember knowing what people were saying before she could talk and she could remember bitterly the humiliation of being helpless. She remembered being carried in her mother's arms to a family reunion and given ice cream for the first time. She had cried over its being too cold and her mother said, "Here, Baby, I'll put it on a stove to warm it." Any fool of even less than two could see it was a table and not a stove, but for some philosophic reason Baby Marcia decided to let the thing pass without protest. If her mother wanted to think a table was a stove, she would just have to wait for a bigger vocabulary to argue the matter. This was the beginning of a series of disillusioning experiences with adult intelligence, and the recurrent question of whether adults were playing a constant game of insulting trickery, or whether they just didn't know much. (*Home*, 22)

Marcia is a truly precocious child. As a preschooler, she shows up her sister at assembly by reciting, with gestures, her older sister's planned recitation; "Even after a punishment for this breach of etiquette . . . Marcia continued to steal Lena's arithmetic or reader and run easily through the homework while Lena was patiently working over one word in her Speller. Marcia could not understand why it took her sister . . . so long to learn things when they were like candy—you saw them, ate them, and that was the end" (*Home*, 24). It is clear, however, that the story is told by someone who now has "a bigger vocabulary." There is, as Edmund Wilson notes, a mix of sophistication and childishness.

However mixed the voice is, it is a truer voice than that of the omniscient narrator in *She Walks in Beauty*. In that novel, Dorrie is Powell's literary twin, but the viewpoint is inconsistent and there is no sense of Dorrie coming to know her world as she grows up. In fact, there is little evidence of Dorrie growing up at all. She is 12 when the story opens and frequently escapes wholly into a dream world. She does not have the force of her expressed childhood to justify this escape from reality, so the resulting portrait is that of a naive adolescent. It is the love known in childhood that gives poignancy to the Willard girls' loss of fortune. For despite the burdens imposed by their father's financial irresponsibility and the sadness of their mother when he is on the road, it is apparent in the first part of the novel that the girls are loved. Life is not idyllic and the girls suffer the indignities of not having things that other children have—a lack that touches Lena most strongly—but there is comfort. Blissfully ignorant of the much rougher road that lies before them, they settled into a somewhat normal routine.

every night Marcia and Lena took opposite sides of the cradle, rocking it and singing at the top of their voices until Florrie, for some reason, would fall asleep. Sometimes their father got out his shining yellow guitar and sang with them, teaching them to take different parts. When Mama had finished the supper dishes they had quartettes. . . . After Florrie had fallen asleep, the girls were allowed . . . to look at their picture books. . . . But the most fun was when their mother told stories. (*Home*, 33–36)

They are, in short, children, enjoying a comfortable family life when their father is at home—and knowing that they are loved still when he is away—unaware that life might ever be different.

The protagonists of Powell's New York novels are unencumbered by family. They have shed their family relations and are either actual orphans or self-imposed orphans. Powell herself lived the life of an orphan in New York City, removed from her family—though able to return when she felt the need. In this novel, Powell confronts the complications of her family: "I want to show the Montague-Capulet war between two families—Aunt Lois and Papa warring over a poor dead woman, accusing each other, blaming everything on the death of Daisy. This hatred mounting, use of the children as a football . . . Both betrayed into cruelty, revenges, etc. and hate themselves for it—but hating themselves, blame it on others" (*Diaries*, 223). Powell acknowledges the strong emotions that infuse her family—a hate born of love that infects all relationships. The New York orphans sometimes provide a glimpse of their past, but they do not admit to any love. Because Powell, like Dickens, had a difficult time not including at least one orphan in a story, there is an orphan in *My Home Is Far Away*. Here the unloved orphan provides the contrast with the sisters' closeness—a closeness that the sisters themselves do not admit to. During their first visit to their aunt and uncle's farm, when their mother is still alive, "Marcia was very happy because Lena had no one else to play with and was forced to make a chum of her sister. They made up secrets, and played school with the cornstalks as pupils" (*Home*, 73). They are content until Almedy, the orphan, chastises Marcia for whipping a cornstalk pupil for misbehavior. Almedy is "pushing sixteen . . . when you get them from the orphanage you can't tell, so we just let Almedy pick her own birthday," their uncle explains (*Home*, 67). Marcia initially observes Almedy with some envy, even muttering in a moment of annoyance with Lena, "I wish I was an only child. . . . I wish I was an orphan with a different birthday every year and no home" (*Home*, 72). But Marcia finds upon closer observation that this fate would not be entirely desirable: "An orphan was different from people. It looked like people, ate like people, and could talk a little, but it was more like a horse or dog. Orphans were nearly always ungrateful and after you gave them a home and raised them they usually got into trouble or ran off with some fellow and you never saw them again" (*Home*, 77). In confronting the reality of orphanhood, Powell confronts her own links to family and seems, in some measure, grateful for them.

After the stay at the farm, the girls reluctantly readjust to life at the London Junction duplex. Marcia goes to school, finally, and "The first thing Marcia got from school was measles, which she passed on to Florrie. In return for this Lena acquired chickenpox and got the whole family quarantined, a condition that lasted a long time, as one would get it just as another was getting well" (*Home*, 85). Their mother manages to stay well through the girls' convalescence, but as they emerge into health, she becomes quite seriously ill. And an evil specter emerges.

Throughout the novel runs a thread of evil. Powell noted that in this book, "I want to trace corruption, private and public, through innocence and love—possibly learning that only by being prepared for all evil can evil be met" (*Diaries*, 214). In the first part, it is a distant evil—barely seen but intensely felt—in the shape of a man attempting to balloon across the county. At the opening of the novel, as the girls arrived at their new home in a borrowed surrey, the horse desperately trying to outrun a gathering storm, they see him. Cast against the billowing darkness is a man in a balloon:

> Marcia and Lena, arms tight around each other, looked upward, frightened and fascinated while the balloon drifted slowly downward. . . . They could see a dark figure outlined in the ship, a fairy-tale monster, omen of thunder and darkness and nightmares to come. The lightning sprang behind it like hell-fire from the Bible pictures, and the horse reared. . . . The children stared helplessly, filled with sick loneliness and fear, as if the creature flying up there had brought the clouds and lightning and the blight to their perfect day, and no one, not even a father and mother, could stop his wicked vengeance. (*Home*, 17–18)

This figure recurs, appearing for the final time as their mother dies, when the mother cries out: "Look, it's the man in the balloon! Look out!" (*Home*, 94).

The frightful balloon man is ushered out of the plot by the dark shapes of the funeral people who arrange themselves at the close of part 1.

> The funeral people suddenly filled the Fourth Street house, their dim unknown faces haunted the dark hallways upstairs and down, the mur-

mur of their funeral voices rose and fell like the sighing of the wind, their catfeet slipped back and forth on whispering errands. The minute a heart stopped beating, these shapes assembled as if this was the cue that brought them to life, and the final clang of the iron cemetery gates would shoo them back into designs in the wallpaper and shadows behind doors. (*Home,* 97)[5]

It is at the funeral that eight-year-old Marcia perceives herself for the first time as different from others. Other people cried; Marcia did not. She considered Lena's ability to cry at anything and nothing a peculiar power that Marcia simply did not have. Not coincidentally, Amanda Keeler Evans of *A Time to Be Born* shares this experience: " 'Why she isn't even crying!' she heard people say at her mother's funeral, as if it was for this moist tribute that people died. People were always wanting children to cry and prove again and again their helplessness, so that they might take advantage of it" (*Born,* 37). Ever wary of sentiment in the satires, Powell pulls readers away with her next line: "She did cry a little, quite suddenly, when she remembered that now she would not get the red snow suit her mother had promised." There is much of Marcia in Amanda. In fact, the description of Amanda's childhood[6] is Powell's childhood in miniature, with a satiric twist—"childhood was a crime painfully remembered," Amanda mutters (*Born,* 34)—as if Powell was making a final effort to rid herself of her own ghosts in the satire.

Apparently failing in that effort, Powell allowed her childhood the full canvas of its own novel, and in the nonsatirical autobiographical novel, Marcia is allowed a less avaricious explanation for her stoicism:

> The little girl named Marcia could be pinched or bruised without feeling pain, because she was filled with the numbing fragrance of death, an immense thing by itself, like a train whistle blowing far off, or an echo in the woods. There were no people in it, not even Mama, here or gone. But nobody knew this. Nobody knew it but Marcia's secret self, and it filled her to the brim with such a tangle of desperate wonder there was room for nothing else. (*Home,* 99)

When their mother dies, the girls find that Marcia's wished-for orphanhood has nearly come upon them. Without the force of their mother to hold them together, they are scattered to various relatives. Marcia experiences a growing awareness of difference during this time, and "it astonished Marcia to discover that other children lived in an almost incomprehensibly different way than they did" (*Home,* 139). In this drifting section, the girls learn to look out for each other, even as they begin to develop differing personalities. This evolution seemed to come unbidden for Powell as she gave over the development of the novel to the characters:

> I am in a curious position about this book, for I haven't the faintest notion of whether it's good or bad but at least now it is going very fast. It pours out spontaneously now that it is more fictionalized. The purity and loyalty of Florrie must be brought out more; the mixture of arrogant self-ishness, pride and bravery of Lena; the complete retreat into dream world of Marcia with surprised shock of contact with reality. (*Diaries,* 226)

Marcia's point of view evolves from the wholly egocentric view of the small child into a growing realization of differing viewpoints held by those closest to her. For instance, when the girls return to the farm briefly, they find that their aunt and uncle do not want them there. So Lena, ever conscious of others' views of her, orchestrates a return to London Junction. The sisters band together, largely under the command of Lena. As they watched their sister plan the move, "Florrie and Marcia watched their competent leader with satisfaction" (*Home,* 142). Realizing their need for one another, they come to appreciate one another.

Marcia and Lena parallel Dorrie and Linda in *She Walks in Beauty,* but the characters are drawn very differently and for different purposes. In the earlier novel, Powell worked with caricatures, rather than characters. The dichotomies are too sharply drawn: Dorrie is too plain and too dreamy, Linda is too beautiful and too vain. Despite the distress imposed by the scene—being on the wrong side of the tracks—the sisters have a loving home, but they do not find strength in each other: "The two girls had little to say to each other, but their silences were precious, since that was all they had ever shared" (*Beauty,* 21). Linda, the older sister, is concerned only with her pursuit of Courtney Stall, along with the attendant needs for that pursuit: appearance, attitude, a sister that doesn't embarrass her. Lena, Linda's parallel character, is somewhat self-absorbed in *My Home Is Far Away,* but she shows compassion for her sisters. Lena admired Marcia's intelligence and defended her at school when teachers gave her low marks on compositions, refusing to believe that she wrote them without assistance. Marcia admits admiration for "the way Lena never got reality and pretending mixed up, but went straight out and did things" (*Home,* 265). This grudging admiration of each other's talents helps them survive their moves.

She Walks in Beauty also lacks the balance of Florrie, the youngest child, who embodies "pure love." Everyone adores Florrie, so she did not have trouble finding a home. Though their father tries to keep the girls together, Florrie is not always with the older sisters on the various moves. But she grounds the sisters with her unwavering devotion to Papa—"Florrie always wept at criticisms of Papa" (*Home,* 141)—and to the memory of Mama. She reminds Marcia and Lena of what is important: the love that holds them together. When Lena is plotting an escape from their stepmother's house, Florrie and Marcia turn to each other for comfort: "Florrie was desperately worried about Lena, but Marcia's concern was for her five-dollar goldpiece" that Lena had borrowed from her (*Home,* 265). Florrie's presence in the novel moderates the emotions of her sisters, softening their responses. In the end, though, they do not have the same fortitude as Florrie, and they leave home.

Like those of nearly every family, the complicated emotions in the novel can be confusing. Powell wanted to lay bare the facts of her childhood, the rawness of being unloved, but she held back by investing Marcia with an adult-like stoicism. Out of fear of hurting her family or her memory of her family, Powell blunted the pain. Most notably, Powell directs no anger toward her father, who surely is the person to blame for the woes of her childhood.[7] In 1936, 10 years after his death, Powell outlined a possible story devoted to her father: "A male 'darling' who was devoted to whatever job or boss he had. Michigan Bed Company salesman. The Star Cookie Company. Cherry factory. Worked with Indians. A radical or a conservative depending on the boss" (*Diaries,* 127). She understood his weaknesses, but did not hold them against him.

Even when he neglects their basic needs, the girls defend him. On the occasions he returns home, he bears such gifts as stale candy, discarded hats, slightly spoiled fruit, and clothing samples not suitable for everyday wear. The girls are thrilled, and "They were unhappy and bewildered that anyone should accuse him of being an indifferent parent, for he brought them, in addition to the scarfs, a bag of oranges and a box of Eugenia Chocolates, discarded from [a] sample case as being a little stale" (*Home,* 109). The girls admire his new suit, and quickly reassure him that their shoes are just fine because "We put paper over the holes. We don't need new shoes anyway because we don't go to Sunday School here" (*Home,* 109). This loyalty remained throughout the Powell sisters' lives. A clue to this continued loyalty may be found in a letter Powell wrote to her husband while sitting at her father's deathbed: "Today I cried thinking that once a dark vivacious woman loved this poor wreck of a man . . . and at midnight I saw her with long brown hair lying beside him on the bed while his second wife slept in the next room."[8] For the sisters, their father was the final real link to their mother and to the family as they knew it. This too may account for the bitter view of childhood, when Marcia/Dawn was ignorant of the fact that this indeed was home. Had she been more aware, she might have embraced that time when the family was whole—now it is much too far away. This link is suggested in the novel, when the sisters are enjoying a rare visit with their father as he sings to them: "He scarcely ever would sing the old favorites. When the girls sang them he would interrupt with a command to go on an errand, or he would himself go out, frowning. It was as if these songs were buried in the Mapleview Cemetery with Mama, all covered with myrtle and graveyard flowers" (*Home,* 157). It is during one of these absences that Aunt Lois comes to the Lesterville boarding-house in response to Lena's urgent letters. Their father, out all night, has not returned by the time the girls had lunch, which was "hot water soup," as Lena explains: "You boil the water and put in salt and pepper and buttered crackers for oysters, so it tastes like oyster soup" (*Home,* 174). Aunt Lois takes them home—to her home.

Throughout the moves, Marcia's knowledge has been broadening, and upon their return to London Junction, she notes wistfully,

> There were different kinds of happiness. . . . The biggest jolt in growing up was to discover that you didn't like what others liked and they thought you were crazy to like what you liked.
>
> Marcia thought the greatest happiness was to be left alone. . . . Lena wanted everything other girls wanted, whether she really liked it or not, and since these were all tangible objects costing money, Lena was unhappy a good deal of the time. Florrie's happiness consisted in having people love her and fondle her and refrain from unkind words about anybody. (*Home,* 179)

All of these kinds of happiness are quenched with their father's final betrayal: marrying Idah Hawkins. Neither the balloon man nor the funeral people could prepare the girls for the tangible evil of the step-mother: "[She] was a careful woman and felt that all possessions were better locked up, since it was regrettably impossible to lock up their owners" (*Home,* 189). She took Marcia's books, Lena's dresses, and Flor-rie's hugs and put them all beyond reach. Finally, the family was together physically—in the house that was promised to their own mother—but Idah had the opposite force of their mother: rather than holding the sisters together, she drove them apart, forcing them to defend themselves, each in her own way.

> Mrs. Idah Willard's "stand" was so elaborate, and involved so many contingencies, that her new family despaired of ever getting it straight. First, they were to stay out of the house except for sleeping or eating. Second, they were not to sit out on the lawn mooning where everybody could see them, nor were they to go visiting relatives or school friends or have them call. They were not to use their school paper for games, because it cost money, nor were they to keep reading in their school readers for fun after their lesson was learned. They were to make themselves useful, instead of ornamental, but on the other hand, She'd rather do all the housework herself than have them singing songs while they made beds or washed dishes. . . .They were not to go places where townspeople would talk about their ragged clothes, but they were not allowed to use their sewing boxes either, because needles and thread cost money. (*Home,* 203)

Powell certainly aimed a lethal pen at her stepmother, though accounts in Powell's diaries and letters, in addition to the family's testimony, indicate that the treatment was not exaggerated.

It would seem that this oppressiveness would bog down the narrative. But Powell had learned the leavening effect of humor in her own life and through writing her satires. Here the humor comes in the shape of the grandmother, who arrives in town not to save the girls as they had hoped, but to rescue the novel from unbearable grimness. In the darkly humorous spirit of David "I was born a posthumous child" Copperfield, the grandmother drolly pronounces: "A grandmother doesn't like children any more than a mother does. . . . Sometimes she's just too old to get out of tending them, that's all, but I'm not. Never felt better in my life" (*Home,* 207). Unlike Aunt Jules in *She Walks in Beauty*—who has all of the loving characteristics of Powell's grandmother and Aunt Lois, but none of their practicality and awareness—Grandma is in full ownership of her character. She appears just occasionally with her friend Mrs. Carmel—armed with her mysterious bag filled with mothball-scented candy, sheet music, fabric remnants, and a catalog of other goodies—to lighten the mood. Eventually, even Grandma finds this task too monumental when she perceives that her "arrival . . . in London Junction had a devastating effect on the Willard girls. A person goes through life accepting his lot with equanimity, till a moment of complete happiness reveals to him that he has up to now had a perfectly wretched existence"

(*Home,* 209). Powell herself felt bogged down by the narrative, noting in the process of writing it: "This oppressive novel never seems to get anywhere in spite of many good things in it. It is like a child that takes so long to grow up and look after itself" (*Diaries,* 232). Florrie, the baby, rescues the girls briefly by seeing the only humane aspect to the Stepmother: " 'I feel sorry for Her because She can't help being mean,' Florrie said guiltily, knowing this confession of weakness would not please her sisters. 'Marcia can't help spilling things and breaking things, and Papa can't help his temper, and She can't help being mean. I guess that's why Papa doesn't get mad at her; it's because he knows She can't help it' " (*Home,* 222). Lena and Marcia cannot summon up any defense of her.

Desperate though they are to stay together, to cling to family, they cannot bear up under the stepmother. Lena was the first to break free: "After her first difficulty with her stepmother, Lena refused to take any orders except from Papa" (*Home,* 197). Lena escapes first to her friend's house, then to Aunt Lois's house. Marcia escapes initially into herself. She cannot leave, but she will not give the stepmother the satisfaction of knowing that she can be hurt. Marcia's stoicism infuriates her stepmother because she is not allowed to see the fruit of her cruelty.

> Stonily impassive during this punishment, Marcia looked contemptuously at the former Miss Hawkins, who sank back flushed and trembling into a chair.
> "Next time you'll cry," she gasped. "I'll get a bigger whip." (*Home,* 210)

This refusal to bow under her stepmother's brutality seems a gesture of wish-fulfillment for Powell, making up for the times that young Dawn responded to her stepmother's cruelty. If there is a flaw in Marcia, it is that she is too cool, too controlled, reflecting Powell's own assertion that "I mustn't ever cry" (Josephson, 50). Marcia's coolness is a sophistication imposed by the adult Powell. Her 1915 journal, written much closer to the wreckage that was her childhood, reveals the truer emotions of "Marcia":

> I have been thinking of home a great deal lately. . . . I never cried so whole-heartedly before in my life. I thought of all the terrible times in my life—of that desperate week at North Olmsted when I was praying and sobbing every minute for someone to take me away—of Phyllis and Mabel and I abnormally subdued, morose, and shut out from the

house—we dare not run and play in the orchard—in the barn or anyplace. Desolate existence for three little girls, motherless and with a mis-
understanding father. And then do you[9] remember that night when
Mabel came out on the car from Cleveland—you know she was staying
there in Jennings Flat with Mrs. Johnston then—and how glad Phyllis
and I were to see her? Then she whispered that because of my desperate
letters to Auntie May—(I'd written nine in the five days I'd been
there)—that Auntie May had sent a special delivery to her to come after
me. Oh how glad I was. ("1915 diary," 20 August)

Marcia's final escape is equally dramatic, but it is much cleaner, less desperate. Marcia, in the process of sneaking a book out of the parlor, is
trapped behind a chair when her stepmother comes in to talk with her
brother. Vance has impregnated a woman who subsequently dies of a
botched abortion, so the stepmother helps him devise a plan to leave
town. Marcia unwillingly hears it all. When the stepmother discovers
her, as she must, she banishes Marcia. Again the Bakhtinian life in death
motif emerges: Marcia's eviction is the start of her new life. On the
train, she muses,

She was still scared, but she felt light-headed and gay, the way Papa did
when he was going away from home. She thought she must be like Papa,
the kind of person who was always glad going away instead of coming
home. She looked out the window, feeling the other self inside her, the
self that had no feelings and could never be hurt, coming out stronger
and stronger. (*Home*, 293)

My Home Is Far Away views events from a distance, controls them.
Powell is able to objectify her experience and write about it, though
even decades later the emotions are fresh enough to come through in the
novel. Readers feel true loathing for Idah Hawkins, and they sympathize
with the girls. Mabel is somewhat colder in the fictional version, but
then, so is Marcia. Conflicted emotions do blur the novel, but the fact is
that they stem from truth. Readers may want to see Roy Powell get his
due, but Powell does not. In one of her final writings, she remains true
to her father, though recognizing her relatives' antipathy toward him:

It's always a picnic or a shore dinner when you're out with the dead in
my family. . . . Sometimes my father shows up, eager to go. This I dread,
for all the women start picking on him right away, and even though he's
just as dead as they are he's never allowed to come along. He looks so
disappointed that I want to cry out, "Never mind, Papa, the basket never

gets opened up, we never really get there, and it's only a dream anyway."
(*Best,* 447–48)

Maybe this is her father's book after all as Powell comes to an understanding of herself through her father's life.

On the day the novel was published, Powell wrote in her diary: "Publication of *My Home Is Far Away,* which I now think is one of my best
books. On rereading it my first feeling was of queasiness over the initial
establishment of a distinctly autobiographical flavor, but after a while
the characters became wholly fictional, increasingly round, and with the
full reality that only created characters have. Certainly few facts are
here" (*Diaries,* 234). Powell seemed to regret identifying *My Home Is Far
Away* as an autobiographical novel because it seemed to her that she
moved further from fact and closer to fiction as she wrote it. "Although I
set out to do a complete job on my family," Powell wrote, "I colored it
and, even worse, diluted it through a fear of embarrassing my fonder
relatives, also a distaste for throwing away my own privacy" (*Diaries,*
222). The public identification of the novel as autobiographical did
expose Powell's family to potential embarrassment. Powell wrote:
"Unusually fearful over book, largely because the skeleton is so close to
life and I hate to bring myself out so openly for censure, also to expose
the family. It made me cringe today when review called it pathetic, etc.,
good-for-nothing people" (*Diaries,* 234). A week later, she lamented:
"Nothing happens about my book—not even ads anymore—so I am
waiting as usual for the Great Review that will put it over" (*Diaries,*
235). And then the Great Review came—Edmund Wilson wrote it for
the *New Yorker:*

> Miss Powell has so much talent and of a kind that is so uncommon that
> one is always left rather disgruntled at her not making more of her work
> than she does. Three of her recent novels—"Angels on Toast" and "A
> Time to Be Born," as well as this latest one—have all been in some ways
> excellent, but they sound like advanced drafts of books rather than fin-
> ished productions. It is not only that they are marred by inaccuracies,
> inconsistencies, and other kinds of careless writing . . . her carelessness
> extends . . . to the organic life of the story. Miss Powell has a way of
> resorting, in the latter parts of her novels, to violent and sudden inci-
> dents which she needs for the machinery of the action but has not taken
> the trouble to make plausible. . . . the whole book . . . gives the impres-
> sion of being merely an all-but-final draft which represents the stage at
> which the writer has got all his material down but has not yet done the

sculptural rehandling which is to bring out its self-consistent contours and set it in a permanent pose. . . .

This is a genuine disappointment, because Miss Powell, like Marcia in her novel, is a born literary temperament, with an independent point of view that does not lend itself to clichés of feeling, and a life of the imagination that makes writing, for her, an end in itself. She will never be a popular purveyor of the daydreams of feminine fiction. She does not hold up the public for laughter, excitement, or sobs. But, as a writer, she has never yet quite grown up. She appeals to the intelligent reader, but she appeals, again, like the perceptive little girl, who entertains you with breathless dashes of talking but whose vivid improvisations betray, by their falterings and their occasional whoppers, that her imaginative world has not yet been developed to include all of adult experience.[10]

Wilson had spoken. Powell was devastated: "If Bunny's review had been offset by a powerful, favorable one the book would have gotten off. As it is, it is very discouraging to have someone (who actually has told me I'm infinitely better than John Marquand and equal to Sinclair Lewis at his best) do me so much genuine damage" (*Diaries,* 237). Wilson had, in fact, hit on the very thing Powell was striving for, but he finds fault with it rather than saying, "Ah, that is the point." Wilson perceives the child-like point of view, but cannot carry it through to understand that, indeed, Marcia "does not know what moral she wants to point [out]"— that is the point. The story is about Marcia's coming into that knowledge. And what possible moral could a human derive from such a wreckage of childhood? That life itself is not "plausible." And, that, finally is Powell's point. You make of your life what you can. You tell the story that you need to tell and move on.

In *A Time to Be Born,* Amanda Keeler divests herself of her past in order to be born again, to move into a new, uncertain life. In a way, the novel was liberating for Powell also, but she recognized that this was not necessarily a good thing. "I think my greatest handicap and strongest slavery is my insistence on freedom," she wrote. "I require it. So I cannot make the suave adjustments to a successful writer's life—right people, right hospitality, right gestures—because I want to be free. So I am tied down and now in middle years almost buried (so far as my career goes) by my freedom" (*Diaries,* 242). Powell unburied herself with more New York satire. Though she continued to write for another two decades, she did not publish another book set in Ohio. It was not, however, for lack of trying. *My Home Is Far Away* was intended to be the first part of a trilogy. As the project grew, she envisioned a saga that bridged her two worlds through the story of three sisters growing up from childhood through adolescence to adulthood:

> The world growing up as fast as they do, the political wrangles and changes in sophistication. Sisters coming together . . . not on virtues but on vices. . . . It seems like an endless job—three volumes anyway. The early separation of provinces and New York; the way vices as much as inventions brought the two parts of America together, and vices, inventions and corruption brought America and the Old World together. (*Diaries,* 211)

Drafts of the second novel, titled *Marcia,* are set in Cleveland. Despite 20 years of sporadic work—she was working to complete it the month before she died—Powell did not finish it.[11] Powell did, in effect, bridge her two lives, but not in a physical way. Instead, she was finally able, at age 43, to exorcise the demons of her past, to bring them back to life in order to put them to rest.

Chapter Five

Out of Place: The Novels Set
Outside New York and Ohio

A few of Powell's novels defy the categorization of this study, drawn along the lines of Powell's primary settings, New York and Ohio. *Angels on Toast* (1940), set in both New York and the Midwest—in addition to numerous points in between and beyond—does not embrace either geographical area, instead relishing the movement from one area to another. Two other "outsider" novels—*A Man's Affair* (1956), a truncated paperback version of *Angels on Toast,* and *A Cage for Lovers* (1957), which divides its setting between Paris and upper-state New York—are works that Powell might well wish left out of her legacy, but they are instructive because their failures help to point up the strengths of Powell's other novels.

Angels on Toast is curiously classified as a New York novel by Gore Vidal, who wrote that it "was the first of Powell's novels to become . . . the book for those who wanted to inhabit the higher, wittier realms of Manhattan where Truman Capote was, later and less wittily, to camp out."[1] Though the novel is furiously paced like the New York novels, Powell conceived of it as a venue for

> another provincial angle—the businessman on planes, trains, buses, private cars, whose business axis is New York; whose homes are Iowa, Chicago, Detroit, Pittsburgh, Alabama. These men have their wandering minstrel, gypsy lives, in and out of hotels—the Stevenson, Chicago, the Fort Sumter, Charleston—tornadoes, wrecks strike them, a life of adventure, a code of their own. (*Diaries,* 151)

Powell's geographic loyalties converge in this novel, expanding the boundaries of the strictly provincial or the focused New York novels. The scene of *Angels on Toast* shifts frequently in accordance with the itinerary of its businessmen protagonists. This feature sets the work apart from Powell's other novels, which have a stable setting (even *My Home Is Far Away* shifts settings only within the confines of Ohio). Locales in *Angels on Toast* include Chicago; New York City; Miami; Danbury, Connecticut; Havana; and occasional train stops. Powell wrote to Max Perkins that she "wanted to convey the sense of speed, changing geography with no change in the conversation, the sense of pressure behind the ever-evanescent big deal, and behind these adventurers."[2] Characters speed along in planes, trains, and automobiles, depending on their mission of the moment. At the novel's opening, Lou Donovan and Jay Whittleby are settling in for a train ride from Chicago to New York:

> Jay was still a little sore because Lou wouldn't wait over for the fight that night and plane out the next day. . . .
> "If we got to take a train, why couldn't we have taken the bedroom train on the Century?" complained Jay. "Give me the New York Central any day. I took the Commodore Vanderbilt out of New York last month and slept like a baby. Not a jolt."
> "Ah, you can't beat the General," said Lou. "You got to admit the Pennsylvania's got a smoother roadbed."[3]

The dialogue reveals intimacy with modes of transport between the cities. The train serves a different role here than in the Ohio novels, where the characters looked longingly at the trains traveling onward to great cities. Here, the train is an adequate vehicle promising no great escape.

The cities themselves become vehicles. They are not as important as the movement between them, as Lou and Jay press on to another job prospect, another lover. In fact, New York takes some hard knocks, as characters blame not themselves, but the city, for their failures. Ebie, a successful commercial artist with a fine apartment on Park Avenue, mutters "the hell with New York," (*Angels,* 95) and flees to a Connecticut home. Lou, on the cusp of a great business deal, exclaims: "What a town, New York, . . . what a beautiful, big-hearted honey of a town. No place in the world like New York" (*Angels,* 96), only to growl when the deal goes bad: "What a lousy town, what a two-timing, ungrateful, ugly, crooked, stinking town New York was. . . ." (*Angels,* 232). In this narrative, there is not the union between character and scene that marks the New York novels; New York is but one whirring backdrop to the perpetual motion of the story.

Occasionally, though, things go awry when characters peculiar to one scene appear in another scene. The resulting mésalliance between character and scene brings forth carnival elements of Menippean satire, as described by Bakhtin: "A free and familiar attitude spreads over everything: over all values, thoughts, phenomena, and things. . . . Carnival

brings together, unifies, weds, and combines the scared with the profane, the lofty with the low, the great with the insignificant, the wise
with the stupid" (Bakhtin, 123). Comedy is born of these mésalliances.
For instance, in the first chapter, Jay's wife greets him at the train's stop
in New York City, perhaps not knowing that Jay was joined by his girlfriend at an earlier train stop. Lou quickly comes to the aid of his friend
by claiming that Jay's girlfriend is his new secretary. Jay's wife then
hints to Mary, Lou's wife, that Lou may be having an affair. (In fact, Lou
does have an affair, but not with the girlfriend/secretary. He has just a
brief fling with her.) This ironic sequence of events is characteristic of
satire.

Another notable instance of "misplacement" involves Mary. In this
case, Mary remains in her home city, Chicago, but she travels from her
refined suburban home to the Spinning Top, "not one of Chicago's better spots; its chief charm for its customers was that it was not popular
and was no place to take a wife" (*Angels,* 175). Lou knows this, which is
why he intended to meet his lover Trina Kameray at the bar, not knowing that Mary overheard him making plans for the tryst. So Mary goes
along with Lou and gets her first taste of the carnival side of life at the
Spinning Top:

> It was a jolly combination of seedy Hollywood glitter and old-time
> honkytonk. It was near enough to the station so that a busy man could
> nip over for a drink and the show between trains, say hello to the girls,
> maybe, and then, after he missed his train, could even be put up in the
> little adjoining hotel. The girls were good-natured, not bad-looking
> graduates of various burlesque wheels, and they sat around at the bar in
> little fig-leaf costumes, fluttering their blue-greased eyelids at strangers,
> and on dull nights at least keeping up a semblance of gayety by their
> perpetual squeals and chatter. . . . Homey, that was the way a traveller
> described the Spinning Top. (*Angels,* 175–76)

Perhaps, but not the kind of home that Mary is used to. The mésalliance
between Mary's refinement and the Spinning Top's clamor is striking.

> "How do you like the place, Mrs. Donovan?" Jay politely asked.
>   Mary turned a pale bright face toward him.
>   "Oh, terribly amusing," she said. "I had no idea there were places like
> this."
>   "I knew it, all right," said Flo. "The only thing is try and get your
> husband to take you to one."

> Ha ha ha, laughed everyone, and then the drinks came, and Lou saw that
> Mary was having plain soda, and to add to this exhibition of good sports-
> manship she was taking a couple of aspirin with it to help endure the
> pain of having a good time. (*Angels,* 182)

Mary is clearly out of her element as she views her husband in this new
atmosphere, puzzling out what it is about this world that appeals to the
man she married. The Spinning Top functions classically as one of
Bakhtin's "carnival squares" in which roles are reversed. Mary's quiet
aristocracy, which shuns bawdy behavior and raucous frivolity, has no
potency here. Bakhtin notes that

> Carnival is the place for working out, in a concretely sensuous, half-real
> and half-play-acted form, a new mode of interrelationship between indi-
> viduals, counterposed to the all-powerful socio-hierarchical relationships
> of noncarnival life. The behavior, gesture, and discourse of a person are
> freed from the authority of all hierarchical positions (social estate, rank,
> age, property) defining them totally in noncarnival life, and thus from
> the vantage point of noncarnival life become eccentric and inappropriate.
> (Bakhtin, 123)

Mary has never experienced carnival and is reluctant to do so now. Lou
moves easily between Mary's refined home and the Spinning Top
(though he is more comfortable at the bar). Lou is unable to form "a new
mode of interrelationship" with his wife in this scene. Mary is a trophy
wife, as Lou admits to himself:

> [The] thing that had won Lou, besides her good breeding, her name, and
> her discreet passivity, a quality he'd never found in any other woman,
> was her youth. She was twelve years younger than he and it seemed to
> give an added piquant flavor to the conquest, as if her youth was a rare
> diamond that he was able to buy and show off. He spoke of her youth
> oftener than necessary because, to tell the truth, she seemed older than
> himself with her restraint and dignity, qualities he was still struggling to
> master. (*Angels,* 155–56)

But in the dim, smoky light of the Spinning Top, her refinement
appears ridiculous to Lou:

> He would have liked to sit here . . . and brag about how his wife never
> went to nightclubs, never drank, loved music and culture and riding,
> that sort of thing, a real lady, and talking he would have sold himself all

over on her. But here she was being a lady in person, and away from her own background, a lady was just a dud on a party, a liability, a wet blanket. (*Angels*, 182–83)

Ultimately, this carnival scene changes Mary. She is, in essence, "decrowned" as a result of the mésalliance, fulfilling another characteristic of menippea as described by Bakhtin: "profanations: carnivalistic blasphemies, a whole system of carnivalistic debasings and bringings down to earth" (Bakhtin, 123). Unable to move easily between the worlds, as Lou is able to do, Mary forsakes her refinement and embraces the profane world of the Spinning Top. While Lou is pursuing "the Kameray" east and south, Mary ponders her future and determines her fate.

> If she was at fault, and she might be, then the fault had been with her at the very start. If all the things he first loved were still there and he no longer loved, then these must now be all the things he hated. She would have to be different, she would be like . . . the women at that nightclub, she would get up with the orchestra and beat the drums, she would talk to strange men, she would drop in at bars by herself . . . and ask other women's escorts to join her at her own table. Those were all the things she was *not* and therefore they must be the things he wanted of women. (*Angels*, 208–9)

Mary sets out to transform herself, not understanding that Lou never loved her, but rather loved her social status, her coolness, her refinement. The exposure to carnival offers Mary an alternative.

In *Angels on Toast*, Powell's satire vibrates beyond New York City, as Americans moving across their own country, working to capture the spirit of capitalism and progress, wholly American characteristics. In *A Cage for Lovers*, Powell shows Americans clinging to their American-ness while traveling abroad, not unlike Henry James in motive, though far from him in execution. Powell wrote best when she knew and understood her scene, so that it became nearly a character in the novel. She could not be in a place for a brief period and know it—as Hemingway, for instance, was able to evoke the sense of so many varied places. She had to absorb it over time. For this reason, *A Cage for Lovers* falls somewhat short of fulfillment as it is based on Powell's recollection five years after her visit to Paris. During her time there, during the rainy season in late 1949, Powell was worried by her usual lack of money and spent some time trying to market stories, including one inspired and written during the journey across the ocean.[4] She wrote an unusually large number of letters during her stay, claiming to embrace her loneliness. Shortly after her arrival, she wrote to her husband: "Everything is working out as I planned so far. I have seen nobody and have not tried to. I celebrate my loneliness and this is a wonderful city to be alone in . . ."[5] And she wrote to Dos Passos, "I do not want to have a gay time at all, I want to get away from disruption and constant dismay."[6] Edmund Wilson noted to a friend, "Dawn Powell, who is in Paris, has been writing gloomy letters saying that she hates the French—but many Americans feel that way when they first go to Europe later in life; later they find that they love it."[7] Years later, Powell viewed this solitary stay differently: "I couldn't breathe in Paris—fear of strange isolation and the financial panic that precludes all comedy" (*Diaries,* 419). Ready for a working vacation, Powell could as well have been in her usual hotel room in Atlantic City. Instead, a ticket to Paris, a gift from Powell's friend Margaret De Silver, provided that opportunity.

The Paris scenes of the novel reflect Powell's slight disinterest and subsequent confusion in the city, which refused to organize itself in the three months that she stayed there. Two months after arriving, she wrote to Joe Gousha:

> I walked for miles and found [a restaurant], . . . It turned out, of course, to be just about behind this hotel, by 100 yards or less, one of those things that make walking in Paris a puzzle. Walk away from Boulevard Raspail and after an hour's walk straight away you come to Boulevard Raspail which mysteriously has hooked on to Boulevard Montparnasse near Le Dome.[8]

The confusion is conveyed neatly in the novel, as Powell describes the confusion of the newly arrived Christine—who also went to Paris merely because it was a convenient place to escape—as she tries to navigate the city:

> Paris was round. No matter in which direction you walked you wound up where you started, and as if that was not frustrating enough, with the same thoughts seesawing in your head that had driven you out in the first place. Signposts meant nothing—the Samaritaine sign lighting up the Right Bank, the Tour Eiffel, the Lion, the heroic statue of Balzac, the pool in Luxembourg Gardens, the Arc de Triomphe—these familiars reared up before you along the way not like milestones but like traveling companions who had started out with you and might drop off gently at

their posts. Crossing bridges, back and forth, threading and braiding *rues* and *boulevards,* beguiled by one more little square, another *place,* you walked your mind away, postponed the answer, tramped out hope and regret, then you were back at your own post, falling into your place just as the Eiffel, the Lion, Balzac and the others had. Tomorrow you would start earlier and in the other direction, but the companions would be the same, looming suddenly before you like the Cheshire smile, then fading behind you, as the hours had, as the city itself had, for you had really seen nothing but the cloud of uncertainties ahead of you.[9]

The scene enriches and underscores the confusion in Christine's head, as she circles around the merits and disadvantages of returning to a life as a companion to a lonely old Miss Lesley in her "little world of pro-grammed duties and pleasures" (*Cage,* 7). She cannot shake the memo-ries and cannot break herself of the habit of transforming the present scene into future stories to tell Miss Lesley (here, she is reminiscent of *The Tenth Moon*'s Connie Benjamin and Blaine Decker, who also live con-tinually in the past and future, but never the present).

Powell did find one place to warm to in Paris. "I prefer Left Bank," she wrote to Dos Passos, "as I want to be in place like the Village where I can meet people after hours without arrangement, and leave them the same."[10] The Left Bank invigorates the novel briefly, but Powell deleted much more material after her editor, Rosalind Baker Wilson, told her: "The general feeling at Houghton Mifflin was hoping this wouldn't turn into another Paris Left Bank sort of book" (*Diaries,* 382). Powell herself found reinforcement for this complaint when she read "*A Room in Paris* [by Peggy Mann] which was extremely profitable for it showed the French Left Bank cliché my novel had fallen into" (*Diaries,* 356). What Powell discovered, though, was that worse than a cliché, she was creat-ing "so far a mere shell of a book and shell of a character. Better to con-tinue it as a shell, then intensify, rather than try to warm up the outside with irrelevant bricks" (*Diaries,* 356). The Left Bank "bricks" are thus cast aside. The shells remained. As one reviewer noted, "Christine is such a mousy girl that it is hard to care whether she makes it or not, but the two broke Americans, scrounging around Paris, are terrifying and very funny. They deserve a book to themselves."[11] Powell consciously eliminated all wit from this novel, and wrote:

I still feel the need to open Christine—or else *dramatize* her. Fortunately there is no wit or humor in this story so it may be successful. Waugh, Huxley, Thurber—none were really able to make a decent living until they lost their sense of humor and practically their ability to feel. I hope for a happy turnabout myself. (*Diaries,* 357)

The happy turnabout did not happen with this novel, largely because of the lack of satire, frequently voiced by the satirist. *A Cage for Lovers* lacks a central satirist, reflecting Powell's unfamiliarity with the scene of the novel. In order to satirize, the author needs to know the scene well enough to know its flaws. *A Cage for Lovers* desperately needs a satirist to save Christine—and the novel—from tedious self-absorption.

In the novel Powell consciously employed flashback, shifting between the present and a past that ranges from the week before to three years earlier. The time shift is paralleled by a space shift: Christine's thoughts move between upper-state New York in the past and Paris in the present. Neither place is integrally linked to the movement of the novel because the backgrounds are static. The flashbacks do not re-create the past chronologically because our minds do not re-create the past chronologically. Rather, Christine's memories are presented in fragments. Triggered by a moment in the present, her thoughts leap back, then forward, then back again to flesh out the original thought. Perhaps the technique does not work because all of the action is occurring in Christine's head, so the reader has the uneasy sensation of eavesdropping. Further, as one reviewer gently noted, "the personality of the heroine remains vague,"[12] so the import of Christine's thoughts do not reach the depth necessary to make the flashback technique work. After writing *A Cage for Lovers,* Powell noted: "No flashbacks! People can reminisce, but openly—no stops and gos" (*Diaries,* 382). In *A Cage for Lovers,* the only goal is for Christine to escape her cage, a negative goal that does not give a clear motive to Christine's recollected past. Christine is not "possessed by an idea," but rather obsessed with indecision. She cannot imagine any possibilities other than either staying with Miss Lesley or running away.

Powell began writing *A Cage for Lovers* in 1955, at Yaddo, the famous writer's colony in upper-state New York. Thought she seemed to draw upon her surroundings for the American locale of the novel, the fictional town of Fairmount could as well be in Ohio in terms of the character of the town (and of the plot: it's not a surprise that Christine's mother runs a boardinghouse, and that Christine's sister is her opposite in features and nature), except that the geological structure of upper-state New York allows for hills and dales that aren't generally found in central Ohio. Thus Christine can move in a classic cliché from the working-class

town up to Miss Lesley's mansion on the hill. Admitting a lack of familiarity with the scene, Powell noted that she wanted to take a writing
vacation in October 1955: "for four days—say, small hotel upstate
where I could be in some atmosphere" (*Diaries,* 350–51), in order to
connect with the novel.

It is odd that Powell chose a non-American locale for the central
location of the novel, since the whole of her career seems devoted to
preserving the America she knows, with all its foibles. Christine indicates several times that she would rather make her escape in New York.
Powell, too, it seems, would rather make her escape in New York.
While writing the novel, she noted that she wanted "to get peculiar
atmosphere of a kind of zombie life—these Americans walking around
against foreign sets, talking America, thinking America, preserving
America, afraid vaguely to go home because in the back of their minds
they know there is no America" (*Diaries,* 351). It seems that in the
back of her mind, Powell knows that there *is* an America. After the pre-
dictable failure of the novel, Powell wrote: "I regard *Cage for Lovers* as a
vacation from myself—a sabbatical from which I return to self,
renewed" (*Diaries,* 382).

Curiously, the failure of *A Cage for Lovers* reaffirmed for Powell the
methods and themes that she knew she could use effectively.

> The English reviews of *Cage* were more helpful than any editing or criti-
> cizing. Everything said indicated how wrongly advised I'd been by
> Houghton Mifflin. The Paris part (as here) was the part most praised and
> regretted more not done there. . . . Also the flashback was criticized,
> however well done (I dislike it myself) and the general character of
> Christine as unimportant. This has made a deep impression on me—
> reminding me of a deep fault of mine. I frequently choose a hero or hero-
> ine I do not like myself purely as a personal exercise in trying to under-
> stand that kind of person. I never end up liking them any better. The
> minor surroundings are always better and more interesting. Dennis
> Orphen in *Wheel* I liked, but the fact is I like raffish characters and might
> as well make them heroes. Also these reviews and my experience in solid
> novel writing teach me at this time to specialize in my specialty—
> Bohemia, raffish people, and satire. (*Diaries,* 382)

In *Angels on Toast,* the lead characters lean more toward sleaziness than
raffishness. The sleaziness is a peculiarly middle-class America version
found in the businessman, and Powell conveys the movement of these
men as they hop from town to town. Powell wrote to Max Perkins:

> I wanted to catch people as I heard them on trains and buses and [in] bars, let them do their own story without any literary frame whatever, without explanations, without author's tricks, in fact without writing. The effect I was after was the after-effect. . . . these characters are presented by their own bare words and their business front—a jovial, open-handed, wise-cracking front that is so seldom let down that they themselves aren't sure what's under it. . . . I expect to be accused of lampooning the American businessman but neither Lou nor Jay are representative of anything but Americans at high pressure. I could certainly satirize the business man, the average business success, but such a pompous, Dale Carnegie . . . type would not interest me.[13]

The idea explored in this narrative is the response of businessmen to high pressure. The central point is an outgrowth of the Ohio novels in their focus on the traveling salesmen who occasionally appear in the small towns: Charles Abbott "The Candy Man" in *Dance Night* and Harry Willard in *My Home Is Far Away,* both of whom neglected their families financially and emotionally. In *Angels on Toast,* the salesmen are fast-moving, fast-talking fellows who abandon their families emotionally, but can afford to maintain them in high style. Powell's writing process paralleled the movement of her characters.

> I myself read *Angels on Toast* recently and found it remarkably good and valuable as a picture of Middlewestern types in high gear and sudden wealth. I was glad to find I enjoyed something of my own—and this one a book I wrote fast and intensely since the mood had to be preserved. (*Diaries,* 220)

The strengths of this novel, and of Powell's other narratives, are apparent by their absence from *A Man's Affair,* the edited version of *Angels on Toast.* Roughly half the length of *Angels on Toast,* this paperback version is stripped of the set pieces and descriptive detail that enrich the narrative. For instance, in the opening train scene of *Angels on Toast,* Lou Donovan meets T. V. Truesdale, a man who later plays a role in Lou's business.

> This was the real music of the rails, some eccentric stranger popping up telling his life story, it passed the time while Indiana slid past the window, towns popped up, announced their names with a placarded station momentarily thrown on the screen, then dissolved into fields, forests, hills. The brown stranger swept through a score of countries, his story was mounted on the wind, it sweetened their drinks, it mingled in Lou's

mind with a picture of Mary's closed door and the house in Winnetka.
(*Angels*, 15–16)

Lou's appreciation of the initial meeting reveals a depth to his character
that is not apparent in his coarse activities. This passage is one of the
casualties of editing, so that Powell is forced to account for Truesdale's
presence later in the novel when he becomes critical to the plot. *A Man's
Affair* provides a hasty bandage in the guise of a flood of telegraphs to
Lou's office midway through the book:

> "Who is this screwball?" Lou angrily demanded.
>   "I knew you'd ask that question," Miss Frye answered. "I was sure you
> were glued at the time. He was that carnival press agent that crashed
> your convention party here. You hired him as an investigator for you and
> paid him two hundred in advance."[14]

The initial romanticism of the encounter is utterly lost and Lou's coarse-
ness remains unchallenged. Further, the zings of the earlier version are
flattened as Powell incorporated the sex scenes requested by her editor.
The original version of chapter 2 closed with a brief view of Lou having
a drink with Jay's girlfriend:

> "I'll bet we had a better time than Jay," she said, her face darkening. "I
> damn well hope so anyway."
>   "Listen, don't be so hard on Jay," Lou laughed. "You can't be that
> mean to a fellow's pal. Have a heart."
>   He put his arm around her. The sun was shining in her bedroom win-
> dow when he woke up. (*Angels*, 26)

The subtlety of the final line is a neat twist, because it is not entirely
expected. The entire affair is conveyed in a single pronoun: "her"—had
the sun been shining in *his* bedroom window or *the* bedroom window,
readers would not know the outcome of the evening. The reedited version in *A Man's Affair* makes the outcome inevitable, and inevitably
tawdry:[15]

> ["I'll bet we had a better time than Jay," she said, her face darkening. "I
> damn well hope so anyway."]
>   ["Listen, don't be so hard on Jay," Lou laughed,] slipping her hand
> into his. ["You can't be that mean *to a fellow's pal*. Have a heart."]

"If he'd only show a little sense once in a while," she said mournfully. "Jay's good-looking and fun, but he's not half the man you are, Lou, and you know it."

It was true, of course, and he had a sudden, overwhelming need to really prove it to her. [He put his arm around her.] From the way her lips clung to his, her arms gently drawing him closer, he got the idea that Ebie felt the same need of proof.

Some time later, [in *her*] Ebie's [bedroom], he was saying, "You know, Ebie, clothes just don't do you justice. I'd like to have a sculptor make a paperweight of you, just like you are now."

"Don't talk," she murmured. "I can't stand a talking lover."

There was nothing halfway about Ebie. The beautiful gown had zipped off in one gesture, the slippers kicked over the bed, and there she was, pale peach body, curvier than you'd ever suspect, on the white taffeta coverlet, arms outstretched, waiting.

Here's a dame that believes in a real production, Lou reflected next morning, the whole works. Ebie sleepily wanted to know why he was chuckling, but he couldn't tell her. He'd just thought what a pity it was he couldn't tell old Jay that his girl was even better in the hay than he'd said she was.

"Oh, Lord, this shouldn't have happened," she sighed, pressing her aching forehead.

"Wrong!" Lou said, gaily. "It ought to happen more often." (*Affair,* 18)

This somewhat lengthy excerpt shows the extent of the damage done to Powell's style and integrity. "Dame?" "In the hay?" This is not Powell's voice. The subtle shaft of sunlight, the single pronoun said far more in many fewer words.

The changes apparently reflect the publisher's demands rather than Powell's intention. Desperate for money—she wrote that she longed for "the luxury . . . of paying all bills" (*Diaries,* 345)—Powell hacked the text in two months. In addition, she apparently was suffering an extended period of writer's block. Her 1954 diary concludes, "A year of practically no writing," (*Diaries,* 344) and her 1955 diary is one of the shortest in the collection, weighing in at a mere eight pages. She cut *Angels on Toast* while she was struggling with the foreign challenge of writing *A Cage for Lovers*—a novel she turned to after abandoning her struggle with the sequel to *My Home Is Far Away.* As she concluded the task, she wrote:

In a familiar tension of weary desperation . . . all on the seemingly all-set
business of cutting and rearranging *Angels on Toast* for reprint. Okay at
first but never any finality—always just one more attempt to "sex" it up,
which at first I thought I could do in a legitimate, true, original way fitting the book, but obviously they must have it in the cliché way. . . .
Turned in *Angels*—revved up and in some ways improved and deperson-
alized. (*Diaries*, 351)

Stripped to the bare bones of plot in the sense of what happens, the
novel loses its spirit. It is the beauty of the journey, the exploration of
the idea that makes Powell's novels live. Fortunately, Powell's writing
strength returned, allowing for one final, strong satire: *The Golden Spur.*

Chapter Six
The Journey:
First and Final Novels

Powell's first novel, *Whither* (1925), and last novel, *The Golden Spur* (1962) both fall under the realm of New York novels, but, separated by nearly four decades, they illustrate Powell's growth as a writer, particularly in her changed plan for unfolding the adventures of a provincial in New York City. She moves from a fairly conventional, though erratically executed, structure in *Whither* to an orchestrated "explosion," as Powell called it, in *The Golden Spur*. The plots of the novels are strikingly similar: In both a provincial heads to New York City to fulfill a quest. *Whither* relays the adventures of Zoe Bourne, "a girl who was breaking off with her family and all the stupidities which Albon represented, for a career in New York. New York!"[1] *The Golden Spur* tells the tale of Jonathan Jaimison, a young man who has come to New York City from Silver City, Ohio, to find his real father. The difference between the two protagonists is primarily one of motive: Zoe is running away from her provincial past toward great fame as a writer, with no working plan for how she will achieve that fame; Jonathan is moving toward a goal, with his mother's notes and diaries from the 1920s to guide him.

These two novels that frame Powell's career show her experimentation with form as she moved from a conventional novel to a marriage of Menippean satire and novel. The scenes in the final novel lead more clearly toward an end than in her first novel. By the last novel, there are far fewer outrageous Menippean characteristics than in the earlier New York novels, though the "carnival laughter" still echoes.

Scene: Down in the Village

As with Powell's earlier novels, New York City is a critical element in the development of both of these novels. In *The Golden Spur,* the plot is a direct result of the relationship between scene and satirist. Jonathan must be in New York City to fulfill his quest of finding his father. What he expects from the city, based on notes that his mother wrote 26 years earlier, is necessarily different from what he experiences. The narrative becomes a vehicle, too, for Powell's own exploration of the city, comparing the city when she first arrived to the city as it has become. As always, Powell wrote best when she knew and understood her scene, so *Whither,* written very shortly after her arrival in New York City, falls somewhat short of fulfillment.

Powell began *Whither* in 1922 and completed it 16 months later, roughly the time frame of the novel itself. Powell wasn't far enough away from her vision of New York to write about the reality of New York, and her provincialism gawks across the novel. She apparently felt that the mere words New York (with an exclamation point!) were enough to explain Zoe Bourne's desire to be there, and so Powell did not supply much physical description of the city. For instance, Zoe's foray into the Village provides an opportunity for Powell to describe the unconventional pedestrians who enliven the streets; however, the description is limited to "The studio was on Bank Street" (*Whither,* 171).

The Golden Spur is set primarily in Greenwich Village, and the plot allows Powell to explore both the Village that she first came to know in the 1920s and the Village that has come to be in the early 1960s. "One importance of living in the Village for a writer," Powell wrote, "is that it keeps him more fluid generally—more *au courant* with the life around him. For a historical novelist it might not be good—constant struggle between contemporary life and a set dead pattern" (*Diaries,* 383). Powell sought to evoke the spirit of the Village and to show that, despite all the external changes, the hope of the Village was essentially the same: "This book must not only be the living Village of today . . . but the reality of Quest for Pure Art and Pure Essence of Beauty, corny as it sounds, rather than quest for kicks," she wrote (*Diaries,* 387). To this end, she seems to have succeeded, judging by the words of her sometimes harsh critic, Edmund Wilson:

> I have said that Dawn Powell must be less at home in the "beat" than in the old Village, yet it is interesting to find that in *The Golden Spur* she has succeeded in modulating without too much strain from the charming Lafayette café to its so much less distinguished successor, and that the beatnik's dread of the "square" comes to seem here the natural extension of the old Greenwich Villager's attitude toward the traditional artist's enemy: "uptown." (E. Wilson 1962, 235)

Here, as in her other New York novels, scene is nearly a character, insinuating itself into the action: "I want the background to be the hero like a river, with the many characters popping into view as people do in this neighborhood, all with one motive—fame" (*Diaries,* 386). The city here has two sides: It is insistently contemporary, trailing wisps of marijuana smoke, and unreliably senile, dusting cobwebs from the memories of other characters. Claire Van Orphen,[2] pressed for information by Jonathan after he finds her name in his mother's diary, realizes that she has no recollection of Jonathan's mother: "All she could do for the young man, Claire thought, was to fill him in on the general background of Greenwich Village in the late twenties, the way biographers did when they ran short of personal facts."[3] Jonathan soon finds himself wallowing in "facts" about the Greenwich Village of old, but with few details to help in his quest for his father.

Zoe's early impressions of New York City are absent in *Whither.* Jonathan's early impressions of New York City are conveyed clearly:

> His window was on a court within hand-shaking distance of other windows, but a wedge of the street below was visible and there rose the contented purr of the city, a blend of bells, whirring motors, whistles, buildings rising, and buildings falling. The stage was set, the orchestra tuning up, and in a moment he would be on, Jonathan thought. Curious he felt no panic, as if his years of waiting in the wings had prepared him to take over the star role. But it was more as if he were released from a long exile in an alien land to come into his own at last. (*Spur,* 2)

The city "purrs" for Jonathan, welcoming him. Not long after his arrival, the city has transformed him, made him one of its own:

> Jonathan recognized New York as home. His whole appearance changed overnight, shoulders broadened, apologetic skulk became swagger; he looked strangers in the eye and found friendship wherever he turned. With the blight of Jaimison heritage removed, his future became marvelously incalculable, the city seemed born fresh for his delight. He took for granted that his mother's little world, into which he had dropped, was the city's very heart. (*Spur,* 51)

For Powell, the Village is the heart of the city, and she views it anew in *The Golden Spur.*

Despite the lack of scenic details in *Whither,* perhaps the most important aspect of this first novel is the fact that it *is* set in New York City, indicating Powell's immediate desire to write of the time and place in which she lived. In this motive she is allied with Dostoevsky, as Bakhtin interprets his work:

Dostoevsky recalls the unique and vivid carnival sense of life experienced
by him at the very beginning of his career as a writer. This was above all
a special sense of Petersburg, with all its sharp social contrasts, as "a fantastic magical daydream," as "dream," as something standing on the
boundary between reality and fantastic invention. (Bakhtin, 160)

In *Whither,* Powell was "standing on the boundary between reality and
fantastic invention." Still at her beginning as a writer and as a resident
of New York City, however, she was not yet able to separate the dream
from the reality. Dostoevsky successfully recalled his youthful time in St.
Petersburg (1837–1843) 20 years later in "Petersburg Visions in Verse
and Prose" (1861). Powell's retrospective did not come until *The Golden
Spur,* and then her youth is woven into her middle-aged observations.

The Golden Spur of the title is a bar, and is a central scene in the narrative. It is, according to the diary kept by Jonathan's mother, the place
where she met her lover. This Village bar lacks the character and refinement of the Café Julien in *The Wicked Pavilion.* It is not legendary and,
indeed, it is a bit surprising to find it still in business after 26 years. One
well-oiled patron notes: "Everybody used to come to the Spur, . . . until
they could afford not to" (*Spur,* 17). Then, it was a place for young,
hopeful writers and artists; now, it is a place for the old, hopeless writers
and artists. Those who did achieve their dreams moved on. For
Jonathan, it marks the focus of his quest:

> The Golden Spur! His mother's Golden Spur, the place she used to go to
> meet the Man, the place she went with her famous friends, but above all,
> the place where the great romance had started, the place, indeed, where
> Jonathan came in.
>
> So the place did exist—not the grand Piranesi palace he had vaguely
> imagined, with marble stairs leading forever upward to love and fame,
> but a dingy little dark hole he must have passed before without noticing.
> . . . If The Golden Spur was real, then all of it was real. His mother had
> stood on this very spot, and suddenly her image leaped up, not the pale
> face on the pillow he remembered from long ago, but the stranger, Con-
> nie Birch, the girl who had written the letters, the girl who had met her
> lover in The Golden Spur. (*Spur,* 11)

Jonathan takes in the bar conversations, which revolve around the current art scene: "A painter can't turn out the stuff they have to do now
without being loaded" (*Spur,* 18) or maybe it's that "they got to paint
sober, then they're so disgusted with what they done they got to get
stoned" (*Spur,* 18). As he listens, Jonathan tries to pry into the conversa-

tion. For Jonathan, this seedy bar is the pot at the end of the rainbow: "He felt as if he had just pushed the magic button that was to open up the gates to his mother's past and his own future" (*Spur*, 19). Indeed, the bar "spurs" connections that shape Jonathan's future. It is here that he finds his future roommates, Darcy Trent and Lize Britten; a potential father, Dr. Walter Kellsey, who once taught his mother; and a notice for a job at the Then-and-Now Café.

The Then-and-Now Café on Bleecker Street serves less as scene than as motif. Jonathan's task at the café is to compile a newsletter filled with bits of information about the Village's past. This information is provided by Dr. Kellsey, who is eager to persuade Jonathan that he definitely might be his father. The café itself was designed to be a transitory scene: it is "in the basement of a Bleecker Street real-estate firm that wanted to siphon off profits for tax purposes" (*Spur*, 51–52). The job serves Jonathan's purposes well because it informs him about the Village that his mother knew, and it provides enough income to pay his portion of the rent. For Powell, the café serves as a thematic focus, allowing her to revisit New York for the first time in a way that she did not do in *Whither.* The café also signals a shift in hangouts for Villagers. This is not the canape-and-liquor café of Powell's youth, but an espresso bar, the preferred digs of the new poets.

Satirist: The Reader Travels Alone

Jonathan is the tour guide for Powell's revisiting of her home. As such, he is an accidental satirist whose provincial view of the city renders it and its inhabitants as curious creatures indeed. Jonathan is the best of Powell's provincial satirists. He is believably naive, but also cool enough not to show surprise at big city ways. As a result, he comes off as being even more streetwise than he is. Part of the humor in the beginning of the novel is derived from Jonathan's accepting as normal events that are rather extraordinary in his effort to avoid appearing too provincial.[4] Jonathan's naiveté is his best and worst enemy as he approaches the city head-on. He moves in with Darcy and Lize because they ask him to, and because he assumes that "It must be a perfectly ordinary New York custom" (*Spur*, 39). When Darcy, then Lize, stumbles into his bed for late-night sex, "he knew it was his provincialism, and he would soon learn city ways" (*Spur*, 55). As it happens, this last gesture, which seems too much even for Jonathan, was encouraged by Malcolm Cowley because, as Powell wrote

Malcolm felt Jonathan didn't have any sex life and should sleep with the girls. I saw his point and did over a scene showing they both used him more or less as a hamburger. Last night I had a strong reaction that this was no good. For Jonathan to be living with two girls is really comic and true—for God knows it happens often. But to be sleeping with them makes him ordinary and unfunny and a cheap convenience. (*Diaries,* 428–29)

This seems, indeed, to be the case. But the scene is short and the sex is so understated that it is difficult to immediately understand what occurred. Ultimately, it reveals more about the nature of Darcy and Lize than of Jonathan, who frets

He had feared that these episodes, in which he blamed himself for taking advantage of their hospitality, would result in a change of atmosphere, but it finally dawned on him that they were no more important or meaningful than the midnight hamburger. City women were wonderful, he decided, but very strange. (*Spur,* 55–56)

Jonathan adopts the laissez-faire attitude of his two housemates with seeming ease. In the process of writing the novel, Powell noted,

I decided that my basic idea of novels is that there is one character, a giant A. who is peeled off like an artichoke into several characters—for each one is but a mood or possibility of the basic one, and a novelist lights up one strip of the artichoke. In *Spur,* as in others, each character represents the hero at another time—in another situation—under different circumstances. The fruit opens, seems several people, then closes into One. (*Diaries,* 441)

Jonathan does reflect nearly every character he encounters. In his quest to find his father, he takes on the characteristics of each candidate, so that he seems to bear paternal resemblance. Jonathan is trying to define himself by finding his father: "If it turns out I'm the heir to a great legal mind, I will know what to expect of myself. . . . All my life before this I didn't think I could count on anything but the Jaimison pigheadedness. Now I can be anything. For instance, if my father was a great writer—" (*Spur,* 68). Jonathan fits the character of the adventure hero:

As regards the adventure hero . . . it is impossible to say who he is. He has no firm socially typical or individually characterological qualities out of which a stable image of his character, type, or temperament might be composed. Such a definitive image would weigh down the adventure plot, limit the adventure possibilities. To the adventure hero anything can happen, he can become anything. (Bakhtin, 102)

Jonathan steps out into the city streets with these very words: " 'I'm not a Jaimison,' he murmured to himself over and over, and his stride grew longer, his head higher. 'I could be anybody—*anybody*!' " (*Spur,* 6). This assertion, born of the knowledge that he was not relegated to living a drab Midwestern life, is the impetus for all the provincials who visit Powell's New York. Having discovered that J. Jaimison Sr. is not his real father, Jonathan sets out to find his father in order to define himself. Of course, Jonathan is really setting out to find himself; in this way, Jonathan's quest is everyone's quest.

The lack of a satirist in *Whither* reflects, in part, Powell's unfamiliarity with the scene of the novel; in order to satirize, the author needs to know the scene well enough to know its flaws. *Whither* was written when Powell could not see any flaws in New York. The salvation that critics found in *Whither*—"a certain engaging air of being deeply and seriously concerned about her characters and their lives"[5]—is the very thing that prevents the book from being satirical. The light parries and thrusts do not hit home because of Powell's obvious affection for Zoe. This affection may be explained by a look at Powell's early letters, which reveal that Zoe is largely Powell's own young self, from the first trembling steps in the city to the bit part in the movie to the storybook whirlwind romance with Joe Gousha. All of these events were too fresh in Powell's memory to have satire roughen the edges. Even Zoe's appearance is that of the young Powell, from the short stature to the olive skin and slightly slanted, brown eyes to the trademark 1920s bob:

> Her hair . . . was cut short and clung in straggly wisps to her head. Zoe had bobbed it herself only the day before she came to New York . . . she had thought to appear unacademic—even modish, whereas she had looked merely immature. Still, there was an inner feeling of tolerant sophistication which short hair gave one . . . It was the suitable gesture for a girl who was breaking off with her family and all the stupidities which Albon represented, for a career in New York. (*Whither,* 5)

Powell's own hair was bobbed, and she wrote to her sister in Ohio: "Is your hair bobbed yet? Mine I still miss, though it's nice not to have to fuss with it. I sort of wish I had it in a way."[6]

In *Whither,* the limited omniscient narrator serves as occasional satirist, and it is in these moments that glimmers of Powell's sword, which she would wield so handily in the late 1930s novels, are seen. One such moment occurs when Zoe picks up a copy of LaBruyere in a bookstore and reads, "There's something more than wit required to make an author," to which she demands of her companion, Christopher Kane, "What more than wit is required to make an author?" Kane responds, "Some say a seat at the Algonquin" (*Whither,* 189). This tart acknowledgment of Dorothy Parker and the Round Table points toward Powell's future novels, where nothing in the contemporary scene is too sacred for a jab.

There are some cynical boarders at Zoe's boardinghouse whose knowledge of the city cuts through Zoe's romantic view. May Roberts, a "very successful" writer who lives in an attic room cluttered with papers, pens, ink, and stamps, plays the "role of the successful author giving advice to the novice." She declares that she has written nearly 30,000 words in the past week. Zoe queries if it is a novel that she is working on.

> May stared. "Heaven forbid," she sputtered. "A novel? Good Lord. Whatever put that in your head? Syndicate stuff is my line. Fashions, household hints, little poems, jokes, trade suggestions—everything."
>
> "Not even any short stories?" Zoe clung weakly to her idea of what an author should be.
>
> "I haven't the physique," dryly answered May. "I tried it once but— Ever see any of my stuff? I'm Johanna Jewell for the syndicates and Henry France for the trade magazines. I might give you a letter to the editor of the 'Dry Goods Economist.'"
>
> Zoe's face plainly and tactlessly revealed her disgust at the idea. May, seeing this, twisted her mouth sarcastically.
>
> "You may as well get this big literary idea out of your head right away, unless you've got enough capital to support it. If you want to earn a living writing, you've got to write selling stuff. You'll save yourself a lot of hard knocks if you start in doing it right away."
>
> "I'd thought of writing plays," faltered Zoe. "I wanted to do something in a big way."
>
> "You didn't want to do anything big," May said in a hard, contemptuous voice. "You're just like all the rest of them. You just want to *be* something big. There's a difference." (*Whither,* 26–27)

Powell did arrive in New York with the hope of writing plays, but she quickly discovered the virtue of publishing small pieces in the newspapers. It was not the romantic life of a writer that she had envisioned, but it allowed her to live in New York City.

Plot: The Adventure of an Idea

Both *Whither* and *The Golden Spur* are adventure novels, but Zoe's adventuring possibilities are far more limited than Jonathan's. Rather than having her own adventures, as Jonathan is allowed to do, Zoe is forced to live Powell's own young life again. In her 1981 dissertation on Powell's work, Judith Faye Pett observed that "the book haphazardly focuses on individual events, flitting from one to another with no apparent purpose. Powell's lack of structure is a perfect technique for her story; even the title ironically emphasizes the lack of a sense of direction" (Pett, 207–8). In fact, there does seem to be a direction, or end point, for the novel, which is reflected in a tiny, bare promotion for *Whither* in the *Saturday Review of Literature:* It depicts a flapper whose cigarette smoke curls up to form the word *Whither* and above the title is the query: "Husbanding or Careering?"[7] Though this may strike modern readers as peevishly trite, it is this question that frames the movement of the novel, and the action is a balance of evidence weighing for either option.

Zoe's adventures are drawn from Powell's own experience, and real life presents events that are more outrageous than anything a writer could invent. One scene depicts Zoe's work on a movie as an extra, along with an aspiring actress who seems drawn into the novel for the sole purpose of presenting this scene. Powell described her own work on the film in a letter to Aunt Orpha May Steinbrueck:

> All this week I've been doing extra work in the movies—a new Selznick picture of Olive Thomas—I guess the name is "Out of the Night."[8] I worked all day Monday over at the Universal Studio at Fort Lee, all day Tuesday, and Wednesday from 8:30 in the morning till 7 o'clock Thursday morning! Four hundred extras—of us—in evening dress supposed to be at a cabaret and we didn't dare leave the set from Wednesday morning till Thursday morning, except to go down and eat. Along about 3 a.m. we all lined up for coffee and sandwiches and staggered home Thursday morning—simply dead. . . .
>   But believe me, I'm through. I never saw such a group of absolute moral degenerates in my life as those movie extras—all the old ham actors that failed on the regular stage hang around the movie studios. . . . I may get a story out of the thing yet for the Sunday Morning Telegraph. I will try to discourage these would-be movie stars.[9]

In every experience, Powell is a writer, observing, taking notes toward writing. And in *Whither,* she packed in as many experiences as she could.

In another unlikely scene, Maisie is wooed by a young man who claims to have inherited a fortune from his late uncle, who lived in Central America. In fact, Powell encountered such a man, as she described in a letter to her college friend, Charlotte Johnson:

> There was the man—Frederick Schneaburg, Jr., University of California, now in Navy—who asked where we were on the subway and because I smiled back he grabbed my arm and told me he had just inherited half a million dollars from an uncle down in the Honduras and it was his guardian, the vice-consul for the Honduras, that he was now on his way to. He was so handsome! And so young! and so—gee! He came to see me twice, then his boat left for the South and I know I'll never see him again.[10]

The fictional beau also disappears after a few dates with Maisie.

Powell's inclination in *Whither* was to write what she knew. Unfortunately, she tried to incorporate *everything* she knew about her early experience in New York City, rather than working out of a few experiences. The effect of this exuberant realism is a fiction that is less than believable. Perhaps Powell's aim was to show just how unbelievably lively life can be in New York City, where one can meet millionaires on the street and put oneself on the big screen without even any acting ability. Nearly 20 years later, Powell reread *Whither* and noted: "Reading *Whither* I was horrified at how completely hopeless and utterly devoid of promise it was—far worse than what I had written at 13" (*Diaries,* 221). In addition to the immature narrative development, the work is weakened by an overabundance of adverbs, adjectives, exclamation points, and dramatic effusions in addition to a decided aversion to using the same word twice.[11]

Charles Norman, a poet and friend of Powell's, was the sole reviewer to give more than a lukewarm reception to the novel, calling it a

> much finer conception of the jazz age than even [John Howard Lawson's] "Processional." Miss Powell has a fine satiric perception of the significances of little things in the affairs of men and women, particularly women. She is thus a dangerous creature to be let free to write of them, for she does so unmercifully, yet withal lightly, so that there is much to laugh with in *Whither.*[12]

This review was a notable exception, though, and Powell was suitably chagrined by the somewhat withering review in the *New York Times:* "All in all, *Whither* should be welcomed by the large public that likes such wholesome and entertaining little yarns."[13] After writing *Whither,* Powell noted,

> Finally it came to me that I cannot work from factual knowledge. A novel must be a rich forest known at the start only by instinct. To have all the paths marked, the trees already labeled, is no more incentive to enter than Central Park is a temptation to explorers.
>
> Such trips through known and classified territory might be an excellent enough challenge to creative ingenuity in someone else. But with me the basic urge to write is neither knowledge nor the desire to expound but pure curiosity, the bottom of all laboratory experimentation. (*Diaries,* 37–38)

It is not "factual knowledge" as much as known arrangement or predestined path that limits the narrative. The adventure itself needs to remain unknown to allow freshness to come through.

By the time Powell wrote *The Golden Spur,* she was well able to entrust the adventure to the hero. Jonathan does not face the limitations that Zoe faces, in no small part because Jonathan is male. Despite Powell's own freedom in life, it seems that she considered herself an exception among women, and that she doubted the freedom-fighting powers of most females. Thus, she allows her male protagonists more freedom than her female protagonists. Further, in the early 1960s, young people of both genders had more freedom, so, rather than limited choices, Jonathan has seemingly endless options.

These narratives unfold differently. *The Golden Spur* "is done in a way like an explosion," Powell wrote.

> A whole world appears—not in orderly sequence but all around with Jonathan in the middle—a spectator in a Theater in the Round. He— like other adventurers—expects to ride over the city. Instead, it overwhelms him. He is a focal point—like a magnet drawing large objects and events to him as center. (*Diaries,* 394)

As characters are drawn to him, Jonathan studies each to determine his or her role in his own life, as a child will egocentrically define others in terms of himself. As the narrative unfolds, Jonathan is continually amazed at how the shards that bombard him in a seemingly haphazard fashion later fit together into a mosaic that completes his understanding of himself. Powell's concept of this arrangement closely parallels Bakhtin's reading of plot:

> Plot . . . is absolutely devoid of any sort of finalizing functions. Its goal is
> to place a person in various situations that expose and provoke him, to
> bring people together and make them collide in conflict—in such a way,
> however, that they do not remain within this area of plot-related contact
> but exceed its bounds. The real connections begin when the ordinary plot
> ends, having fulfilled its service function. (Bakhtin, 276–77)

Powell orchestrates the fragments so that they are linked by the end of
the narrative. For instance, very early in the novel, Jonathan "collides"
with "a ruddy-faced, agate-eyed man, bare-headed, with gray-streaked
pompadour and mustache, carrying an attaché case and a rumpled blue
raincoat over his arm" (*Spur*, 9). This man is, like Jonathan, drawn to
watch the destruction of the old Wannamaker's. He later becomes one
of the prime candidates for Jonathan's father. The effect of this arrangement is not a feeling of being manipulated by a too-clever author but
rather a sharing in the surprised response of Jonathan. In the process of
writing the novel, Powell noted:

> I am working on this book in a somewhat different way. I am doing the
> sketches and scenes before blocking out the complete mural—as an artist
> does. In fact I may use these in a new way—not tightly chaining them
> but allowing a distant perspective of a whole design, made up of minor
> complete scenes—no actual linking as the real ones are generally more
> dramatic. (*Diaries*, 383)

The final mosaic is not tightly chained, but rather it is something like
the product of the 1960s artists: It is a happy circumstance that all the
pieces somehow ended up on the same canvas.

The sketches and scenes make up Jonathan's adventure as he comes
together with various people to piece together the truth of his past.
Bakhtin describes the movement of the adventure plot:

> the adventure plot relies not on what the hero is, not on the place he
> occupies in life, but more often on what he is not, on what (from the van-
> tage point of the reality at hand) is unexpected and not predetermined.
> The adventure plot does not rely on already available and stable posi-
> tions—family, social, biographical; it develops in spite of them. (Bakhtin,
> 104)

Jonathan defines who he is not as he eliminates the potential paternal
candidates. Further, although Jonathan does not recognize this immediately, he does not have to adopt the characteristics of his father once he

finds him. Although the plot comes to an end when Jonathan discovers
his father's identity, the story itself does not end. Jonathan's adventuring
possibilities have begun anew and on a different level since he has inherited a generous fortune. Jonathan does try a few steps in his father's
shoes, but he finds that the style does not suit him. He discovers that he
can define himself on his own terms, that he does not need paternal her-
itage to define it for him.

As Jonathan considers his options, the narrative moves backward and
forward in time, as Jonathan consults his mother's notes on her past and
tries to envision his own future. Here, Powell includes something of her
own past, as she incorporates Ohio in the narrative. Originally, she had a
full Ohio chapter, but Malcolm Cowley, who was editing the book,
apparently did not care for Powell's "Ohio stuff", so she reduced the
material. What remains is a glimpse of Jonathan's aunt, a figure similar
to Aunt Lois in *My Home Is Far Away:* a wise, witty woman who knows
the family's secrets and reveals just enough of them as is necessary.
There is also a glimpse of Jonathan's stepmother, not in her home but in
New York City. Jonathan's father and stepmother bear strong resemblance to Charles and Idah Hawkins Willard in *My Home Is Far Away,* in
their eagerness to get their hands on Jonathan's money. The criticizing
nature of Jonathan's stepmother is revealed as "her little brown eyes
shopped over his person busily, price-tagging his corduroy slacks and
checked shirt, recognizing his old sport jacket and mentally throwing it
out" (*Spur,* 230). Jonathan suffers this glance, certainly a mild affront
compared to the evils of the stepmother in *My Home Is Far Away.*
Jonathan takes in his stepmother's attire: "A closer look at his stepmother showed that she had gotten herself up to hold her own in the
great city. The effect was not a New York look but the small-town look
multifold. The rouge was redder, the jaw firmer, the coiffure browner
and kinkier, the bracelets bigger and noisier, the Alice-blue silk dress
bluer and tighter, the patent-leather sandals higher-heeled" (*Spur,* 231).

Powell here has stripped the stepmother of her innate horror and
made her a ridiculous figure, one that does not inspire fear as much as a
snicker. Powell, it seems, has gained the distance necessary to put her
own stepmother in her place.

In *The Golden Spur,* the polyphony of voices is orchestrated in a wholly
natural fashion, so that the arrangement is not forced or farcical. The
unfolding of the narrative is dependent upon various rhetorical forms,
both written and spoken. Jonathan's mission is revealed by his Aunt
Tessie, who reveals to Jonathan that Jaimison is not his real father and

advises him: "Keep thinking of all those stories your mother used to tell you every night, stories about people and places she knew in New York, like that Golden Spur where she met all those famous ones" (*Spur,* 12). Aunt Tessie admits that she herself never kept the stories straight: "Used to go in one ear and out the other like all those stories girls tell about their good times away from home, all those beaux, all fine men, all better than the hometown boys" (*Spur,* 12). Jonathan must rely at the outset on his own memory and the diaries and letters of his mother. The written clues cannot be taken at face value because they are tinted with the romantic outlook of a provincial in her 20s exploring the city. The quest continues based on the spoken word, recollections of an earlier time by a variety of individuals who, admittedly, have but a dim recollection of Connie Birch. Powell lets us into the speakers' heads, revealing the dual nature of Jonathan's mother: the shy girl and the streetwise young woman. Threads of memory are teased out, woven into stories, and the narrative unfolds through the words of many characters.

Nearly everyone Jonathan encounters opens conversation by telling him, "You remind me of somebody." Initially, this excites Jonathan, until he recognizes his capacity to emulate the mannerisms of the person he is with. He eagerly absorbs the stories of the people he traces from his mother's journal, unaware that the stories have been altered by time, decorum, and the needs of the person speaking. For instance, Claire Van Orphen remembers little about Connie Birch except that she was shy and obliging. Also, Claire discovered, Connie frequently stopped for a beer after work and once, during a literary tea, Connie was found passed out cold. Claire quickly decides that she can't reveal these details to Jonathan. During the interview with Jonathan, Claire recalls that Major Wedburn sent Constance to her:

> Claire suddenly interrupted herself, overjoyed to have found one small nugget, and in her relief invented words of admiration the Major had used at the time. Claire was ordinarily truthful, but she did want to prolong the interview. She made a bold decision to invent other little tidbits as coming from the late Major. (*Spur,* 64)

In her exuberance, Claire mentions George Terrence, who becomes a prime candidate for paternity and proves to be as unreliable a narrator as Jonathan's other acquaintances.

George Terrence piques Jonathan's interest by declaring that he knew Constance Birch "perhaps in some ways even better than his wife [Connie's then-roommate] had" (*Spur,* 154). He then hastily backsteps:

"George realized that, in his anxiety to detain his caller, he had gone too far. He had only the vaguest memory of Connie; all he remembered was his disappointment when the door used to open on Hazel's roommate instead of Hazel herself" (*Spur,* 154). The embellishments of George and Claire, invented for the purpose of making them appear to be reliable sources, lead Jonathan down some fruitless paths, and finally, "It occurred to him that there was truth in every lie if you waited long enough, and you might as well believe everything while you waited" (*Spur,* 122).

Jonathan's reward for waiting is one of Powell's few comic endings. Jonathan receives an enormous legacy from his late father, and the world opens before him. He does not step into his father's work, but has instead the freedom to pursue his own dreams, whatever they turn out to be. This latter uncertainty is a Powell touch, as she never fully seals the fate of her characters.

Shoring Up

The Golden Spur may be Powell's ultimate Menippean satire, as she shores up the elements of her life's work in this final, extraordinarily comic novel. Ghosts of characters assemble to act out variations of themes that Powell explored in earlier novels. Jonathan hails from Silver City, the hometown of Prudence Bly in *The Happy Island.* Powell originally had a chapter set in Ohio, but took it out at the urging of Malcolm Cowley. The male homosexuals of *The Happy Island* are replaced with "dykes" romping across Washington Square. Rather than being an isolated focal group, homosexuals are now a casually accepted part of life in the city. Abortion, too, has toned down from the critical plot turning in *My Home Is Far Away* to "the usual agonies" of a young woman in the city. The Peggy Guggenheim figure is back, but not on center stage. Here she is played by the aptly named Cassie Bender, who was "forty-three—well, all right, forty-eight, if you're going to count every lost week end" (*Spur,* 206). Even the ghost of Dennis Orphen is summoned up, in the name of Claire Van Orphen.

Like Dennis, Claire serves as an alter ego for Powell. The friendship between Claire Van Orphen, a stately relic of the early Greenwich Village, and Earl Turner, "ageless, jaunty, wearing his faded bohemian uniform with the calm assurance of the true belonger" (*Spur,* 16) is unlikely, and seems to play out the carnival relationship: "Carnival is the place for working out, in a concretely sensuous, half-real and half-play-acted form, a new mode of interrelationship between individuals, counter-posed to the all-powerful socio-hierarchical relationships of noncarnival life" (Bakhtin, 123). This "new mode of interrelationship" is critical to Powell's portrayal of the Village. Her aim is to show not only that relics of the 1930s—Powell included—can coexist with the beatniks of the 1960s but that they can also learn from each other, sharing their art in order to find new forms suitable to new media. True to his name, Earl Turner helps Claire Van Orphen turn her stories around so that they fit into current expectations and media: "in the old days the career girl who supported the family was the heroine, and the idle wife was the baddie, . . . And now it's the other way round. In the soap operas, the career girl is the baddie, the wife is the goodie because she's better for business" (*Spur,* 118). Claire makes a deal with CBS for two of the stories and Hollywood wants the rights. Together, Claire and Earl renew each other, as they play out a "dialogic relationship" in which both are changed as a result of the interaction.

By the close of the narrative, Claire's success is complete. She is making money, enough to purchase a natty, modern black wool suit, and has moved to a different, more deluxe apartment, furnished by its previous late owner. Claire notes: "I've been budgeting and scrimping for so many years I can't enjoy splurging unless I balance it by doing without something else" (*Spur,* 242). In some ways, Powell was writing her own future in Claire: After the dismal response to *A Cage for Lovers* (1957), Powell's final novel, *The Golden Spur,* won high praise and was nominated for the National Book Award. Powell fills *The Golden Spur* with "Bohemia, raffish people, and satire," and she seems to have chosen a hero whom she genuinely likes, as with Dennis Orphen. Through Jonathan's eyes, New York is viewed afresh, a remarkable feat for a writer who had lived in the Village for more than three decades. In fact, the writing of *The Golden Spur* followed closely on the heels of Powell's homeless state in late 1958, and Powell wrote to Sara and Gerald Murphy: "I am always delighted to find new sides of New York and this is a lot of fun—every two blocks a new city. . . . We have a vague sensation of being tourists and really enjoying the town instead of dozing in our old rut."[14]

Powell's beloved city was literally tumbling about her as she wrote *The Golden Spur.* Her life, too, was fragmenting. During the time that she worked on the novel, from 1958 to 1962, she was forced from her home; her longtime housekeeper, Louise Lee, died; Jojo suffered several severe episodes; Joe Gousha died; Powell began radiation treatment;

and Margaret De Silver died. Her diary bears terse testimony to the effects of these trials: "Weepy in house and imprisoned and paralyzed. Need air and sun" (*Diaries,* 438). Writing was itself a trial: "Days of so much blood washing, etc., that I come to office and fall into deep drenched sleep with fascinating dreams—very plotful due to rather drained conscious mind. Effort to re-enter novel knowing it's not right but knowing I have a dull knife to cut it with" (*Diaries,* 430); "Fatigued, numb, brainfagged yet must reassemble novel" (*Diaries,* 432). The writing, though, gave her reason to surface from the doom; "I dread the dictatorship of loneliness, the collaboration compelled because that's all there is" (*Diaries,* 437); Powell found her strength in laughter. During a time that threatened to crush her, she found the fortitude to write her most comic novel.

Like Jonathan, Powell came to New York City to find her identity. She found it and a home to love. In *The Golden Spur,* Powell aligns the plot with the movement of a world larger than that inhabited by the character alone. Powell wanted to show the change in the Village, as well as the change in art, in order to demonstrate, finally, how much has stayed the same. The artists' appearance and works are different than they were 30 years earlier, but they came to the Village to seek the same freedom that the earlier artists sought.

Epilogue: "The Hope of Being Discovered and the Fear of Being Found Out"

Late in her life, Powell herself wistfully noted the conundrum of "The artist['s} . . . two-headed bogey: the hope of being discovered and the fear of being found out" (*Diaries,* 452). Powell has at last been found out, and in 1996, Richard Selzer declared in the *Wilson Quarterly* that "It is no longer possible to make a study of 20th-century American literature without considering Powell."[1] So why did it take 40 years to invite Dawn Powell to the literary fete? The answer, like Powell's literature, refuses to be neatly summarized. It reaches from such banal sources as lack of publishers' advances to the very structure of Powell's fiction, and woven through it all is a series of poor decisions and bad luck.

Powell noted in her diary: "One reason for literary situation is that writers do one of two things—either write or make a name for themselves. Making a reputation takes all their time, so they have none left to write" (*Diaries,* 379). Powell spent her time writing. In her final novel, Powell ushered in the next generation of artists in Greenwich Village. Yet another generation would pass through before Powell's work received the acclaim that was largely missing in Powell's lifetime. Powell was nominated for the National Book Award in 1963 for *The Golden Spur.* As she awaited the verdict, she pondered, "Will Success Spoil Dawn Powell? I don't see why not. I'm no better than anybody else, never said so" (*Diaries,* 444).

Even in 1940, when Powell was near the height of her career, an interview with her is titled, "Dawn Powell, Whose Witty Novels Find Too Small a Public, Discusses Her Trade." Wilson suggests that Powell's small following could be attributed to

> her complete indifference to publicity. She rarely goes to publishers' lunches or has publishers' parties given her: she declines to play the great lady of letters, and she does not encourage interviews or the appearance of her photograph on book jackets. No effort has been made to glamorize her, and it would be hopeless to try to glamorize her novels. (E. Wilson 1962, 233)

In truth, Powell's various publishers didn't always offer to throw a party for her. In her diaries, she cited continual frustration with lack of advance publicity for her novels: "Book appeared with no ad or review. If I had not been blessed with flu, I would have been devastated" (*Diaries,* 376). At times, it must have seemed a conspiracy, as with the publication of *My Home Is Far Away,* which coincided with the publication of *Young 'Un* by Herbert Best, a novel with a nearly identical plot.[2] And Powell's fantastic send-up of the publishing industry in *Turn, Magic Wheel* may not have endeared her to publishers.

Powell lacked good sense when it came to dealing with publishers. Rather than ask for the hefty advance that her novels deserved, she would ask for tiny amounts of money. Powell lamented in an interview with Robert Hethmon that "Those old, fine old firms are the worst about money of anybody. . . . They will gladly spend fifty dollars for lunch for you to make unconscious and at the time explaining why they cannot give you twenty-five dollars on your advance." But she said: "It really doesn't matter, I've decided. It used to be you were supposed to be loyal to your firm, but then you're loyal to them and the person you're loyal to has quit and gone to another firm anyway, so that tradition is gone completely nowadays. You might as well hop for every five dollars more you get anyplace."[3] At the time of the interview with Hethmon, two months before her death, Powell had hopped from Viking to Random for her next book, the last of many moves in her effort to find a publisher who would support her style of writing. Twenty years earlier she had written, "I think my great handicap and strongest slavery is my insistence on freedom. I require it. So I cannot make the suave adjustments to a successful writer's life—right people, right hospitality, right gestures—because I want to be free. So I am tied down and now in middle years almost buried (so far as my career goes) by my freedom" (*Diaries,* 242).

Powell had the misfortune of being a witty woman in New York at the same time as Dorothy Parker, whose reputation persisted long after Parker ceased writing her poems, short stories, and reviews. In a review of one of Powell's novels, Diana Trilling wrote: "Miss Powell, one of the wittiest women around, suggests the answer to the old question, 'Who really makes up the jokes that Dorothy Parker gets the credit for?' "[4] This is, of course, unfair to both Powell and Parker. The comparison particularly rankled Powell: "If people said she was another Dorothy Parker, she'd hit them," Jacqueline Miller Rice, the former executor of Powell's estate, told John Guare. "Dawn was a Village person. Not an

Algonquin person. . . ." (Guare, x). In 1931, when Dorothy Parker was still the toast of the town, Matthew Josephson said that Dawn Powell was "the wittiest woman in New York" (*Diaries,* 34). And Ernest Hemingway once said, "Dawn is a better wit than Dottie Parker . . . who cries too much" (Josephson, 20).

Powell's work captures the characters and lifestyle of New York City from the 1920s when young hopefuls rushed from the Midwest to the big city, hoping to take it by storm, into the early 1960s, when Powell's beloved Greenwich Village had undergone a sea change, from bohemian to beatnik. Powell maintained that she was a "permanent visitor" in New York, and her Midwestern protagonists have that same sense of impermanence. Her novels often focus on an outsider trying to fit in. It might be this alienated feeling, this desperate plea for uniqueness that draws Powell's audience. It might be, ironically, the thing that kept Powell in obscurity because, as in life, in Powell's novels there are no heroes, just survivors.

Powell herself is a survivor, even in death. *My Home Is Far Away* (1944) has sold more copies since its reprinting in 1995 than in the previous 50 years. Her New York novels have waiting lists of readers ready to purchase copies as soon as they are printed. Her dramas, too, are receiving attention; four were reprinted in fall 1999. Perhaps, with the proper production, they will find new life on the stage, also. Audiences may find the wisdom, finally in Robert Benchley's lonely praise of her drama in which he sheepishly admitted: "My reaction to 'Big Night' was apparently one which marked *me* as not only obtuse but calloused. I liked it."[5]

The initial embracing of Powell's works in the 1990s might be attributed to a nostalgia for works by and about the 1930s and 1940s—a nostalgia played up by the publishers with two-color photographs of New York City on the covers. The continued allegiance to Powell, however, suggests a long-overdue appreciation of her innovative style. Perhaps Powell's own words best sum up the rewards of the discovery:

> Sometimes a new face appears, someone fresh from yesterday's obituary page, a New York friend, and this is a problem. It's hard to mix friends with family, live or dead, and I'm torn between them. Wait for me at the corner bar till I get rid of the folks, I whisper . . . I won't be forever. Wait for me and I'll tell you how I ran away from home. (*Best,* 448)

The fine story was well worth waiting for. My initial feeling when I was first swept away by Powell's novels was that this was a woman ahead of her time. Others have since concurred. Among them, Fran Lebowitz wrote of *A Time to Be Born:* "I am torn between the enthusiast's urge to spread the word and the collector's inclination to hoard. Uniquely, the truth serves both ends: this book is extremely funny, exceptionally intelligent, and still, despite the fact that it was originally published in 1942, much too modern for the likes of you."[6] Powell's equal-opportunity satire exposes all—men, women, and, occasionally, children, of all classes, but especially of the readers' own (presumably) middle class—as ridiculous. And the satire has found an audience. The time has come to welcome the break of Dawn.

Notes and References

Preface

1. Gore Vidal, "Queen of the Golden Age," *New York Review,* 21 March 1996, 4.
2. Fragment of proposal for Guggenheim Fellowship, ca. early 1940s, Collection Tim Page, the Estate of Dawn Powell, Columbia University Archives.
3. Dawn Powell, *The Diaries of Dawn Powell 1931–1965,* ed. Tim Page (South Royalton, Vt.: Steerforth Press, 1995), 213; hereafter cited in text as *Diaries.*
4. "Dawn Powell, Novelist, Is Dead; Author of Witty, Satirical Books," Obituary, *New York Times,* 16 November 1965, 47.
5. Judith Faye Pett, "Dawn Powell: Her Life and Her Fiction" (Ph.D. diss., University of Iowa, 1983; Ann Arbor: UMI, 1992 [8128448]), 207–8; hereafter cited in text.
6. John Updike, "An Ohio Runaway," *New Yorker,* 20 & 27 February 1995, 262–71.
7. Cover, *New York Times Book Review,* 26 November 1995.
8. Matthew Josephson, "Dawn Powell: A Woman of Esprit," *Southern Review* 9, no. 1 (1973): 18; hereafter cited in text.

Introduction

1. Rosalind Baker Wilson, *Near the Magician: A Memoir of My Father, Edmund Wilson* (New York: Grove Weidenfeld, 1989), 202; hereafter cited in text. R. B. Wilson (1923 –) was also Powell's editor at Houghton Mifflin.
2. It should be acknowledged that Powell made this assertion in a fellowship proposal that she never submitted, which casts some doubt on her assertions here. Of course, it's possible that she simply missed the deadline for the proposal and that it is all nevertheless true.
3. Dawn Powell, *Dawn Powell at Her Best,* ed. Tim Page (South Royalton, Vt.: Steerforth Press, 1994), 445; hereafter cited in text as *Best.*
4. Eudora Welty, "Place in Fiction," in *The Eye of the Story* (New York: Vintage, 1983), 129; hereafter cited in text.
5. Powell disavowed this novel and cited *She Walks in Beauty* as her first novel.
6. Dawn Powell, *The Story of a Country Boy* (New York: Farrar & Rinehart, 1934), 159; hereafter cited in text as *Boy.*

7. Marion Capron, "Dorothy Parker," in *Women Writers at Work: The Paris Review Interviews,* ed. George Plimpton (New York: Penguin, 1989), 115; hereafter cited in text.

8. Edmund Wilson, "Dawn Powell: Greenwich Village in the Fifties." *New Yorker,* 17 November 1962, 235; hereafter cited in text as E. Wilson 1962.

9. Powell to Max Perkins, 6 June 1942. Collection Tim Page. This wayward boosterism of *A Time to Be Born* must have particularly rankled Powell because of the complexity of the satire involved in this work, which satirizes not only Clare Boothe Luce (a satirist in her own right), but also American war-profiteers, all in fast-paced, immensely amusing prose.

Chapter One

1. Dawn Powell, *My Home Is Far Away* (New York: Scribner's, 1944), 105; hereafter cited in text as *Home.*

2. A persistent factual error, perpetuated by Powell herself, is that she was born in 1897; Powell apparently shaved a year off her age during the 1930s.

3. Harry Redcay Warfel, "Powell, Dawn," in *American Novelists of Today* (New York: American Book Co., 1951), 344.

4. John F. Sherman to Marcelle Smith Rice, 13 January 1997.

5. Powell, address at Lake Erie College (Painesville, Ohio, 1958), Collection Tim Page.

6. Powell, address, Collection Tim Page.

7. Tim Page, introduction to *Dawn Powell at Her Best* (South Royalton, Vt.: Steerforth Press, 1994), xii.

8. Powell to Charlotte Johnson, August 1918, Collection Tim Page.

9. Powell to Charlotte Johnson, 6 December 1918, Collection Tim Page.

10. No known copies of this film exist.

11. Powell to Orpha May Steinbrueck, 23 November 1919, Collection Tim Page.

12. Powell to Charlotte Johnson, 6 December 1918, Collection Tim Page.

13. Powell to Charlotte Johnson, 12 January 1919, Collection Tim Page.

14. Powell to Charlotte Johnson, Easter 1919, Collection Tim Page.

15. Charles Norman, *Poets and People* (New York: Bobbs, Merrill, 1972), 51; hereafter cited in text.

16. Powell to Mabel Powell Pocock and Phyllis Powell Cook, 3 September 1921, Collection Tim Page.

17. Powell to Phyllis Powell Cook, 30 April 1961, Collection Tim Page.

18. Powell to Joseph Gousha, 25 June 1925, Collection Tim Page.

19. Powell to Joseph Gousha, July 1925, Collection Tim Page.

20. John Guare, introduction to *The Locusts Have No King,* by Dawn Powell (New York: Yarrow, 1990), x; hereafter cited in text.

21. *The WPA Guide to New York City: The Federal Writers' Project Guide to 1930s New York* (New York: Pantheon, 1939, 1982), 136.

22. Dawn Powell, *The Wicked Pavilion* (Boston: Houghton, 1954), 306; hereafter cited in text as *Pavilion.*

23. Edmund Wilson, *The Sixties* (New York: Farrar, 1993), 64; hereafter cited in text as E. Wilson 1993.

24. John Dos Passos. *The Best Times* (New York: Signet, 1968), 154; hereafter cited in text.

25. Diana Trilling, review of *The Locusts Have No King,* by Dawn Powell, *Nation,* 29 May 1948, 611–12; hereafter cited in text.

26. Powell to John Dos Passos, 17 September 1947, "Letters of Dawn Powell to John Dos Passos," John Dos Passos Papers (#5950), Special Collections Department, University of Virginia Library. All citations and quotations from Dos Passos's letters are from manuscripts in this collection.

27. Virginia Spencer Carr, *Dos Passos: A Life* (Garden City, N.Y.: Doubleday, 1984), 466.

28. Powell to Phyllis Powell Cook, 11 April 1963, Collection Tim Page.

29. Carlos Baker, ed., *Ernest Hemingway: Selected Letters 1917–1961* (New York: Scribner's, 1981), 195.

30. Carlos Baker, *Ernest Hemingway: A Life* (New York: Scribner's, 1969), 236; hereafter cited in text.

31. Townsend Ludington, *John Dos Passos: A Twentieth Century Odyssey* (New York: Dutton, 1980), 377.

32. Louise Lee (ca. 1890–1960), Powell's housekeeper for more than 30 years.

33. Powell to Phyllis Powell Cook, 7 June 1960, Collection Tim Page.

34. De Silver (1890–1962) was an heiress and a patron of the arts and liberal causes. She was the widow of Albert De Silver, founder of the American Civil Liberties Union.

35. The apartment building was becoming a co-op and the Goushas did not want to buy their space. They neglected, however, to find a new home before the deadline.

36. Josephson, E. Wilson, and Norman all speculate about this relationship. T. Page agrees that the relationship was probably a close friendship.

37. Powell wrote and appeared on *Music and Manners* from August 1939 until February 1940. Taken on as a lark, the job soon overwhelmed her as it "took up more time than [she] should have thought a mere half-hour radio show would do" (Powell to Max Perkins 14 October 1939, Collection Tim Page).

38. Powell to Charlotte Johnson, 20 April 1919, Collection Tim Page.

39. Robert Van Gelder, "Some Difficulties Confronting the Satirist," in *Writers and Writing* (New York: Scribner's, 1946), 132.

40. Powell to Phyllis Powell Cook, 20 August 1924, Collection Tim Page.

41. Powell to Lee Covici at Viking Press, 9 March 1959, Collection Tim Page.

42. Powell to John Dos Passos, 12 November [1950].

43. Powell to Dos Passos, 14 August [1936(?)].

44. Powell to Dos Passos, 14 August [1936(?)]. United Artists eventually dropped the project. MGM made the classic film five years later.

45. Malcolm Goldstein, *The Political Stage: American Drama and Theater of the Great Depression* (New York: Oxford Univ. Press, 1974), 86.

46. Steerforth Press (South Royalton, Vt.) published four of Powell's plays in Fall 1999.

47. John Nerber, "The Unguarded Moment," review of *Sunday, Monday, and Always,* by Dawn Powell, *New York Times,* 29 June 1952, 5.

48. Dawn Powell, "The Elopers," *Saturday Evening Post,* 31 October 1963, 56–59. This story is included in a revised edition of Powell's short stories published by Steerforth Press in Fall 1999.

49. Dawn Powell, "What Are You Doing in My Dreams?" *Vogue,* 1 October 1963, 153, 212–13. This story is included in *Dawn Powell at Her Best* (South Royalton, Vt.: Steerforth Press, 1994) and is included in a new edition of Powell's short stories.

50. Dawn Powell, "Staten Island, I Love You," *Esquire,* October 1965, 120–25.

51. Powell to Dos Passos, 19 March 1963.

52. Malcolm Cowley, "The Last of the Lost Generation," *Esquire,* July 1963, 77.

53. Powell to Dos Passos, 19 March 1963.

Chapter Two

1. "Powell, Dawn," in *American Novelists of Today* (New York: American Book Co., 1951), 345.

2. See Carl Van Doren, "The Revolt From the Village: 1920," *Nation,* 12 October 1921, 407–12.

3. Anthony Channell Hilfer, *The Revolt from the Village 1915–1930* (Chapel Hill, N.C.: Univ. of North Carolina Press, 1969), 4–5; hereafter cited in text.

4. Review of *My Home Is Far Away,* by Dawn Powell, *Nation,* 6 June 1928, 652.

5. Review of *My Home Is Far Away,* by Dawn Powell, *New Yorker,* 7 April 1928, 108.

6. Review of *My Home Is Far Away,* by Dawn Powell, *Saturday Review of Literature,* 12 May 1928, 869.

7. These two authors have been largely overlooked in American letters. Winslow (1893–1961), like Powell, divided her stories between her native state, Arkansas, and New York City. Winslow and Powell knew each other and met occasionally in the city. Suckow (1892–1960) specialized in stories set in Midwestern towns.

8. "Powell, Dawn," in *Contemporary Authors,* eds. Barbara Harte and Carolyn Riley (Detroit: Gale Research Company, 1969), 5–8:915.

9. In the final novel discussed in this chapter, *The Story of a Country Boy,* Powell moves closer to the structure of the New York novels as she moves closer to her contemporary time.

10. Dawn Powell, *The Tenth Moon* (New York: Farrar, 1932), 3; hereafter cited in text as *Moon.*

11. Dawn Powell, *She Walks in Beauty* (New York: Brentano's, 1928), 1; hereafter cited in text as *Beauty.*

12. John F. Sherman to Marcelle Smith Rice, 13 January 1997.

13. Dawn Powell, *The Bride's House* (New York: Brentano's, 1929), 6; hereafter cited in text as *Bride's.*

14. Dell River seems to be modeled after Painesville, Ohio—locale of Powell's alma mater Lake Erie College—situated near Ohio's "nursery belt." It suits the theme for Powell to draw upon a time in her life when she, too, was somewhat shielded from the real world, free to pursue her own studies and interests.

15. Dawn Powell, *Dance Night* (New York: Farrar, 1930), 235; hereafter cited in text as *Dance.*

16. Powell provides a closer look at a similar apartment in her short story "Ideal Home" (originally published in *Story* magazine and reprinted in *Sunday, Monday and Always*), a focused, ironic portrait of a family trying to live in "the wonderful modernistic Ideal Co-operative Apartment House" (*Sunday, Monday and Always,* 184–96).

17. Powell to Joseph Gousha, ca. 27 June 1933, Collection Tim Page.

18. Ellipses are in text and do not indicate breaks or omissions.

19. This unpublished journal, addressed to Mr. Woggs, was kept in July and August 1915 after Powell's first year at Lake Erie College when she was working as a waitress at the Shore Club near Painesville to earn money for college; hereafter cited in text as "1915 diary."

20. Phil Stong, review of *The Story of a Country Boy,* by Dawn Powell, *New York Herald Tribune,* 25 March 1934, 4.

21. Review of *She Walks in Beauty,* by Dawn Powell, *Saturday Review of Literature,* 12 May 1928, 869.

22. On a visit with Powell's relatives in Ohio in July 1997, I was struck by their commitment to Ohio. Powell's sisters never left Ohio: Mabel settled in Shaker Heights, outside Cleveland, and Phyllis settled in Canton. One of Phyllis's daughters lives in Massillon, just 20 minutes from Canton, and the other

lives in Oxford. Mabel's daughter did leave the state and lives in Royal Oak, Mich., linked to Ohio by the shores of Lake Erie. Powell's favorite cousin, Jack Sherman, never left Shelby, where he has lived with his sister Rita for 50 years. Despite various talents among them, none felt the absolute drive to leave that Powell felt.

23. Ellipses are in text and do not indicate breaks or omitted words.

24. In fact, Powell entertained the idea of having Morry make a return in *The Story of a Country Boy,* discussed later in this chapter.

25. Mikhail Bakhtin, "Characteristics of Genre and Plot Composition in Dostoevsky's Works," chap. 4 in *Problems of Dostoevsky's Poetics,* trans. Caryl Emerson. (Minneapolis: Univ. of Minnesota Press, 1984), 122–23; hereafter cited in text.

26. Powell to Michael Sadleir, 30 December 1947, Collection Tim Page.

27. Curiously, 15 years after writing this novel, Powell characterized it as following a "conventional straight pattern" (*Diaries,* 211). This observation may reflect a contrast with the experimentation with structure in subsequent novels.

28. Review of *My Home Is Far Away,* by Dawn Powell, *Nation,* 6 June 1928, 652.

29. Harold E. Stearns, review of *The Tenth Moon,* by Dawn Powell, *New York Herald Tribune Books,* 4 September 1932, 6.

Chapter Three

1. Joan Zlotnick, *Portrait of an American City: The Novelists' New York* (Port Washington, N.Y.: Kennikat Press, 1982); hereafter cited in text.

2. Blanche Housman Gelfant, *The American City Novel* (Norman, Okla.: Univ. of Oklahoma Press, 1954); hereafter cited in text.

3. Neither Gelfant nor Zlotnick cite Powell's works in their bibliographies of city novels.

4. The last category was created essentially as a way of defining the novels of John Dos Passos, the originator and master of the synoptic novel.

5. Dawn Powell, *The Happy Island* (New York: Farrar, 1938), 40; hereafter cited in text as *Island.*

6. While Powell was working intermittently on *Turn, Magic Wheel,* she wrote and published two Ohio novels.

7. Eugene P. Kirk, *Menippean Satire: An Annotated Catalogue of Texts and Criticism* (New York: Garland Publishing, Inc., 1980), xiii; hereafter cited in text.

8. Gore Vidal, "Dawn Powell, the American Writer," introduction to *Angels on Toast; The Wicked Pavilion; The Golden Spur* (New York: Quality Paperback Books, 1989), 242.

9. The *Satyricon's* influence is not wholly unknown in literature. An early ad for F. Scott Fitzgerald's *The Great Gatsby* notes: "Like Trimalchio, who

staged his magnificent entertainments in the reign of Nero, The Great Gatsby lavished his wealth on invited and uninvited guests on his estate at West Egg" (*Saturday Review of Literature,* 25 April 1925, 709).

10. Dustin Griffin, *Satire: A Critical Reintroduction* (Lexington: Univ. Press of Kentucky, 1994), 193; hereafter cited in text.

11. Northrop Frye, *Anatomy of Criticism* (New York: Atheneum, 1966), 313; hereafter cited in text. Following a brief discussion of Robert Burton's "Anatomy of Melancholy," Frye writes: "The word 'anatomy' in Burton's title means a dissection or analysis, and expresses very accurately the intellectualized approach of his form. We may as well adopt it as a convenient name to replace the cumbersome and in modern times rather misleading 'Menippean satire' " (Frye, 311–12).

12. Kirk's catalog "attempts to list exhaustively all Menippean satires written before 1660 in the languages of Western Europe, and all the criticism published in those same languages about Menippean satire, up to the present time" (Kirk, ix).

13. Kirk notes that: "Frye has been mistaken, by some readers eager for a definition or prescription of necessary and sufficient characteristics for Menippean satire, as a provider of a set of exact rules for the genre, and a number of explicatory studies of modern works have been the result. Whether all the works that Frye's remarks seem to illuminate have in fact any connection beyond psychic similarity with the consciously imitating tradition of Menippus remains to be seen. But it is indisputable that Frye's remarks have promoted awareness of the genre. As he himself stated, with gentle irony, 'When I started writing on such subjects there was not one in a thousand university English teachers of *Gulliver's Travels* who know what Menippean satire was: now there must be two or three' " (Kirk, xxxi).

14. Alvin Kernan. *The Cankered Muse* (New Haven: Yale Univ. Press, 1959), 35; hereafter cited in text.

15. Kernan himself applies this model to English Renaissance literature.

16. Powell to John Hall Wheelock, 18 September 1950, Collection Tim Page.

17. Powell called *Turn, Magic Wheel* "very likely my best, simplest, most original book" (*Diaries,* 336).

18. Powell adored the Empire State Building, completed in 1931. When out-of-town visitors came, they made the trek to the roof of the building, and there are frequent references to the building in her diaries. The passage cited, in fact, came to the novel nearly intact from her diaries (*Diaries,* 54).

19. Dawn Powell, *Turn, Magic Wheel* (New York: Farrar, 1936), 189, 193; hereafter cited in text as *Wheel*.

20. Dawn Powell, *The Locusts Have No King* (New York: Charles Scribner's Sons. 1948), 3; hereafter cited in text as *Locusts*.

21. Dawn Powell, *A Time to Be Born* (New York: Scribner's, 1942), 312–13; hereafter cited in text as *Born*.

22. The portrayal of Julian's contempt for mental illness reveals Powell's contempt for this character. Because of her son, Jojo, Powell had tremendous insight into the workings of the mad mind, as the passage cited reveals. For a truly sympathetic account of the inmates of an asylum and the mothers who visit them, see Powell's short story "The Elopers," *Saturday Evening Post*, 31 October 1963, 56–59.

23. Powell was a great fan of Charles Dickens's works and his influence shows in her names that are, like those of Dickens's characters, indicative of the characters' traits.

24. Powell to John Hall Wheelock, 18 September 1950, Collection Tim Page.

25. While writing the novel, Powell noted: "Reshape first chapter showing more dream quality. Frederick like White Rabbit in a rush, not knowing where or how, already late" (*Diaries*, 256).

26. Two other novels do share this theme: *Whither*, Powell's first novel, and *The Golden Spur*, her last novel. There is a good chance that Wilson never read *Whither*, because Powell all but buried the book. Wilson's piece was written on the occasion of the publication of *The Golden Spur*, so it may be that the novel cast its glow over Wilson's recollection of Powell's earlier New York novels and caused him to forget her Ohio novels altogether.

27. Powell noted a similar disbelief in her own fame when a visiting Midwestern relative said, "Dawnie, you won't believe this but there's a real famous writer same name as yours, lives right in New York, too. I seen books by her. My wife's always thinking how funny it would be if you run into her" (*Diaries*, 436).

28. It is quite possible that the model for this aspect of Prudence Bly was Dorothy Parker.

29. William Soskin, "Laughing Amid Cafe Society," review of *The Happy Island*, by Dawn Powell, *New York Herald Tribune*, 11 September 1938, 3.

30. In her review of the novel, Diana Trilling wrote that Powell "cries out to be quoted, not one sentence at a time . . . but whole paragraphs and pages" (*Nation*, 19 September 1942, 244).

31. Apparently the Luces decided that the best defense was a good offense: *A Time to Be Born* is one of only two Powell books ever reviewed in *Time* (the other is *The Happy Island*). The review, which does not mention the obvious satire of the Luces, is noncommittal, providing some summary and concluding: "Cracks and gags are Authoress Powell's speciality. This novel crackles with them. As social comment it is a feast of peanut brittle" (*Time*, 7 September 1942, 115).

32. Edith H. Walton, "Cafe Society," review of *The Happy Island*, by Dawn Powell, *New York Times Book Review*, 4 September 1938, 7.

33. Review of *The Happy Island*, by Dawn Powell, *Saturday Review*, 24 September 1938, 20.

34. Powell, open letter about *The Wicked Pavilion* ca. Summer 1954, Collection Tim Page.

35. Powell, open letter, Collection Tim Page.

36. Gore Vidal, "The Woman Behind the Women," *New Yorker,* 26 May 1997, 73.

37. Powell, open letter about *The Wicked Pavilion* ca. Summer 1954, Collection Tim Page.

Chapter Four

1. Penciled in the margin by Powell, presumably at a later date, is "My Home Is Far Away."

2. Powell to Carol Brandt, 30 March 1944, Collection Tim Page.

3. Kenneth Fearing, review of *My Home Is Far Away,* by Dawn Powell, *New York Herald Tribune,* 19 November 1944, 2.

4. Fuffy, the nickname given to Powell's youngest sister Phyllis, was the name Powell used in drafts; it was later changed to Florrie.

5. The funeral scene, which is powerful and eloquent, caught readers' attention: "I sat next to Van Wyck Brooks at 'Inside U.S.A.' the other night," Powell wrote, "and he said he had just read *My Home Is Far Away*—thought it was a perfectly wonderful work, and description of funeral was one he could never forget. I was so dazed by this belated encouragement of a work that almost threw me completely by the indifference of its critical reception, that I found the very bad, noisy but genial show very fine" (*Diaries,* 271).

6. See *A Time to Be Born,* chapter 1, part 4 (32–39).

7. Though Marcia's mother dies of consumption in the novel, family lore holds that Powell's mother died of a botched abortion. (In 1997, Powell's nieces related this information as the story they had been told of her death.) This would make Roy Powell responsible not only for the daughters' erratic upbringing but also for the death of their mother. It is not clear, however, whether Powell was aware of this story.

8. Powell to Joseph Gousha, 5 July 1926, Collection Tim Page. Powell's diary notes about the deaths of loved ones are, as her response at the funeral, remarkably stark. Of her father's death, for instance, she noted simply on 8 July 1926: "Papa died at 4 p.m." But she wrote remarkably evocative letters from the deathbeds of various relatives and friends.

9. The entry is addressed to Woggs, Powell's imagined audience in this diary.

10. Edmund Wilson, review of *My Home Is Far Away,* by Dawn Powell, *New Yorker,* 11 November 1944, 93–94.

11. The second novel may be drawn in part from the life of Mabel, Powell's oldest sister, who moved to Cleveland to live. During a time of working on the novel, Powell wrote to her editor: "The sequel to *My Home Is Far*

Away . . . has undergone considerable revision. . . . the death of my sister [Mabel] last year paralyzed that background for me in a curious way, and it only became workable a short while ago, but the novel will be a very good one. . . ."(Powell to John Hall Wheelock, 18 September 1950, Collection Tim Page).

Chapter Five

1.   Gore Vidal, introduction to *Angels on Toast,* by Dawn Powell (New York: Quality Paperback Books, 1989), xiii.

2.   Powell to Max Perkins, 4 August 1940, Collection Tim Page.

3.   Dawn Powell, *Angels on Toast* (New York: Scribner's, 1940), 2; hereafter cited in text as *Angels.*

4.   The *New Yorker* expressed an interest in this story, "The Pilgrim," but the sale didn't happen. The story was published in Powell's collection *Sunday, Monday and Always* (1952).

5.   Powell to Joseph Gousha, 24 October 1950, Collection Tim Page.

6.   Powell to John Dos Passos (n.d. ca. Fall 1949).

7.   Edmund Wilson to Philippe Thoby-Marcelin, 19 December 1950, *Letters on Literature and Politics,* ed. Elena Wilson (New York: Farrar, 1977), 494.

8.   Powell to Joseph Gousha, 22 November 1950, Collection Tim Page.

9.   Dawn Powell, *A Cage for Lovers* (Boston: Houghton Mifflin, 1957), 133; hereafter cited in text as *Cage.*

10.   Powell to Dos Passos (n.d. ca. Fall 1949).

11.   Review of *A Cage for Lovers,* by Dawn Powell, *New Yorker,* 2 November 1957, 190.

12.   Review of *A Cage for Lovers,* by Dawn Powell, *Booklist,* 1 December 1957, 201.

13.   Powell to Max Perkins, 4 August 1940, Collection Tim Page.

14.   Dawn Powell, *A Man's Affair* [abridged paperback version of *Angels on Toast*] (New York: Fawcett, 1956), 59; hereafter cited in text as *Affair.*

15.   Original words are retained in brackets, and the cuts are italicized.

Chapter Six

1.   Dawn Powell, *Whither* (Boston: Small, Maynard and Co., 1925), 5; hereafter cited in text as *Whither.*

2.   No apparent relation to Dennis Orphen.

3.   Dawn Powell, *The Golden Spur* (New York: Viking, 1962), 43; hereafter cited in text as *Spur.*

4.   The young Jimmy Stewart would be perfect in Jonathan's role.

5.   Review of *Whither,* by Dawn Powell, *Saturday Review,* 18 April 1925, 694.

6. Powell to Phyllis Powell Cook, 20 August 1924, Collection Tim Page.

7. Advertisement, *Saturday Review of Literature,* 21 March 1925, 621.

8. The film was released as *Footlights and Shadows* in 1920.

9. Powell to Orpha May Steinbrueck, 23 November 1919, Collection Tim Page.

10. Powell to Charlotte Johnson, 8 December 1918, Collection Tim Page.

11. Here is a sampling of synonyms for the word "said" in the first 20 pages of the novel: reflected, questioned, applauded, guessed, queried, murmured, negatived, speculated aloud, explained, admitted, sighed, snapped, solemnly averred, exclaimed, grumbled, meditated aloud.

12. Charles Norman, review of *Whither,* by Dawn Powell, *Literary Review,* 11 April 1925, 5.

13. Review of *Whither,* by Dawn Powell, *New York Times,* 15 March 1925, 17.

14. Powell to Sara and Gerald Murphy, 28 November 1958, Collection Tim Page.

Epilogue

1. Richard Selzer, "Keepsakes of a Satirist," *Wilson Quarterly* (Spring 1996): 78.

2. Though William Poster noted in the *New Republic* (1 January 1945) that Best's novel was not as well written as Powell's novel.

3. Dawn Powell, interview by Robert Hethmon, New York City, 24 August 1965.

4. Diana Trilling, review of *A Time to Be Born,* by Dawn Powell, *Nation,* 19 September 1942, 243–44.

5. Robert Benchley, review of *Big Night,* by Dawn Powell, *New Yorker,* 28 January 1933, 24.

6. Fran Lebowitz, blurb on *A Time to Be Born,* by Dawn Powell (New York: Yarrow Press, 1991).

Selected Bibliography

Primary Works

Published

Whither. Boston: Small, Maynard and Co., 1925.

She Walks in Beauty. New York: Brentano's, 1928.

The Bride's House. New York: Brentano's, 1929; South Royalton, Vt.: Steerforth Press, 1998.

Dance Night. New York: Farrar, 1930; South Royalton, Vt.: Steerforth Press, 1994, 1999.

The Tenth Moon. New York: Farrar, 1932; as *Come Back to Sorrento,* South Royalton, Vt.: Steerforth Press, 1997.

Jig Saw. New York: Farrar, 1934.

The Story of a Country Boy. New York: Farrar, 1934.

Turn, Magic Wheel. New York: Farrar, 1936; South Royalton, Vt.: Steerforth Press, 1994, 1999.

The Happy Island. New York: Farrar, 1938; South Royalton, Vt.: Steerforth Press, 1998.

Angels on Toast. New York: Scribner's, 1940; New York: Quality Paperback Books, 1989; South Royalton, Vt.: Steerforth Press, 1996.

A Time to Be Born. New York: Scribner's, 1942; New York, Yarrow, 1991; South Royalton, Vt.: Steerforth Press, 1996.

My Home Is Far Away. New York: Scribner's, 1944; South Royalton, Vt.: Steerforth Press, 1997.

The Locusts Have No King. New York: Charles Scribner's Sons, 1948; New York: Yarrow Press, 1990; South Royalton, Vt.: Steerforth Press, 1995.

Sunday, Monday and Always. Boston: Houghton Mifflin, 1952. Stories. Expanded edition, South Royalton, Vt.: Steerforth Press, 1999.

The Wicked Pavilion. Boston: Houghton, 1954; New York: Quality Paperback Books, 1989; New York: Vintage, 1990; South Royalton, Vt.: Steerforth Press, 1997.

A Man's Affair. [abridged paperback version of *Angels on Toast*] New York: Fawcett, 1956.

A Cage for Lovers. Boston: Houghton Mifflin, 1957.

The Golden Spur. New York: Viking, 1962; New York: Quality Paperback Books, 1989; South Royalton, Vt.: Steerforth Press, 1997.

The Diaries of Dawn Powell 1931–1965. Edited by Tim Page. South Royalton, Vt.: Steerforth Press, 1995.

The Letters of Dawn Powell. Edited by Tim Page. New York: Holt, 1999.

Unpublished

"Big Night: A Play in Three Acts." 1932.

"The Journal of D[awn]. P[owell]." Summer of 1915.

Letters of Dawn Powell. Collection Tim Page, the Estate of Dawn Powell, Columbia University Archives.

"Letters of Dawn Powell to John Dos Passos." John Dos Passos Papers (#5950), Special Collections Department, University of Virginia Library.

"Women at Four O'Clock." Drama.

Secondary Works

Biography

Dawn Powell. Interview by Robert Hethmon. New York City, 24 August 1965.

"Dawn Powell, Novelist, Is Dead; Author of Witty, Satirical Books." Obituary. *New York Times,* 16 November 1965, 47.

Feingold, Michael. "New York Stories: Dawn Powell's Acid Texts." *Voice Literary Supplement,* June 1990, 12–14.

Gousha, Joseph. "My Book of Memories of My Mother Dawn Powell."

Guare, John. Introduction to *The Locusts Have No King,* by Dawn Powell. New York: Yarrow, 1990.

Josephson, Matthew. "Dawn Powell: A Woman of Esprit." *Southern Review* 9, no. 1 (1973): 18–52.

"My Home Is Far Away." *The New York Times Book Review,* 26 November 1995, 1.

Nerber, John. "The Unguarded Moment." *New York Times,* 29 June 1952, 5.

Norman, Charles. Review of *Whither,* by Dawn Powell. *Literary Review,* 11 April 1925, 5.

Page, Tim. *Dawn Powell: A Biography.* New York: Holt, 1998.

————. Introduction to *Dawn Powell at Her Best.* South Royalton, Vt.: Steerforth Press, 1994.

Pett, Judith Faye. "Dawn Powell: Her Life and Her Fiction." Ph.D. diss., University of Iowa, 1983. Ann Arbor: UMI, 1992 (8128448).

Poster, William. Review of *My Home Is Far Away,* by Dawn Powell. *New Republic,* 1 January 1945, 28.

"Powell, Dawn." In *American Novelists of Today,* by Harry Redcay Warfel. New York: American Book Co., 1951, 344–45.

"Powell, Dawn." In *Contemporary Authors,* eds. Barbara Harte and Carolyn Riley. Detroit: Gale Research Company, 1969.

Review of *Angels on Toast,* by Dawn Powell. *New Yorker,* 9 November 1940, 79.

Review of *Angels on Toast,* by Dawn Powell. *New York Times,* 20 October 1940, 6.

Review of *A Cage for Lovers,* by Dawn Powell. *Booklist,* 1 December 1957, 201.

Review of *The Happy Island,* by Dawn Powell. *Saturday Review,* 24 September 1938, 20.

Review of *The Happy Island,* by Dawn Powell. *Time,* 19 September 1938, 69.

Review of *My Home Is Far Away,* by Dawn Powell. *Nation,* 6 June 1928, 652.

Review of *My Home Is Far Away,* by Dawn Powell. *New Yorker,* 7 April 1928, 108.

Review of *My Home Is Far Away,* by Dawn Powell, *Saturday Review of Literature,* 12 May 1928, 869.

Review of *She Walks in Beauty,* by Dawn Powell. *Saturday Review of Literature,* 12 May 1928, 869.

Review of *A Time to Be Born,* by Dawn Powell. *Time,* 7 September 1942, 115–16.

Review of *Whither,* by Dawn Powell. *New York Times,* 15 March 1925, 17.

Review of *Whither,* by Dawn Powell. *Saturday Review,* 18 April 1925, 694.

Selzer, Richard. "Keepsakes of a Satirist." *Wilson Quarterly* Spring 1996: 77–78.

Soskin, William. "Laughing Amid Cafe Society." Review of *The Happy Island,* by Dawn Powell. *New York Herald Tribune,* 11 September 1938, 3.

Stearns, Harold E. Review of *The Tenth Moon,* by Dawn Powell. *New York Herald Tribune Books,* 4 September 1932, 6.

Stong, Phil. Review of *The Story of a Country Boy,* by Dawn Powell. *New York Herald Tribune,* 25 March 1934, 4.

Teachout, Terry. "Rediscovered Once More." *New York Times Book Review,* 26 November 1995, 9.

Trilling, Diana. Review of *A Time to Be Born,* by Dawn Powell. *Nation,* 19 September 1942, 243–44.

———. Review of *The Locusts Have No King,* by Dawn Powell. *Nation,* 29 May 1948, 611–12.

Updike, John. "An Ohio Runaway." *New Yorker,* 20 & 27 February 1995, 262–71.

Van Gelder, Robert. "Some Difficulties Confronting the Satirist," In *Writers and Writing,* 132–34. New York: Scribner's, 1946.

Vidal, Gore. "Dawn Powell: The American Writer." In *At Home,* 241–71. New York: Vintage, 1990.

———. "Dawn Powell, the American Writer." Introduction to *Angels on Toast; The Wicked Pavilion; The Golden Spur,* by Dawn Powell. New York: Quality Paperback Books, 1989.

———. "Queen of the Golden Age." *New York Review,* 21 March 1996, 4–7.

———. "The Woman Behind the Women." *New Yorker,* 26 May 1997, 70–76.

Walton, Edith H. "Cafe Society." Review of *The Happy Island,* by Dawn Powell. *New York Times Book Review,* 4 September 1938, 7.

Warstler, Debra. "Dawn Powell's Journal of 1915: A Prelude to Her Ohio Novels." Master's thesis, Northeastern University, 1996.

Wilson, Edmund. "Dawn Powell: Greenwich Village in the Fifties." *New Yorker,* 17 November 1962, 233–38. Reprinted in *The Bit Between My Teeth,* 526–33. New York: Farrar, 1965.

————. Review of *My Home Is Far Away,* by Dawn Powell. *New Yorker,* 11 November 1944, 93–94.

Background

Acocella, Joan. "After the Laughs." *New Yorker,* 16 August 16, 76–81.

Baker, Carlos. *Ernest Hemingway: A Life.* New York: Scribner's, 1969.

Baker, Carlos, ed. *Ernest Hemingway: Selected Letters 1917–1961.* New York: Scribner's, 1981.

Bakhtin, Mikhail. "Characteristics of Genre and Plot Composition in Dostoevsky's Works." Chapter 4 in *Problems of Dostoevsky's Poetics.* Trans. Caryl Emerson. Minneapolis: Univ. of Minnesota Press, 1984.

Brooks, Van Wyck. *From a Writer's Notebook.* New York: Dutton, 1958.

Capron, Marion. "Dorothy Parker". In *Women Writers at Work: The Paris Review Interviews.* Ed. George Plimpton. New York: Penguin, 1989.

Carlisle, Henry C., Jr. *American Satire in Prose and Verse.* New York: Random, 1962.

Carr, Virginia Spencer. *Dos Passos: A Life.* Garden City, N.Y.: Doubleday, 1984.

Clurman, Harold. The Fervent Years: The Story of the Group Theatre and the Thirties. New York: Hill and Wang, 1945, 1957.

Cowley, Malcolm. "The Last of the Lost Generation." *Esquire,* July 1963, 77–78.

————. *A Many-Windowed House.* Southern Illinois Univ. Press, 1970.

————. A Second Flowering: Works and Days of the Lost Generation. New York: Viking, 1973.

Donaldson, Scott. By Force of Will: The Life and Art of Ernest Hemingway. New York: Viking, 1977.

Dorman, Robert L. *Revolt of the Provinces: The Regionalist Movement in America, 1920–1945.* Chapel Hill, N.C.: Univ. of North Carolina Press, 1983.

Dos Passos, John. *The Best Times.* New York: Signet, 1968.

————. *The Fourteenth Chronicle: The Letters and Diaries of John Dos Passos.* Ed. Townsend Ludington. Boston: Gambit, 1973.

Feinberg, Leonard. *Introduction to Satire.* Ames, Iowa: Iowa State Univ. Press, 1967.

————. *The Satirist.* Ames, Iowa: Iowa State Univ. Press, 1963.

Fenton, Jill Rubinson, et al. *Women Writers From Page to Screen.* New York: Garland, 1990.

Frye, Northrop. *Anatomy of Criticism.* New York: Atheneum, 1966.

Gaines, James R. *Wit's End.* New York: Harcourt, 1977.

Gelfant, Blanche Housman. *The American City Novel.* Norman, Okla.: Univ. of Oklahoma Press, 1954.

Gill, Brendan. Introduction to *The Portable Dorothy Parker.* New York: Penguin, 1976.

Goldstein, Malcolm. *The Political Stage: American Drama and Theater of the Great Depression.* New York: Oxford Univ. Press, 1974.

Griffin, Dustin. *Satire: A Critical Reintroduction.* Lexington: Univ. Press of Kentucky, 1994.

Guilhamet, Leon. *Satire and the Transformation of Genre.* Philadelphia: Univ. of Pennsylvania Press, 1987.

Hilfer, Anthony Channell. *The Revolt from the Village 1915–1930.* Chapel Hill, N.C.: Univ. of North Carolina Press, 1969.

Keats, John. *You Might as Well Live.* New York: Paragon, 1970.

Kernan, Alvin. *The Cankered Muse.* New Haven: Yale Univ. Press, 1959.

Kinney, Arthur F. *Dorothy Parker.* Boston: Twayne, 1978.

Kirk, Eugene P. *Menippean Satire: An Annotated Catalogue of Texts and Criticism.* New York: Garland Publishing, Inc., 1980.

Ludington, Townsend. *John Dos Passos: A Twentieth Century Odyssey.* New York: Dutton, 1980.

Mellow, James R. *Hemingway: A Life Without Consequences.* New York: Houghton, Mifflin, 1992.

New York Panorama: A Companion to the WPA Guide to New York City. New York: Pantheon, 1938, 1984.

Norman, Charles. *Poets and People.* New York: Bobbs, Merrill, 1972.

Ohio Guide, The. WPA. New York: Oxford Univ. Press, 1940.

Rabkin, Gerald. Drama and Commitment: Politics in the American Theatre of the Thirties. Bloomington: Indiana Univ. Press, 1964.

Seidel, Michael. *Satiric Inheritance: Rabelais to Sterne.* Princeton, N.J.: Princeton Univ. Press, 1979.

Thurber, Helen, and Edward Weeks, eds. *Selected Letters of James Thurber.* Boston: Little Brown, 1980, 1981.

Vidal, Gore. "The Woman Behind the Women." *New Yorker,* 26 May 1997, 70–76.

Waldau, Roy S. *Vintage Years of the Theatre Guild 1928–1939.* Cleveland: The Press of Case Western Reserve University, 1972.

Welty, Eudora. "Place in Fiction." In *The Eye of the Story.* New York: Vintage, 1983.

Wilson, Edmund. *Letters on Literature and Politics.* Ed. Elena Wilson. New York: Farrar, 1977.

———. *The Forties.* New York: Farrar, 1983.

———. *The Sixties.* New York: Farrar, 1993.

———. *The Thirties.* New York: Washington Square Press, 1980.

———. *The Twenties.* New York: Bantam, 1975.

Wilson, Rosalind Baker. *Near the Magician: A Memoir of My Father, Edmund Wilson.* New York: Grove Weidenfeld, 1989.

WPA Guide to New York City, The: The Federal Writers' Project Guide to 1930s New York. New York: Pantheon, 1939, 1982.

Zlotnick, Joan. *Portrait of an American City: The Novelists' New York.* Port Washington, N.Y.: Kennikat Press, 1982.

Index

The Author

Marcelle Smith Rice earned her B.A. in English at Albertus Magnus College, M.A. in English at Wake Forest University, and Ph.D. in English at The University of North Carolina at Greensboro. Her interests include twentieth-century American literature and the study of rhetoric and composition. She is an editor at the *News & Observer* in Raleigh, North Carolina, and a lecturer at North Carolina State University.

The Editor

Joseph M. Flora earned his B.A. (1956), M.A. (1957), and Ph.D. (1962) in English at the University of Michigan. In 1962 he joined the faculty of the University of North Carolina, where he is professor of English. His study *Hemingway's Nick Adams* (1984) won the Mayflower Award. He is also author of *Vardis Fisher* (1962), *William Ernest Henley* (1970), *Frederick Manfred* (1974), and *Ernest Hemingway: A Study of the Short Fiction* (1989). He is editor of *The English Short Story* (1985) and coeditor of *Southern Writers: A Biographical Dictionary* (1970), *Fifty Southern Writers before 1900* (1987), and *Fifty Southern Writers after 1900* (1987). He serves on the editorial boards of *Studies in Short Fiction* and *Southern Literary Journal*.